Kill the Documentary

INVESTIGATING VISIBLE EVIDENCE

INVESTIGATING VISIBLE EVIDENCE

New Challenges for Documentary

Series editors

Jane Gaines

Faye Ginsburg

Michael Renov

Brian Winston

A new series addressing the most pressing questions for documentary studies today.

Kill the Documentary

A Letter to Filmmakers, Students, and Scholars

Jill Godmilow

Foreword by Bill Nichols

Columbia University Press   New York

Columbia University Press
Publishers Since 1893
New York   Chichester, West Sussex
cup.columbia.edu
Copyright © 2022 Jill Godmilow
All rights reserved

Library of Congress Cataloging-in-Publication Data
Names: Godmilow, Jill, author. | Nichols, Bill, 1942– author of foreword.
Title: Kill the documentary: a letter to filmmakers, students, and scholars / Jill Godmilow; foreword by Bill Nichols.
Description: New York : Columbia University Press, [2021] | Series: Investigating visible evidence: new challenges for documentary | Includes bibliographical references and index.
Identifiers: LCCN 2021036419 (print) | LCCN 2021036420 (ebook) | ISBN 9780231202763 (hardback) | ISBN 9780231202770 (trade paperback) | ISBN 9780231554701 (ebook)
Subjects: LCSH: Documentary films—Philosophy.
Classification: LCC PN1995.9.D6 G553 2021 (print) | LCC PN1995.9.D6 (ebook) | DDC 070.1/8—dc23/eng/2021107
LC record available at https://lccn.loc.gov/2021036419
LC ebook record available at https://lccn.loc.gov/2021036420

Cover design: Lisa Hamm

When I sit down to write a book, I do not say to myself, "I am going to produce a work of art." I write it because there is some lie that I want to expose, some fact to which I want to draw attention, and my initial concern is to get a hearing.

▸ GEORGE ORWELL

Contents

Manifestly Radical: A Foreword   xi
  ▸ BILL NICHOLS
Acknowledgments   xvii
I Call This Book a Letter   xix

Introduction—a Letter to Filmmakers   1

1. Abandon the Conventional Documentary—Reject Realism as the Only Authentic Nonfiction Form   7
   The Pedigree of the Real   8
   The Pornography of the Real   13
   The Imperialism of the Real   21

2. Take Action—Make Useful Postrealist Films   27
   What's in This Name *Postrealism?*   31
   Follow Buñuel—Refuse the Codes That Encourage Useless Empathy   37
   Poetry—a "Best Practice" for the Nonfiction Filmmaker   40

3. Forty Postrealist Strategies to Learn from and Borrow   57
   Resist—an Essential Postrealist Stance   57

The Author of the Film Is Always Present, One Way
or Another 62

Defamiliarize by Making Substitutions—Try Rats 62

Decontextualize 64

"Preposturize" (That's Not a Real Word—I Know) 66

Try Camp—There Are Many Routes to Useful Experience 68

Demolish It, Burn It Down 69

Syncopate It, Unwrap It 70

Dwindle, Diminish, Chop It to Dust 71

Decompress Gender Relationships 74

Create Radical New Space; Perform the Unthinkable There 75

Suck Out the Pornographic—Interrogate the Apparatus 76

Recalibrate a History 77

Perform What Could Have/Should Have Been 78

Promote Criminal Behavior with a Straight Face 80

Recast the Terms . . . the Poetry 81

Pirate from Films and Texts to Examine and Remap Them 82

Jiggle and Juggle It Around 85

List Everything That Pertains—Reveal the Essence of All 87

Record Social Rituals, What They Offer, Whom They Ignore 88

Postrealist Film as a Koan 90

Make Maps So the Lay of the Land Can Be Grasped 91

Reject Pessimism—Collaborate with Other Filmmakers 93

Reject the Westerncentric Games Anthropologists Can Play 94

Reject the Clichés of Journalism 95

Dodge the Privileged Gaze 96

Excessify It—I Mean Blow It Up Big and Let Us Ponder It 97

Animation Anyone? 99

Mix Indigenous Humor with Colonial Nightmare—
Blend Carefully 99

Collaborate Intensely with Your Social Actors   101

Make Us Stare at It—Make Us Count the Time   105

Misaddress an Audience; Produce a New Uninhibited One   108

Shoah, an Education in Impossible Filmmaking   109

Want More? Study This Superb Postrealist Film   111

Ten Thousand More Strategies: Here's a Good One   115

When You're Forbidden to Make a Film, Get Started Making It   116

Exploit Sound and Its Absence   118

Can You Dance a Nonfiction Film? Can You Drum a Useful Tale?   120

What Is the Political Usefulness of the Postrealist Film?   121

Finally, Some Useful Notes from the Poets   124

Afterword   125

4. The Toolkit   127

The Questionnaire: For Doing a Close Reading of a Documentary Film   128

Definitions of the Documentary Over the Years   133

The Unspoken Pleasures of the Documentary-as-We-Know-It   135

The Documentary Writ Broad in Just Five Sentences   136

Where to Find All the Postrealist Films I've Mentioned (Though Some, at Times, Tend to Disappear)   137

Teach Yourself Poetry . . . Just the Basics   141

Five Superb Hybrid Feature Films to Study   155

A Brief Review of the 2017 Burns/Novick PBS Series *The Vietnam War*   160

"Kill the Documentary as We Know It," Jill Godmilow, 2001   163

What Happened to Jill in Poland and How Postrealism Entered Her Life   164

I Want to Be Useful   166
144 Feature Films You Should See Before You Croak   169
Filmography   173

Notes   177
Bibliography   185
Index   191

Manifestly Radical

A Foreword

▶ BILL NICHOLS

Jill Godmilow calls her extraordinary book a "letter," and it is one heck of a letter. I prefer to call it a manifesto. It is not the first, but it is, to my knowledge the first by an exemplary woman director of documentaries whose own films are not, in her terms, documentaries so much as warnings, provocations, and fully in the post-realist spirit she urges us to embrace.

Cinema has its manifestos. In abundance. Scott McKenzie compiles 175 of them in his superb *Film Manifestos and Global Cinema Culture* (Berkeley: University of California Press, 2014). His is an eclectic, wide-ranging assembly of public declarations of intent and methods (the root meaning of *manifesto* stems from *manifestare*, Latin for "make public"). Best known are the handful that were produced by well-known, male directors like Sergei Eisenstein and Dziga Vertov in the heady days of silent Soviet cinema, and, later, Dogme 95 by Danish directors Lars van Trier and Thomas Vinterberg, who accompanied it with their tongue-in-cheek "Vows of Chastity" about what acts were permissible in the making of a film. In documentary, Werner Herzog offered his "Minnesota Declaration," a fierce attack on observational cinema as tourist cinema.

Many of the films of Jean-Luc Godard, from *Two or Three Things I Know About Her* to *Letter to Jane,* qualify as manifestos, as well as essay-fictions, given their radical reworking of the image and our assumptions about it. Maya Deren's *An Anagram of Ideas on Art, Form, and Film* comes close to one and is among the few written by a woman. And, in addition to the rousing manifestos by André Breton and Filippo Marinetti, celebrating surrealism and futurism, respectively, there is that most famous of all manifestos, Marx and Engels's *The Communist Manifesto*. All of them are sweeping, polemical declarations of what a transformed reality might be like if we take the path they mark out. They are inevitably calls to action as well as statements of principles.

Godmilow marks out another radical path, one that would leave much of the established documentary production, distribution, and reception apparatus in shambles. Such is the work manifestos set out to do.

All these manifestos want to step outside the standard operating procedures that govern the maintenance of reality as it is commonly understood, including, in Godmilow's case, the way conventional documentaries conform to a reality we already know. The reality we think we see and occupy is, for Godmilow, but the myths our society teaches us to (mis)take for reality. The issue becomes not simply a matter of a bolder, more radical content, but a transformation of form and how we think about that form as well. We need to see anew, to see through smokescreens and myths, subterfuges and illusions. For Godmilow, like many other radical filmmakers, form *is* the content, and those well-intentioned works that take up the vexing issues of the day in the form of a realist display of life, its problems, and the solutions that await our support are doomed to failure.

Jill Godmilow's films put into practice what she preaches. Her description of how she came to make *Far from Poland* is a capsule version of the principles and practices she advocates throughout this "letter" to us. (It is described in the toolkit portion of this book: "What Happened to Jill in Poland and How Postrealism Entered Her Life.") Godmilow's description of this new postrealist approach has basically two parts: what it is not (realist or conventional documentary) and what it is (postrealist, formal, or, most crucially, useful film).

Her attack on realist documentary is merciless, fully in the no-holds-barred spirit of most manifestos. Since the time of Robert Flaherty's *Nanook of the North* (1922), realism in documentary has meant falsification. Dominant conventions of realism move toward pornography in which the people in a documentary, like the women in a *Playboy* centerfold, are reduced to their usefulness to the filmmaker and his vision (these works are predominantly by men). This, she argues, is pornography. A pornography of the real. And any rebuttal that says, No, such images and the people represented in them evoke empathy, enlighten viewers, and alert us to the pressing issues of the day, is a mere diversion for Godmilow. It is empathy for the individual subject not understanding of the systemic issue shrouded beneath a feel-good liberalism.

Conventional documentaries typically exhibit a narrative with a beginning that demands an ending which resolves the issue identified at the start, a resolution that belongs fully to the world of fiction rather than to a reality where problems persist long after the completion of the film. Real issues cannot be reduced to the damage incurred and obstacles faced in individual cases and specific instances, nor can they be resolved within an hour or two of screen time. Standard issue documentaries, which the films of Ken Burns may epitomize as pointedly as any, from *The Civil War* (1990) to *The Gene* (2020), point us outward toward the world around us, to a "there, then, it" rather than draw our attention to another reality, the one actually in front of us, a "here, now, us."

The Vietnam War series, made by Burns and Lynn Novick, earns a scathing, carefully argued condemnation. Such documentaries use the images that address us to urge us to look through the screen on which they appear; they encourage us to forget about the "here, now, us" of what it means to watch a film. They draw on "common sense" as the fertile soil for vivid descriptions and rhetorical exhortations and they thereby leave all the assumptions that say commonsense realism can readily represent the world unquestioned. Godmilow will have none of it.

This is heady stuff and clearly meant to shake us up. But Godmilow has an alternative to propose, and this is where her manifesto takes us down a road that moves through less well-known terrain, the postrealist landscape of films that focus less on what we must attend to out there in the world and more on what we must attend to about the process of watching documentaries that claim to represent that world. Resist, refuse, rebel might be her mantra. Resist conventional strategies, refuse realist pretenses, rebel and find a better way.

The postrealist way leads us back to the Russian formalists of the 1920s, in those heady days when Constructivism in art had paved the way for a radically new form, which the silent Soviet filmmakers of that period embodied. The formalists championed *ostranenie*, a defamiliarization of the familiar. Art depended on it. To see what we were already conditioned to see simply repeated the dominant ideology. Defamiliarization, exemplified by Sergei Eisenstein and Dziga Vertov, taken up later by Bertolt Brecht, makes our familiar world less so. It took hold of the stick from the other end and jarred our assumptions free from their apparent bedrock in the way things are (when, in fact, they could be otherwise).

Far from Poland, Godmilow's first film of this sort, reported on the Solidarity movement in Poland, but not as a realistic, journalistic report from the frontlines. She could not get to Poland to make her film so instead she made her film *Far from Poland* in New York City, with coal mining sequences in Pennsylvania, and with numerous devices that defamiliarized the customary ways of interviewing, observing, and providing evidence from the field. It made us think about how what we were seeing and hearing was constructed as well as what was happening in Poland. It propelled Godmilow in a new direction that all her subsequent films have pursued, the result of which now arrives before us in the form of a manifesto.

Defamiliarization—montage for Eisenstein, the alienation effect for Brecht, postrealism for Godmilow—stresses the difference between a map and the territory it represents. Realism reduces the difference. As Alfred Korzybski once said, "The map is not the territory," but realism encourages us to mistake a representation for what it represents. Godmilow wants all the various markers that identify a map as a map, a *guide* to reality, to be front and center, reminding us of the distinction and drawing our attention to the "mapness" of the map or the "sounds and images-that-appear-before-us" quality of the documentary. Her many examples demonstrate what this means in practice, since there is no one universal map for reality but many distinct maps that reveal the perspective of the individual filmmaker just as a Mercator projection shows us the world from the perspective adopted by Geradus Mercator in the sixteenth century. It could be otherwise. It is just a map. Or, as René Magritte might put it, were he to paint such a map, its title might be "This is not a map" (it is now a painting of a map, not the map itself, just as a map is not the territory it represents).

This is a bold, provocative manifesto, cutting through subtleties and qualifications as most manifestos do. It is not meant to be an academic treatise or a carefully nuanced analysis (although it has elements of both). It sets out to grab us by the lapels and shake us up. This is a common goal of the manifesto. *The Communist Manifesto* was a terse, combative, rousing, and oversimplified call for revolution that would destroy capitalism. It lacked the analytic sophistication that Marx provided in his three-volume tome *Capital*. But it inspired a response that his detailed analysis never could. Likewise, Godmilow sets out to advocate and inspire. She does, however, offer concrete examples and detailed analysis along the way; it is not just advocacy. But it does draw as sharp a distinction as possible between the conventional, pornographic documentary that she urges us to kill and the postrealist one she wants us to embrace.

As a result, there is quite a bit of wreckage under the postrealist bus described here. Godmilow tosses out everything that smacks of conventional documentary aesthetics from Robert Flaherty's *Nanook* to Errol Morris's *The Fog of War*. These are not useful works in Godmilow's terms. They admit a realist perspective through the front door and do little to get us thinking about their assumptions. Instead they simply display their presumption to hold before us a truth about the world.

So much wreckage. But Godmilow clearly has a rich array of alternative, postrealist documentaries to champion—and what models they are! From Luis Buñuel's *Land Without Bread* and Georges Franju's *Blood of the Beasts* to Jafar Panahi's *This Is Not a Film* and Harun Farocki's *Inextinguishable Fire*, she marshals a pantheon of hard-hitting, tough-minded films that refuse to be herded into the realist corral.

Godmilow's letter, or manifesto, like most manifestos, draws a line in the sand. Which side are you on becomes the question. Stay put and miss the point, or step on through to the other side and restore for yourself some of the nuance and subtlety that is foreign to the spirit of a manifesto.

As Godmilow might say, we deserve more. We deserve better. We need jarring reminders that the myths we live by could be otherwise. We deserve documentaries that urge us to think about their assumptions, limitations, and perspective. We need the kind of perspective and the type of extant but underappreciated works that Godmilow gathers together into a movement, a postrealist movement that can upset apple carts. Manifestos put new horses in front of the carts they envision. Werner Herzog makes the case in a bold style, characteristic of manifestos when he declares during an interview in *Burden of Dreams*, a documentary about the making of his film *Fitzcarraldo*, "We have to articulate ourselves. Otherwise we would be cows in a field." All we have to do is decide whether Godmilow's cart is the right cart for us and then, if so, climb aboard.

Acknowledgments

Boy, did I have a lot of help with this book—you know who you are. First there was Lauren Hamersmith, then there was Ricky Herbst again and again, then Scott MacDonald, Deirdre Boyle, Martha Gies, Jane Banks, Beth Corzo-Duchardt, and Brian Winston. For courage and fortitude, I must thank my Polish friend Joanna Krakowska, who insisted I keep going.

Then there are the countless filmmakers whose work inspires me and the critics who have written so usefully about nonfiction filmmaking, especially dear James Agee, who started it all.

And there are my two friends, no longer with us, whom I must thank: Milos Stehlik of Facets Multimedia, a good friend who distributed almost all my films for forty-four years; and another good friend, Jonathan Kahana, who, twenty-six years ago, helped me rationalize making a somewhat outrageous film . . . a perfect replica, in color and English, of Harun Farocki's *Inextinguishable Fire*.

And let me also acknowledge my gratitude to Bill Nichols, who started me thinking about documentary back in 1981 and hasn't stopped.

My thanks to the University of Notre Dame, which kept me writing, teaching, and filmmaking for twenty years.

Thanks to all.

I Call This Book a Letter

I call this book a letter, and I mean it to be. Calling it a letter accounts for my avoidance of academic prose and theoretics—rather writing often informally and personally to filmmakers about my experience and criticism of documentary cinema as it has been practiced since Robert Flaherty's 1922 film *Nanook of the North* until today—and likely through tomorrow.

Twenty years ago I called upon filmmakers to "kill the documentary as we know it." Here I sound that call again, then advocate for a *postrealist* cinema. Once you've read this letter, you will have some good strategies for making a useful nonfiction film. Perhaps more important, you will understand how to watch the documentary-as-we-know-it with eyes that can shatter brick walls and build from those shards an effective and useful cinema for today. (Note: to avoid too much repetitive typing, from here on I'll often refer to the "documentary-as-we-know-it" as the DAWKI, which is fun to say and only five letters.)

I am not at all interested in trashing all documentaries, but I am interested in examining the assumptions they operate under, primarily that these are necessary and useful truths a citizen is entitled to. I am interested in how they implicitly describe us, the viewers, as caring citizens. I write to disclose what assumptions about us are not examined, and how the explicit use of realism covers all these sins. You could call it a *handbook* . . . for correcting these errors and for suggesting other ways to use your cinema voice to ask the right questions without cover of "realism" and "truth." And I propose that practicing poetry writing could help loosen the ties that bind us to our cameras and microphones in unthinking ways. Central to my thesis is what Adorno wrote in *Prisms* in 1967, "A successful work of art is not one which resolves contradictions in a spurious harmony, but one which expresses the idea of harmony negatively by embodying the contradictions, pure and uncompromised, in its innermost structure."

I hope you can learn from this letter, and enjoy it. Be sure to watch many of the alternative forms of postrealist films I discuss. Write some poems too.

Kill the Documentary

Introduction—a Letter to Filmmakers

In 1945, James Agee, film critic for the *Nation* magazine, pointed out the documentary's tragic tendency toward pornography, what I call *pornography of the real*.

PORNOGRAPHY is the objectifying of a graphic image, reducing it to some essential aspect of itself so the thing or person depicted can be commodified, circulated, and consumed without regard to its status as a subject—that is, turning it into something useful for someone else.

The paragraphs I offer here are from Agee's March 24, 1945, review of two different documentary films about the battle of Iwo Jima, both constructed from footage supplied by the Navy, Marines, and Coast Guard. Agee praises one film over the other for its "unusually intelligent job of editing, writing and soundtracking" . . . and good use of flat silence, and he mentions a pan down a photograph of a dead man *for whom time no longer moved*.[1] Then he offers this provocation:

> Very uneasily I am beginning to believe that, for all that may be said in favor of our seeing these terrible records of war, we have no business seeing this sort of experience except through our presence and

> participation. I have neither space nor mind yet to try to explain why I believe this is so; but since I am reviewing and in ways recommending that others see one of the best and most terrible of war films, I cannot avoid mentioning my perplexity. Perhaps I can briefly suggest what I mean by this rough parallel: whatever other effects it may or may not have, pornography is invariably degrading to anyone who looks at or reads it.
>
> If at an incurable distance from participation, hopelessly incapable of reactions adequate to the event, we watch men killing each other, we may be quite as profoundly degrading ourselves and, in the process, betraying and separating ourselves the farther from those we are trying to identify ourselves with; none the less, we tell ourselves sincerely that we sit in comfort and watch carnage in order to nurture our patriotism, our conscience, our understanding and our sympathies.[2]

In 1980, when I first read Agee's review, it started me thinking about what intelligence and what pleasures, especially pornographic pleasures, the documentary has to offer its audience—and what it should not offer and why not. Agee seems to be challenging filmmakers as to what we represent, for whom, and, most important, how. His observation about the pornography of battle films eventually made me a much different filmmaker than I'd been. For me, useful filmmaking boils down to these questions: what relationship do we construct between the viewer and the material; how does documentary film address and construct the viewer? How does the film satisfy the viewer? Should it satisfy, or should it do something else? Finally, are there ways to avoid a potentially pornographic relationship in the conventional documentary as it has been practiced at least since Robert Flaherty's 1922 *Nanook of the North* and John Grierson's 1929 *Drifters*?

I've been thinking for a long time that what is commonly understood as the liberal documentary is an inadequate form—a relatively useless cultural product, especially for political change. Its basic strategy is description, and it makes its argument by organizing visual evidence, expressive local testimony, and sometimes expert technical testimony into a satisfying emotional form. Though the liberal documentary takes the stance of a sober, nonfiction vehicle for edification about the real world, it is trapped in the same matrix of obligations as the fiction film:

to entertain its audience; to produce fascination with its materials; to achieve closure; to satisfy, and to assure the audience of informed and moral citizenship. My question is: is that of any political use?

Now, forty-one years on, I am writing this letter, advocating for a cinema whose trustworthiness and usefulness is dependent not on documentary's pedigree nor pornography of the real, but rather on the strength of the performance of its ideas. To that end, I intend to be as provocative and subversive as I can. To some it will sound like a reproach, although I mean for it to be in part a lament about the conventional documentary, as well as a set of propositions concerning what I call *postrealist* nonfiction. (I used to think of these postrealist films as *antidocs,* given that they resist the systematic strategies of the conventional documentary. Sometimes that old name pops up again. I like the punch of it and can't refuse it when it appears.)

I'm arguing for a necessary intervention in documentary practice, as we know it, and for an artisanal cinema (artisanal as in material objects made partly or entirely by hand), one that resists the allure of *realism* of the documentary as it's practiced today. The risk of arguing for a postrealist, nonfiction cinema is not lost on me, since most audiences have come to believe that the conventional documentary offers a useful, truthful experience. I will take that risk.

> REALISM: in film, that stylistic mode best suited to create the illusion that what is happening on screen is a neutral and natural recording of objective events. Realism in documentary film implies a temporary belief in the "transparency" of the presented footage, in the three-dimensionality of the space projected on the screen and in the "presence" of the events unfolding (as if for the first time) before our eyes.[3]
> —E. ANN KAPLAN

How can we use the machine of film to do something like that? How can we disrupt our existing relationships to old useless ideas of who we are? We need a cinema practice of intervening in the institutional formation of knowledge. There are a thousand ways, but none are routed through realism. We need to sidestep the electronic hallucination that is realism to produce useful intelligence and a fruitful transaction with the film's audience.

I also want to help you read the conventional documentary—to see past its surface, to decipher how audiences are constructed and prepared by it to receive the experience of its text.

I offer instruction in how to piece together a film's *ideology* for yourself, to see what it's telling—and selling. I want to show you how to read these documentary texts *aberrantly*, that is, against their grain.

IDEOLOGY is any or all of the following: a method of social control without the exercise of force, the system of ideas and images that operate to enlist the oppressed in their own subjugation; the deployment of false ideas in the direct interest of the ruling class; a way to placate social tensions and respond to social forces so that they cease to be dangerous to the established social system of inequality. Ideology doesn't refer to the beliefs people consciously hold, but to the myths that a society lives by, as if these myths referred to some natural unproblematic "reality."

Every text, be it a novel, a news story, a cartoon, a film, or even a cereal box, is ideological: "Coke—the Taste That Refreshes," or "Wheaties—the Breakfast of Champions." Who are we? Do we need to be "refreshed?" Do we all want to be "champions?" Like the Coke and Wheaties taglines, documentary texts are ideological, but in much less evident and more seductive ways. Almost all of them address us as caring citizens and project an empathetic relationship to the materials represented in the film.

My ideas and opinions come from my own political experience in the civil rights, antiwar, and feminist movement, from my fifty-one years of experience making nonfiction films, from teaching documentary cinema at a university for more than twenty years, and from reading—among others, Hayden White, Brian Winston, Bill Nichols, Harun Farocki, Michael Renov, Trinh T. Minh-ha, Luis Buñuel, Andrei Tarkovsky, Jorge Luis Borges, Edward Said, James Agee, Béla Tarr, James Baldwin, Susan Sontag, Tacita Dean, Elizabeth Cowie, Deirdre Boyle, Vivian Sobchack, Martha Rosler, Gilberto Perez, Ernie Larsen and Sherry Millner, Jeff Skoller, and many more, from whom I will sometimes quote. Alongside the postrealist filmmakers, these writers are my teachers.

Moreover, my ideas and opinions are reaffirmed by a rich canon of postrealist filmmakers who have made useful films in different places and during different times that still remain useful today. Buñuel did it in 1933 with *Land Without Bread*. Georges Franju did it in 1948 with *Blood of the Beasts*. Alain Resnais did it in 1956 with *Night and Fog*. Harun Farocki did it in 1969 with *Inextinguishable Fire*. Carolyn Strachan and Alessandro Cavadini did it in 1981 with *Two Laws*. Trinh T. Minh-ha did it in 1982 with *Reassemblage*. Harun Farocki did it again in 1991 with *Videograms of a Revolution*. Rithy Panh did it in 2002 with *S-21: The Khmer Rouge Killing Fields*. And the Mumbai-based CAMP collective did it with their 2013 *From Gulf to Gulf to Gulf*. These are all masterpieces of what I call postrealist film, although hardly anyone calls them that but me. They are not just antimimetic, but blatantly interventionist and interactive. In this book, I want to show you an armory of strategies for making something similarly useful and enduring.

I assume my readers are independent thinkers if not yet already independent filmmakers. Of course, to call yourself a filmmaker all you have to do is to make your first film, and I encourage you to do so. If you have a great idea, then it will find a way. The postrealist film, or antidoc, is usually made with small or limited means, using a poverty of materials. You could say that to make one you have to sidestep the power of the cinema, its ability to enthrall, delight, amaze, and seduce. In postrealist cinema, there is no snow job. Begin to think, to plan it, and to write. Start now, or finish reading this book, think it over, then start to conceptualize your first, or next film.

At the end of this letter there is a chapter I call the toolkit, which contains a variety of useful items or tools:

The Toolkit

The Questionnaire: For Doing a Close Reading of a
    Documentary Film
Definitions of the Documentary Over the Years
The Unspoken Pleasures of the Documentary-as-We-Know-It

6 Introduction—a Letter to Filmmakers

    The Documentary Writ Broad in Just Five Sentences
    Where to Find All the Postrealist Films I've Mentioned
        (Though Some, at Times, Tend to Disappear)
    Teach Yourself Poetry . . . Just the Basics
    Five Superb Hybrid Feature Films to Study
    A Brief Review of the 2017 Burns/Novick PBS Series
        The Vietnam War
    "Kill the Documentary as We Know It," Jill Godmilow, 2001
    What Happened to Jill in Poland and How Postrealism Entered
        Her Life
    I Want to Be Useful
    144 Feature Films You Should See Before You Croak
    Filmography

1
Abandon the Conventional Documentary—Reject Realism as the Only Authentic Nonfiction Form

We are drowning in nonfiction film today, especially since the digital revolution. Many filmmakers are lazy. They entrench us in some situation or another, but they don't enlighten, provoke, or even heal us. They always say in some way: now you've been there—to some war-torn country, to some art gallery, to some famous person's home, to the shacks and tents of some poverty-stricken immigrants. Now we have met the real people who live in these situations, who perform themselves in these films (I call them social actors), and now we *understand*. Not good enough, I say.

A warning: in 1966 the filmmaker Robert Bresson, addressing Jean-Luc Godard in a 1966 *Cahiers du Cinéma* interview, warned, "I, like you, believe that the camera is a dangerous thing—meaning it's too easy, too convenient, we have to almost forgive ourselves for it."[1] With digital cameras and editing programs that you can slip into your laptop and settle onto your kitchen table, digital filmmaking is fast and easy. Easy could seem like a good thing—why not? But before you start shooting, slow down and think. If you don't, you will probably make a conventional documentary (what now can be considered an institutional mode of representation), tracking situations and presenting testimony by social actors, eliciting expert opinions, arousing your audience into a kind of concerned attention as good citizens of the world. But films like these are fictions—fictions about who the social actors are, about who the viewers are, and how that separation can be closed by watching and caring. These films overwhelm our analytical minds with *the real*.

Simply by virtue of its stance as a documentary, such a film says that only real visual and auditory facts have been assembled into this film text. Seeing is believing, right? But this seeing/believing obscures an embedded ideology and all its conceits. In particular, it obscures the us/them configuration. The first step for making a useful film is to recognize and abandon three powerful and insidious conceits pervasive in nonfiction films: the pedigree of the real, the pornography of the real, and the imperialism of the real.

THE PEDIGREE OF THE REAL

Realist documentaries are premised on the concept that, in order to change consciousness, the filmmaker must *show* a situation—the world as a *show*, thus *showable*. The world is an event that can be repeated in art, that is, in documentary film. But what does it mean to show a situation? Is a situation showable? The French critic Roger Munier writes, "Language is discourse *about* the world—photography and cinema are languages *of* the world. The world speaks through its images in an inarticulate way, and each sequence of moving icons is either illusionary or stripped of all meaning, because void of all discourse. These are mere images whose eloquence confers a power of illusion."[2]

You could call the pedigree of the real a *guarantee*—that, since all footage was shot by a trustworthy filmmaker in real life and real time, the film offers a true, useful picture of the situation. You could also call it a *warranty*, such as a full, money-back warranty, or a *certification*, in advance, that the real as represented, is yes—no doubt about it—the truthful real or, at the least, an adequate and useful representation of the real.

What does this pedigree look and sound like? Conventional documentaries almost always have a beginning, middle, and end. The "problem" is announced early on, and events are usually presented chronologically. Sound and image are aligned in perfect synchrony. In the cinema verité style, the run-and-gun shooting, shaky camera, natural lighting, diegetic sound, and long takes convey the sense that the filmmaker was there: just following the events, not creating them. The film's truth claims are based on only what took place in front of the camera without rehearsal or prompting. Anything else, we are taught, is a fabrication, especially any appearance or statement by the author/filmmaker. Thus the documentary-as-we-know-it is able to announce its neutrality and bury its ideology under its found-in-nature guise.

Regarding "the real," consider Robert Flaherty's famous 1922 documentary, *Nanook of the North* (figure 1.1). You probably already know that the romantic "primitive" star of the film, the man who performs Nanook, was actually not an "Eskimo" but an *Inuit* named Alliakariak. You might also know that while Nanook is presented in the film as monogamous, in fact he had two wives, which was common in Inuit society. Consider also that, by the time Flaherty shot his film, "Eskimo blankets" came from a department store in Toronto, the Inuit sold their skins to opportunist traders flying in from New York, and harpoons had been replaced by rifles. (Flaherty did not allow his subjects to shoot a walrus with a nearby shotgun. He insisted they use a harpoon instead.)

INUIT: many consider the term *Eskimo* to be derogatory due to its common usage by racist colonizers; the word itself possibly translates to "eater of raw meat," understood as violent and perhaps barbaric. Though some native groups still call themselves Eskimos, the 1982 Canadian Charter of Rights and Freedoms recognized the Inuit as a distinctive group of "Aboriginal peoples in Canada."

Contrary to the film, many "Eskimos" had seen a phonograph before 1922. The scene where a confused Nanook attempts to discover where the phonograph's music is coming from, putting the vinyl record in his mouth and biting down, was staged (figure 1.2). It's a degrading sequence, but perhaps necessary, in Flaherty's eyes, to lock in the notion that the primitive and humble Eskimo has a lot to learn from us and might someday enjoy the benefits of industrialized society, not to mention recorded music. *Nanook of the North* is a fiction film—a rousing, even inspiring enactment of ancient conceits about the wonderful, skillful primitives (who, like other Indigenous peoples, have managed to

FIGURE 1.1
Nanook of the North,
Robert Flaherty, 1922

FIGURE 1.2 *Nanook of the North*, Robert Flaherty, 1922

survive our campaigns of removal and genocide). We admire the competence of the primitive Eskimo and wish him well, and maybe even, in our unconscious heart of hearts, promise to love and protect him. Flaherty's Nanook charms us. Any tall tale can be told this way.

The French filmmaker Jean Rouch offers this useful story: "My mother told me all movies were just made-up stories. 'But, I asked her, last week I saw *Nanook of the North*—was that fiction too? Ask your father, she said. My father tried to explain that there was no difference between fiction and real film. The fact was that those small dogs in the snow were very cold, and in the film the actors were very good."[3]

What we normally think of as "the real" in documentary films is a construction, made up of how well the look and the sound of the film *simulates* the actual. Documentary filmmakers should become quite comfortable sidestepping the pedigree of the real.

JG: I LIKE TO RELATE A FRIEND'S STORY . . . a useful, fictional tale. "In his late Cubist period, Picasso was painting a portrait of a woman. One afternoon, the husband of the woman came by the artist's studio to take her home. He asked Picasso to see the painting of his wife, and Picasso showed it to him. The husband studied it awhile and said, 'It doesn't look much like my wife.' Picasso considered this, then asked, 'What does your wife look like?' The husband reached into his pocket and brought out his wallet. From his wallet he took a snapshot of his wife and handed it to the painter, who studied it for a long time, then turned to the husband and said, 'I didn't realize she was so small.'"

Rouch says that *Nanook of the North* was the first film he ever saw, and that it inspired him. But study Rouch's films and you'll see that he was more inspired by his Nigerian collaborators in his films *Jaguar, Me, a Black, Petit à Petit*, and all the rest. Rouch crossed fiction and ethnography, which was called *shared anthropology* or *ethnofiction* at the time, and made what I call tales of the possible. Instead of simulating, he said *We were trying to stimulate reality . . . to provoke it*. He did.

You may already know that the Lumière brothers' famous film *Workers Leaving a Factory* (1895), considered the very first documentary, was shot three times before they got the lighting right. Wikipedia tells us, "These versions are often referred to as the 'one horse,' 'two horses,' and 'no horse' versions, in reference to a horse-drawn carriage that appears in the first two versions pulled by one horse, then two horses in the first retake." Which season, what lighting, how many horses may become more important than the lives of the workers themselves going home after their labors.

With the conventional documentary, we are securely ensconced in "spectacle," where our eyes, our ears, and our understandings can be focused on all the people we could not otherwise meet, in places we have never been, nor shall ever visit. To transport us there is to put us in a dream state—not the best place to learn something useful. Dream states are imaginary places where anything goes, including half-truths, omissions, and lies. Theoretically, there's nothing wrong with dream states, unless the dreamers don't know they're dreaming.

As theorized by Joel Agee, "In the documentary dream state, we grant the effortless consent of our eyes and enjoy the power to move in and out of proximity to a given object, or to soar above it, or to change location abruptly. That we are not controlling these movements does not diminish their appeal. On the contrary, there is pleasure in being relieved of own's volition, in being asked to dream while awake."[4]

Sight as a mental process depends on much more than optical information received by the eye. Memory is central to vision in that what we see is in large part seen because we already know it for what it is. The "new" is very difficult to see until organized into our visual conventions. Optical stimuli only become information when they "make sense to us," when we recognize them again. Hilary Roberts writes, "Whatever its ambiguities and possible pornographic appeal, the photograph is compelling enough, convincing enough, to shock disinterested observers into wanting to know more of the event it purports to depict."[5]

The soundtrack of a *conventional documentary* puts us in the represented time and space of the image, bringing the image to life in this (ongoing) moment. Without any soundtrack, a silent film would simply be a recovery act of people and things once photographed—back then. Though we can follow a silent narrative, we are never in that represented time and place where and when it's happening. In a film with synchronized sound, we are in the living, breathing time and space of the film's representations—with the farmer and his corn field, with the refugees in their boats.

When considering the pedigree of the real, never forget that every film, all films, are written—no different than any other text. They are plotted. They are designed, either while shooting or in the editing room. Yet the conventional documentary pretends that it hasn't been plotted and designed. Here's my favorite definition of the doc by the Vietnamese filmmaker Trinh T. Minh-ha: "Documentary, because reality is organized into an explanation of itself."[6] She is saying that the reality footage, what's included and what's not, what's been conveniently ignored or repressed, has been organized into the appearance of a whole. Isn't there's something fishy about that? Don't play that game.

I would argue that the only reality in/of a film is the reality of the spectator's experience and the importance of that experience in their lives—not the ability of film to capture reality "out there" for us "back here."

THE PORNOGRAPHY OF THE REAL

As I wrote earlier, pornography is the objectifying of a graphic image, reducing it to some essential aspect of itself so the person depicted can be commodified, circulated, and consumed without regard to its original status as a person.

Just as the pornography of the *Playboy* centerfold no longer represents a "female person" but a fetishistic object for sexual excitation and/or for magazine sales, so the overcirculation of nature close-ups of "wild animals" in advertising turns the cougar, chimpanzee, or polar bear into consumable friends that can promote the sale of clothes made of natural fabrics. The overcirculation of images of war, such as the naked nine-year-old Vietnamese girl on fire with napalm fleeing down a road, becomes both an exciting memory of the war and an emotional trigger for generalized human grief, as opposed to an actual understanding of the issues of the Vietnam War. (The Vietnamese call it the *American War* or the *Resistance War Against America*).

Pornography produces inert objects, matter without spirit, from those who were once, in fact, living, feeling beings. Charming, courageous, skillful Nanook becomes consumable. *Nanook of the North* is charming pornography.

14   Abandon the Conventional Documentary

The conventional documentary can and often does operate as a *Playboy* centerfold does. Rather easily, it can deliver up for our pleasure the excitement, the visual tits-and-ass of climate destruction, corrupt corporate power, or the constraints on teenage girls in any number of Muslim countries. It can deliver pornography of the "welfare mother." Or the pornography of a farmer whose land has become toxic because it gets its water from a river full of pig manure from a nearby CAFO (concentrated animal feeding operation). Or the pornography of that famous network television documentary *Hunger in America* (1968), which presents, one after another, newborn babies almost too weak to live because of their mothers' insufficient diet: one African American baby, one Native American baby, one Hispanic baby, and one baby of poor white sharecroppers. At birth, one of these babies is too weak for the doctors to save. She or he dies on camera, before our eyes. Viewers gasp, hold their breath, blink, and feel extremely sad. As viewers, we're constructed as those who care very much about this sudden death and the shame of these parents—as those who would fix the problem *if only we could*. This is poverty porn. Or trauma porn. Or welfare porn. Or Black-family-Hispanic-family-Native-American-family-poor-white-family porn. But watching this film is like an express ticket to personal exoneration. "We watched and we cared" seems sufficient. The problem is no longer ours.

But how is it that watching victims of slavery, crime scenes, or extreme hunger on film can be pleasurable? There's this sort of deep, hardwired thing in us that seems to draw us to carnage. One useful proposition: "We eat chilies and bitter greens, and drink bitter tonics and bitter coffee, for the same reason that we ride roller coasters and watch horror films: to fool the body into thinking it's in danger, and then enjoy the adrenal ride," says psychologist Paul Rozin.[7]

To watch war death, babies dying, or social struggle in Hong Kong in nonfiction cinema offers a kind of benign, pleasurable masochism. A conventional documentary gives all that a name, a face, and a place. The film's plea for empathy and then the promotion of emotional resolution underscores and legitimates our pleasure in witnessing the abject, the tormented, the distressed, the miserable, and the afflicted. All these films come to some sort of resolution. *Hunger in America* shows us how government-supplied food stamps are reducing the hunger problem. Another film, *Harlan County, USA (1976)*, about a coal miners' strike in Kentucky, can finally draw to a close when the miners' strike against the Duke Power Company succeeds. Such pleasure. Such proof of our fellow feeling, our humanity—all delivered directly to us in the comfort of your local cinemas, your living room, bedroom, or, now, even your cellphone.

The problem with such resolution is that although the immediate situation may have had a satisfactory and gratifying ending that deserves celebration, the outstanding, multiple issues and circumstances of the situation are repressed. The four families of *Hunger in America*, unable to provide food for their families through their own labors, have to purchase food using only the monetary equivalent of what a family that size would receive in the U.S. federal government Supplemental Nutrition Assistance Program (SNAP). Today, in 2020, that is $194.00 per person per month, or $6.37 per day. The situation of the undernourished babies is not produced by a lack of ready cash but by inadequate education and poorly paid labor. This documentary has nothing to say about that. Instead, *Hunger in America* calls out for our compassion and our pity.

The critic Freddy Bauche writes, "Pity is the sister of resignation and the very basis of moral dishonesty: it provides every individual who is too cowardly to engage in revolt with a weighty, yet specious alibi."[8] In James Baldwin's essay "Everybody's Protest Novel," about Harriet Beecher Stowe's novel *Uncle Tom's Cabin*, he writes, "Sentimentality, the ostentatious parading of excessive and spurious emotion, is the mark of dishonesty . . . the wet eyes of the sentimentalist betray his aversion to experience, his fear of life, his arid heart; and it is always, therefore, the signal of secret and violent inhumanity, the mark of cruelty."[9]

The essential gesture of the traditional nonfiction film is to produce *us-watching-them* in an effortless way—not traveling to where they are, not learning their language, not smelling their food, and, most important, not being in their time. There are a million variations of us-watching-them in the seemingly innocent contexts of photographic accuracy and unmediated truth for our education and the elevation of our senses, so that we can be good, knowledgeable citizens.

The conventional documentary offers special opportunities for the liberal middle class. Why? Perhaps because middle-class viewers are secretly self-conscious and possibly ashamed of their privileged position, because they are educated and value knowledge, and because they have the means and the time to watch. The middle class goes to the documentary to get more comfortable in their own skin, to experience the momentary satisfaction of concerned citizenship. For the length of the film, the middle-class spectator is transfixed in an elevated sense of citizen-self.

This is something historian and journalist Thomas Frank (*What's the Matter with Kansas?*) calls the "liberal class virtue-quest." He writes about the middle class imagining themselves in "the international goodness community."[10] The liberal documentary offers our goodness community an imitation of politics through a kind of fraudulent intimacy. As filmmaker Martha Rosler pointed out decades ago, "a film addressed to the liberal spectator has the effect of naturalizing the asymmetry between an audience and the disempowered victims. It naturalizes and sustains."[11] I tell my students that the unspoken, unconscious (but essential and necessary) viewer response to the documentary filmmaker can be characterized this way:

Thank you for this information.
Thank you for a chance to meet these interesting people and learn
 and care about their situation.
And (sotto voce or whispered to oneself) Thank God that's not me!

Empathy, the capacity to understand or feel what another person is experiencing from within their frame of reference, is the mainstay of the liberal documentary. Empathy permits one to feel psychologically enhanced, that is, to feel morally ennobled with an expanded sense of self. But empathy can make the moral compass go wonky. It can and does cause us to elevate individuals over groups, so that we care more about these ten slaves than those thousands in bondage, or these two teenage basketball players instead of the uneducated, underpaid, and impoverished Black communities in this country that produced them. (Just for scale, consider this note from a recent edition of the *New Yorker*: "The brains of sperm whales are six times larger than our own, and are endowed with more spindle neurons, cells associated with empathy and speech."[12] I like to hypothesize about sperm whales watching *Hoop Dreams*. They would probably weep for the loyal mothers of the basketball boys.)

By embracing the pornography of the real and calling for our empathy, the conventional documentary is the perfect medium for personal exoneration. Consider *Hoop Dreams* (1994), the film by Steve James for the independent Kartemquin production group in Chicago, and what it tells us about the Black working poor in the ghettos of Chicago, and why, for these families, it seems that only with superior basketball skills can young Black boys rise up and out of poverty. No other route is examined. *Hoop Dreams* initiates us to feeling that we

1. fervently care about the education of Black boys in the ghettos;
2. maintain high hopes for these Black boys through their demonstrated skills in competitive high school basketball;
3. wait patiently to see if these boys will make their supportive mothers proud;
4. hope that the boys are good enough to get a scholarship to one of the top ten basketball schools, and then maybe a chance at the NBA, then untold wealth for them and their families.
5. However, finding the focus and determination to stay in school and keep your mind on the game and grades (and not on girls and clothes and drugs) is hard for African American kids, and when it doesn't work out for these sweet sons (especially in the exploitative system of professionalized amateur athletics), the least we can know and feel is that they tried, and we can continue to hope that someday, miraculously, just maybe, one (or even two) of these deserving African American kids, those who have gotten a bit more education than they would have without basketball skills, might be able avoid the pitfalls of the Black inner-city life that brought their fathers and brothers down so low and finally climb out of the underclass to comfort and security. Someday.

The narrative is a linear story form, which involves an introduction of characters and setting, presentation of a disturbance, puzzle, or lack, a goal-oriented line of causally linked situations and events, followed by a resolution of the disturbance or a solution to the puzzle. An essential, reduced narrative containing all important narrative elements could be characterized thus: two men set off across a valley, had many adventures, met and overcame many obstacles, and returned home safely. Of course, they returned home safely, so that viewers can go home relieved and satisfied.

Most narrative docs run away from loss and tragedy. The narrative *Hoop Dreams* needs to reward we viewers for our patient attention. Though it can't quite achieve closure, resolution, or redemption—neither protagonist quite makes it to the NBA and endless wealth—nevertheless, the film suggests that it still seems worthwhile investing in the NBA dream. This is a weak resolution considering our now weary eyes and souls, and our emotional investment for 171 minutes in the personal struggles and basketball careers of young William Gates and Arthur Agee. We are left dreaming/hoping that perhaps the next two kids can get into a top basketball university, the NBA, and fame and riches, making their parents proud. When you're making your documentary, avoid the lure of narrative. You need your viewers to think on, and further . . . to think better, past the drama, to the realities of the situation and its causes.

Narrative filmmaking, and especially narrative documentary filmmaking, demands returned-home-safely closure. Closure closes off the possibility of change, which must occur outside the film. No redemption in nonfiction. It isn't true or useful. Simply put, it's dishonest.

Hoop Dreams offers the audience an ideal opportunity for personal exoneration and absolution. The film offers tacit forgiveness for our past and current racism and economic oppression. After all, we viewers didn't create the hood. We didn't *personally* deliver the crack cocaine that led the boys' fathers into addiction. We didn't encourage their parents' failures. These things somehow just happen to Black folks in inner-city Chicago.

AS FOR CLASS, THE SAME GOES FOR RACE. David Halperin speaks of "the remarkable ease with which socially authorized individuals can communicate certain 'truths,' about a gay person, a black person, a Muslim, an Asian, a Native American, a working-class person, an immigrant, or any other marginal subject. If the message is already waiting at the receiver's end, it doesn't even need to be sent; it just needs to be activated."[13]

These films never hint that our racist history produces the underclass and all its dilemmas. Even after 246 years of brutal Black slavery and roughly 99 more years of Jim Crow, then the mandated segregation of public schools and transportation, and the segregation of restrooms, restaurants, swimming pools, libraries, and drinking fountains, the redlining of housing, then police brutality and mass incarceration—we are nevertheless exonerated because we watched this film and cared about these two boys' futures, delighting in their basketball skills and feeling compassion for their mothers . . . for three hours of our valuable time. The appeal for empathy is intense. But should watching *Hoop Dreams* absolve us from our political inaction? Are we active enough in our political lives to support and protect these mothers and their sons? Not yet, for sure.

Hoop Dreams offers intensely competitive basketball, famous people, dramatic pleasure (will either one or both make it to the NBA?), and a front row seat to observe the abject, the cast-off, the unwanted, the miserable in excruciating detail. Could you call this pornography? I do.

The film lacks the will to address the problems of African American inner-city life or the guts to speak about a complex issue with any rigor. That cowardice cloaks the racialized economic/social problems of the inner-city with "hoop dreams" and produces nothing for its audience but the pleasure of being transported via an exciting, safety-belted ride through Black Southside Chicago. These well-meaning Kartemquin filmmakers have the right to make any film they want, and we have the right to see past it, find it lacking and irresponsible—part of a dreaming world and not a real world.

The primary action of the conventional documentary is seduction. It asks you to go there to that landscape and, once fascinated with what you find there, to keep watching, anxious for more, and finally find some kind of resolution of the problems presented. The doc asks you to enjoy, weep, celebrate, have pity, gasp, perhaps dread, and finally be released from care when the credits roll and you can go back home and go to bed. Instead, documentary film ought to *decolonize* us, help us to become a more responsible, aware, self-conscious audience, capable of thought and action.

> JG: I'VE READ RECENTLY THAT, BY THE TIME THEY'RE IN FOURTH GRADE, children growing up in low-income communities are already three grade levels behind their peers in high-income communities. About 50 percent of students in low-income communities will not graduate from high school by the time they're eighteen years old. Those who do graduate will perform on average at an eighth-grade level. What does *Hoop Dreams* say to that?

My friend Ava Tomasula y Garcia, a labor organizer in Chicago's working-class and immigrant neighborhoods, always asks herself, "Who would this person be, if not for . . . If this person were not 'illegal,' who would they be? If this person were not incarcerated, who would they be? If this person were not standing in an unheated warehouse, folding cardboard pizza boxes for twelve hours at a time, who would they be? If this person were not fighting for fifteen years of stolen wages, scraping by on lousy pay, with a dread of termination should any complaint be raised."[14]

A conventional documentary never asks questions like these. Rather, it actively limits the possibilities of its viewers' conclusions—and their imaginations. We need forms of nonfiction that rupture the fixed identity politics that blind us and spark the kind of intellectual and ethical understanding that compels one to take responsibility, that compels one to act.

A useful film should confront what the cartoonist and graphic novelist Art Spiegelman once described as our particular, peculiar *social imaginaire*: He wrote, "We Americans, poor fish, have a perpetually recurring case of amnesia, trying to wriggle off the hook when it comes to facing our history as a Rapacious Capitalist Empire. We prefer to think of ourselves as wide-eyed innocents with perpetually renewing hymens."[15]

The conventional documentary-as-we-know-it facilitates the hymen-renewing process, or, at the least, it's the Vaseline. It weakens the political imagination of both maker and spectator, making it virtually impossible to speak of or listen to useful ideas. Watching a documentary is like being in a chauffeured car where nothing—not even driving—is required of you. You just sit back, relax, and enjoy the ride, knowing that by the end of the film your attention will be rewarded by a new, informed, caring sense of self.

Gertrude Stein once said, "I am I because my little dog knows me."[16] I say that we are ourselves because the cinema knows us—and produces us. The conventional documentary, in particular, *knows us* by imagining and projecting our values, our cares, our sense of community, our citizenship, our righteousness. It creates our identities in crude, familiar dreams of self, and we've grown comfortable wearing those toxic skins.

I've lost track of the author of this sentence, but offer it here as I could not say it better, or quicker: "Actually traditional documentaries are exploiters of the truth, operating in the rhetorical medium of 'common sense' . . . making judgments that it suggests are shared by an entire class, an entire nation or the entire human race . . . without reflection." "Without reflection" says it all.

THE IMPERIALISM OF THE REAL

In his book *Culture and Imperialism*, Edward Said argued that it is the job of the *artist-in-exile* to undo the substrate of ideological exceptionalism that undergirds U.S. imperialism. Said contends that

> "imperial power is constructed on a bedrock not only of force but of culture as well. Culture provides the crucial underpinning, justification and validation of empire. . . . The U.S. carries out its imperial policies behind the facade of democracy and freedom. Culture and politics produce a system of control that includes a hierarchy of representations and images that dominate the imaginations of both the oppressor and the oppressed."[17]

Most conventional documentaries produce a common mindset, an egotism that eternally places the citizen/viewer at the center of the universe, looking out into the represented world, discovering the problems

22   Abandon the Conventional Documentary

of other peoples. It's a kind of cultural imperialism, as if our new knowledge exempts us from having had any part of the damage we find there. The documentary's primary mode—a description of them, there, and then—leaves us exempt from criticism and, of course, from action. Unreceptive to interrogation, the documentary cannot tolerate new ideas or fill the baffling silences we may find. Instead, imperialism proceeds apace. (Between 1950 and 2000, the U.S. government has overthrown sixty democratically elected governments, dropped bombs on over thirty nations, and attempted the assassination of over sixty foreign leaders. Millions have died in undeclared wars. One out of five U.S. children doesn't get enough food to eat.)

> CARL SAGAN, the American astronomer, astrophysicist, and science communicator, has said, "For me, the most ironic token of [the first human moon landing] is the plaque signed by President Richard M. Nixon that Apollo 11 took to the moon. It read, "We came in peace for all Mankind." As the United States was dropping seven and a half megatons of conventional explosives on small nations in Southeast Asia, we congratulated ourselves on our humanity. We would harm no one on a lifeless rock.[18]

One might wonder how neoliberal capitalism can produce and circulate (and honor with an Academy Award for Best Documentary Feature), a film like Errol Morris's *The Fog of War: Eleven Lessons from the Life of Robert S. McNamara* (2003). The film serves as a deferential platform for Robert McNamara, the United States secretary of defense from 1961 to 1968 and chief architect of the U.S. war in Vietnam. It offers him an opportunity to personalize his own battered revisionist history of that war. It clearly identifies the war crimes McNamara orchestrated, but never mentions his complete underestimation of the Vietnamese intense and unwavering will for national liberation, which accounts for the U.S. defeat after ten long years of fighting and bombing. Perhaps unwittingly, it functions as an attempt to end our *Vietnam Syndrome*, to explain away the first U.S. war that ended in complete defeat and killed more than fifty-eight thousand U.S. soldiers.

VIETNAM SYNDROME RATIONALE: the North Vietnamese were well versed in guerrilla warfare, sabotage, atypical and asymmetric battlefield moves, infiltration, etc., but their unsustainable casualty count would not have survived a protracted engagement in the absence of major American political interference and Communist-funded antiwar propaganda in the United States, which eroded popular support for the conflict.

The Fog of War is a distracting, imperfect attempt to soften the blow of that defeat in Vietnam, while arousing our curiosity and sympathy for the man, Robert McNamara, who orchestrated and rationalized it. It elicits a kind of respect and understanding for this sad character. It restores America's best intentions and innocence—the narrative that the U.S. is a unique force for good in the world. McNamara, held harmless in this version of events, has become our wise teacher while U.S. imperialism and its current and future military adventures rush on.

I like Mark Fisher's term *capitalist realism* to describe our current political-economic-cultural situation. Capitalist realism expresses the impossibility of imagining an economic system different from what we have now, where it is impossible to imagine a coherent alternative. "In this world, where ultra-authoritarianism and capital are by no means incompatible, but an absurd and deadly concoction that persists, where internment camps and franchise coffee bars can co-exist . . . where only senseless hope makes sense, and where superstition and religion, the first resorts of the helpless, proliferate."[19]

CAPITALIST REALISM might be a most apt replacement for the word *documentary*, or documentary-as-we-know-it. Alas, most of these docs operate without any sense of a world after now . . . after the present. The embedded now/realism of these docs seems to make it impossible to project or struggle into a future

What can be done? To be what Said calls an *artist-in-exile*—an ethically grounded artist—is to refuse to use cinema to manage the world for the middle class, so that documentary consumers can sidestep their guilt and fear of the dark. Rather, I am proposing a nonfiction film that doesn't colonize its viewers by a specific kind of address and an unspoken appeal to their liberal class position. We need new original knowledge that will encourage the imagination, without which every attempt to change the world is doomed to failure. And we need inspiration.

Consider some of the following specific strategies to release the documentary-as-we-know-it's clutch on the nonfiction film.

For starters, never situate your viewer in the there/then of what is represented. Instead of putting us within it, put us *à côté de*, next to it, by examining its underpinnings, its ideological premises, its various representations. When we are not in it, but rather next to it, we can see its smooth conceits. Don't put us "there"—there in McNamara's mind or there in 1972 in Vietnam. If we are there, we are positioned to forgive McNamara's failures and to feel compassion for his sad dilemma.

In her article on *Las Hurdes* (also known as *Land Without Bread*), Vivian Sobchack quotes Luis Buñuel from a lecture at the University of Mexico:

> I will let Frederick Engels speak for me. He defines the function of the novelist (here read filmmaker) thus: The novelist will have acquitted himself honorably of the task when, by means of an accurate portrait of authentic social relationships, he will have destroyed the conventional idea of those relationships, shattered the optimism of the bourgeois world, and forced the reader to question the permanency of the prevailing order, even if the author does not offer us solutions, even if he does not clearly take sides.[20]

The useful postrealist film could help us break out of our imperialist chains. It could shatter *the optimism of the bourgeois world and force the reader to question the permanency of the prevailing order*. Sad to say, this useful film of yours probably won't get served up on Netflix, or any other profit-producing platform. It won't be nominated, most likely, for an Academy Award. Economic forces reward imperialistic documentaries that reinforce our economic system. Postrealist films undermine that system and thus are not welcomed into the celebrated fold.

Imagining how to break down that system through new forms of nonfiction film helps us to identify the *imperialism of the real*, expose its worldview, recognize its limits, and weaken its presence and power. How otherwise could films speak to us? There are other ways, and that's what this letter is about. A useful film must disrupt and destroy the "you" that the conventional documentary has nurtured for so long.

In 2002, I wrote in an article,

> The documentary filmmaker should always, somehow, as Buñuel did in *Land Without Bread*, be setting into operation a second track of meaning, a track about ourselves, so that we, watching the film, don't melt into pure disembodied spectators, spectators who seem to have no designs of our own upon the world, no personal interests, no class interests, no national interests. My own strategy for making the second track—and it means something different in every case—is to reframe the footage somehow. To reframe the footage means to renegotiate it, and in the renegotiating, to raise all possible questions about its representations.

2
Take Action—Make Useful Postrealist Films

Those who do not move, do not notice their chains.

▸ ROSA LUXEMBURG

Are there ways to avoid a potentially pornographic relationship in documentary film? Can films be provocative performing ideas, nothing less? (From here on I will refer to the conventional documentary, the "documentary-as-we-know-it," as the DAWKI, my five-letter abbreviation for describing the documentary as it has been practiced since Flaherty's 1922 *Nanook of the North* and John Grierson's 1929 *Drifters,* and is still practiced today—for example, in the eighteen-hour *The Vietnam War* (2017) by Ken Burns and Lynn Novick.

Instead of conventional realist documentaries, which could be referred to as landscape films, useful films might be something more like maps, postrealist maps. Maps don't suck you in, rather they configure the lay of the land. The map is analytical. It allows for and encourages examination, understanding, reason, and the possibility of action. A useful film—a film map, let's say—is always an invitation to rethink and rewrite personal, class, or national relationships. It opens up spaces and provides avenues to move forward. The film artist's vocation is to be the true chronicler of who we were and where we came from, making the invisible visible. In times of distress like ours, culture is not a luxury but a life raft.

Consider a new type of documentary filmmaking—not just antimimetic or antirealist, but blatantly interventionist and interactive. Consider the antiwar film *Winter Soldier* (1972), which chronicles what was spoken at a Detroit conference sponsored by the Vietnam Veterans Against the War in 1971. The film is a simple record of a conference that took place over a long three-day weekend, six months after news of the My Lai massacre of five hundred Vietnamese peasants became public. One hundred and fifty combat veterans gathered to testify about war crimes they themselves and others had committed in Vietnam. Their entire three-day testimony was recorded by a collective of more than twenty independent filmmakers, but the final edit is only ninety-three minutes long (figures 2.1–2.4).

FIGURES 2.1–2.4 *Winter Soldier*, Winterfilm Collective, 1972

Clearly, a selection was made of the most dramatic and painful testimony in order to show that U.S. policies in Vietnam led to gross violations of the terms of the Geneva Convention and that actions like the massacre in the hamlet of My Lai happened not once, but routinely. The soldiers speak of their suffering. And they continue to suffer for having testified to their crimes and to the crimes they witnessed.

Even the simplest documentary is shot, edited, and organized into the most persuasive text possible. *Winter Soldier* is the simplest film document I know—a record only of what was spoken there in that Detroit motel. Nevertheless, this "mirror held up to reality" is something more than a reflection. It is a text, an invitation to witness some very distraught and courageous veterans going on record about their killing of civilians and their children. They confessed to rape, mutilating bodies, throwing prisoners out of helicopters, of indiscriminate razing of villages. The veterans were testifying truthfully, and not without personal cost (figure 2.5). They were trying to stop a war.

FIGURE 2.5 *Winter Soldier,* Winterfilm Collective, 1977

30   Take Action—Make Useful Postrealist Films

> AN IMAGE HAS NO LIFE OF ITS OWN outside the institutions that exist to fix its meanings. Film does not exist as a neutral medium to convey messages which are independent; rather it finds its meanings in a series of social relationships that position producer and consumer so that only certain meanings are possible.[1]
> —JEAN-LUC GODARD

Winter Soldier is unforgettable, it's transfixing, and also pornographic. There's a thrill in discovering the worst and most heinous crimes committed by U.S. soldiers in Vietnam. We suck on these revelations. Perhaps, secretly, we are grateful that we weren't there to commit these crimes or to witness them. Somehow, through the film's address to us as moral, competent citizens, we are reassured that we would have resisted such tendencies. These courageous soldiers were the first to acknowledge such crimes in Vietnam. As witnesses to their testimony we might feel as though these crimes, now revealed, will never reoccur now that they have been told.

> POLITICALLY AMBITIOUS, THE FORMAL FILM seeks to divert our attention from the spectacles of transgression which the agencies of normalization routinely stage—spectacles who's intended effect is, in part, to render unspectacular, if not invisible, by contrast, the agencies responsible for staging them—and instead to dramatize the conventionally more discreet operations of the disciplinary mechanisms themselves.[2]
> —DAVID HALPERIN

As I write, I'm dreaming of a new postrealist film where veterans of the Iraq and Afghanistan wars (maybe members of Iraq Veterans Against the War and others) might reenact some of this 1971 *Winter Soldier* testimony. Perhaps we would watch them rehearsing. Perhaps they would fumble some words and start over again. This reenactment could implicitly speak to the unending cascade of U.S. wars and the commitment of these younger vets to continue in the *Winter Soldier* tradition. It could be called *Again, Winter Soldiers.*

It could ignite renewed interest in the 1971 film and suggest that there will be more war crime testimonials—and more, and still more. This would be a postrealist film, not dependent on the actual but on the urgent necessity of reenacting what was done and said in 1971.

WHAT'S IN THIS NAME *POSTREALISM*?

What is this postrealist film—sometimes referred to as formal film, or performative film—perhaps all inadequate names? I conjured up this postrealist term, suggesting "after realism," to identify films that strategically pop the lid on the conventional documentary by refusing to exploit the pedigree, the pornography, and the imperialism of the real. Instead, they have invented a radical new form to provoke new thinking and, on the strength of their filmmaking strategies, to probe and question.

Now I can define it further. The postrealist film is an antispectacular form that refuses documentary transparency, evidentiary arguments, classic narrative structure, psychological explanations, and the sympathetic identification systems that posit us/them symmetries. It might exploit any or all of these in a self-reflexive, traumatizing way to produce a critique of traditional filmic representational systems and structures and, through that critique, offer a previously unimaginable and radical experience. Most important, postrealism always addresses an audience that doesn't yet exist but that could be produced through understanding provided by the film's experience.

Experience—that's all that films have to offer. The crucial question: what kind of experience? The postrealist film comes in many forms, but always seeks to crack the code of the status quo, to drill even small holes in our social imaginaire, our naturalized worldview that suggests what is understood as normal, reasonable, commonsensical, and generally accepted by all.

To think better, to think for ourselves, to think beyond the social construction of our minds, is to resist the social imaginaire or what seems like common sense. Consider how the eighteenth-century Italian philosopher Giambattista Vico, defined it—judgment without reflection, shared by an entire class and an entire nation or the entire human race.³

> THE SOCIAL IMAGINAIRE is that set of values, institutions, laws, and symbols common to a particular social group and the corresponding society through which people imagine their social whole. The dimension through which human beings create their ways of living together and their ways of representing their collective life . . . an imagined political community or nationness.

You need the arts (literature, music, sculpture, painting, dance, and film) to say the subtlest things a mind can understand. This intelligence of the ineffable, the inexpressible, can be communicated through the arts in the most precise way. Nothing else can do that.

Sad to say, we live with too many images. Still images. Moving images. Images on our phones. Advertising images plastered everywhere in sight, most recently, and improbably, on the turnstile bars you have to push past to enter a New York subway station. The *New York Times* online cannot manage to post an article without a photo next to the headline, often a meaningless one that has little to do with the article. Russell Banks, in his book *The Lost Memory of Skin*, writes, "I have a 9-year-old grandson. He has no memory of life without it being located on the screen. It's frightening because it alters one's brain and whole perceptual apparatus of the world."⁴

In contrast, postrealist films are performative utterances, acts of resistance, and aesthetic rejoinders to a world drowning in its own image. To that end, they invite speculation on the properties and operations of the motion picture medium itself. Sometimes they operate irrationally or anarchically, but they always defamiliarize their subjects, invariably refusing the discourse that usually contains and limits them and continually opening possibilities of what could and what might be. Artists make the invisible visible, shattering the clichés and narratives used to mask reality. These antidocs are the heretical bad children of the family who will not stop pestering us to wake up. Just as important, they are generally witty, exuberant, despairing, engaged, and sometimes apocalyptic.

To give you an idea of how this works, let's begin with the following paragraph—the most profound and amusing antidocument I've ever read. It's from Jorge Luis Borges's story, "El idioma analítico de John Wilkins" (The analytical language of John Wilkins). Borges tells us: "In a certain Chinese Encyclopedia it is written that 'animals are divided into: a. belonging to the emperor, b. embalmed, c. tame, d. sucking pigs, e. sirens, f. fabulous, g. stray dogs, h. included in the present classification, i. frenzied, j. innumerable, k. drawn with a very fine camel's hair brush, l. et cetera, m. having just broken the water pitcher, n. that from a long way off look like flies.'"[5]

I'm pretty sure you're smiling at this fine takedown of the encyclopedia—purportedly the summation of all human knowledge. Borges completely bamboozles the encyclopedia entry, its factual claims, even the established hierarchical structures that constitute its basic foundations. He fools with it to the point of absurdity. The idea that anything can be divided into just so many units in just such a way is demolished, made ludicrous. *That from a long way off look like flies.* Ridiculous! Borges's Chinese Encyclopedia is a delicious text, poetic and transformative. It invites us to laugh at ourselves for the trust we have always offered this great book of knowledge.

> JG: WHEN I WAS GROWING UP IN THE FIFTIES, every middle-class family had on their bookshelves either *The World Book Encyclopedia* or, if they were wealthier, the *Encyclopedia Britannica*. That's where we went to prepare our school reports and gain knowledge of the world.

Can the artist-in-exile, in film, also speak about the world (perhaps as provocatively as Borges does) to an audience that has been made conscious of itself and its attachments? The tactics of Borges's encyclopedia entry could be transposed into a cinema that could scatter our presumed collective knowledge into self-consciousness by destroying the coherence of the political, economic, social, and military arrangements of our state. How should we go about this? Can we change the way images and sounds signify?

For the long view, here's my last and best argument for making useful postrealist films: as artistic productions, they last longer than DAWKIs and they keep on giving. Consider that Buñuel's 1933 film, *Land Without Bread*, still works for us eighty-six years later, as does Alain Resnais's 1956 film, *Night and Fog*, sixty-three years later. (I would never teach a course on nonfiction film without teaching both these films.) Useful films don't fall down the rabbit hole of the "now culture" the way that conventional documentaries do. Except for paintings and sculpture by famous artists and artifacts stolen from indigenous cultures now displayed in museums, and except perhaps for music, films last longer than anything and continue to teach us—maybe forever.

There are thousands of ways to make useful films—films that are formally unique, as good poems always are. Let's start with the idea of sincerity, a necessary state of mind for making useful film (in fact for any and all useful art practice). *Sincerity* as I am using it doesn't mean sober, humorless, or even spiritual. Sincerity describes a certain approach to the truth—candor—and a generous practice that could be sober or rollickingly humorous or terrifying or devastatingly beautiful. Susan Sontag reminds us that sincerity can turn a mere spectator into a witness, and that it is the heart rather than fancy rhetoric that can lead the mind to understanding.[6]

That is the heart of the matter: to produce a witness who can receive uncommon wisdom. The goal of the postrealist film is a witnessing at the highest level of perception.

Put your heart into it. Why are we are still listening to Satchmo sing "Dream a Little Dream of Me"? And Willie Nelson, Stevie Wonder, Smokey Robinson, and Aretha Franklin—they all sang with sincerity and heart. Listen to Ray Charles's "Sail Away." It's as patriotic a song as there ever was, made painful with an intelligent heart. Our films should have some sort of vibrating heart too . . . not heart through a sentimental haze, but heartful intelligence about the arrangements of our lives.

As art forms, postrealist films possess longevity due to a second strength: their potential to be ethical. I quote from Viet Thanh Nguyen's recent book, *Nothing Ever Dies: Vietnam and the Memory of War*.

Art is crucial to this ethical work of just memory. The writing, photography, film, memorials, and monuments that I include in this book are all forms of memory and of witnessing, sometimes of the intimate, the domestic, the ephemeral and the small, and sometimes of the historical, the public, the enduring, and the epochal.... Art is the artifact of the imagination, and the imagination is the best manifestation of immortality possessed by the human species, a collective tablet recording both human and inhuman deeds and desire.... I remain optimistic that in the centuries yet to come, what people will remember of this or any other war will most likely be a handful of outstanding works of art that resist power and war (as well as a history book or two).[7]

Viet Thanh Nguyen's text about a *just memory* reminds me of two outstanding and ethical films, full of heart: John Huston's 1945 documentary *The Battle of San Pietro*, the only one of the U.S. government-sponsored films about World War II that details the costs of war, and Stanley Kubrick's 1957 film *Paths of Glory*, about a French colonel in World War I who refuses to order his men to continue what would be a suicidal attack. The officer attempts to defend his soldiers against a charge of cowardice in a court-martial but fails. Three soldiers are executed. The corruption in the French high command is made appallingly visible. A film that does the same work in a different way is another film by Kubrick: *Dr. Strangelove, or How I Learned to Stop Worrying and Love the Bomb*. All three films, each in its own way, etch for us a just memory and will remain in our archive for at least another hundred years.

After World War II—after the horrors of the fire-bombed cities, the Nazi death camps, and the nuclear bombs dropped on Hiroshima and Nagasaki—some European philosophers and intellectuals argued that after that war, after all that, art would be impossible, even obscene. They argued that representation means making sense of things, and that making sense of things is impossible because World War II had destroyed sense, that the sophisticated culture and art of civilized Europe had produced only death, devastation, and obscenity. As Theodor Adorno offered in his famous dictum, "to write poetry after Auschwitz is barbaric."[8]

And here is a filmmaker, George Franju, whom I call the "mama" of the necessary postrealist film. (I call Luis Buñuel the "papa" for his *Land Without Bread*). Franju's film, *Blood of the Beasts* (1949), takes up the question of modernity and the systems that create comfort zones for the citizens of industrialized countries. Franju sensed that industrialized killing had now penetrated the nervous system and the culture not just of Germany but of France and other countries forced to cooperate with the Nazis during the war.

Franju worried that the industrialization, mass production, mass annihilation, and all the systems that had produced war would be forgotten and could come back again, worse than before, in spades. He feared that no one would see it coming.

Blood of the Beasts was made just four years after the end of World War II, when France was already rebuilding, already writing myths of national greatness, already complacent, and already forgetting, even after the Vichy police state deported 75,000 Jews to Nazi concentration camps, the infamous Vel' d'Hiv Roundup (code named "Operation Spring Breeze"), a Nazi operation in which the Vichy French government played a key collaborationist role in the internment and extermination of Europe's Jews. The raid began on July 16, 1942, when French police arrested and confined 13,152 Jews, including 4,051 children and 5,802 women, in the insufferable summer heat, virtually without food, water, or sanitary facilities at the Vélodrome d'Hiver, a bicycle velodrome and stadium. After five days the survivors were deported to Auschwitz.

The French were beginning to forget the discomforts and compromises of German occupation. Franju's film critiques the development of mid-twentieth-century modernity by demonstrating how efficiently butchers dismember horses, cows, and sheep in the slaughterhouses of Paris. He's speaking about killing-without-anger and takes us to the slaughterhouses to show us how it's done. And so we watch mass killing and dismembering and wonder what it has to do with us.

Franju refrains from confronting this problem directly. He treats the Paris slaughterhouses with great respect and without irony. He tells about the celebrated butcher who can split a cow in two during the twelve strokes of the noonday clock. He shows us the cysts on the butchers' hands. He notes that some butchers even sing opera when they work. Franju says, without any irony, don't fret—here's where it happens, quite out of sight, in serene, well-organized spots on the outskirts of Paris. Don't fret—here are the fine men and women who provide us our meat. Don't fret—here are some nice stories we can tell about how and what they do. He shows us the rows of calves' heads, how all parts are accounted for, how the refuse is made to disappear, how scraps of fat are carried off by Sisters of Charity to make candles. Neat, clean killing, not unlike the processing of prisoners at Auschwitz-Birkenau, Majdanek, Belzec, and Treblinka.

He is showing us, ever so discreetly, how killing has been sucked into the genes of the French working class so that they can purchase and eat pork chops with no thought of the killing of animals. It's a warning about who we have become and how modernity has turned us into unconscious accomplices to murder. The more Franju politely enumerates the skills of the butchers and the efficient order of the slaughterhouse, the more we are sucked into conflicted self-consciousness for our part in the destruction. We recognize modernity for what it is: a system that propagates structures of annihilation. See how what Art Spiegelman said about Americans fits here with the French and their pork chops, *We prefer to think of ourselves as wide-eyed innocents with perpetually renewing hymens.* Franju reminded the French of their "perpetually renewed hymens," and, as we watch his film today, of ours.

We need a new type of nonfiction cinema—not just antimimetic but overtly interventionist and interactive, like Franju's interactive *Blood of the Beasts*.

FOLLOW BUÑUEL—REFUSE THE CODES THAT ENCOURAGE USELESS EMPATHY

Study Buñuel's very useful film *Land Without Bread* (1933), also called *Las Hurdes*. Here, in perhaps the grandfather of all postrealist films (sometimes referred to as an ethnofiction), the anarchist/surrealist Buñuel takes us on a "touristic" excursion to some remote, impoverished villages in Spain. He combines the style of the travelogue film with geography lessons of the kind encyclopedias usually offer, but cut with dispassionately photographed illustrations of debasement, pierced by affectless, ironic narration. He shows us the mountainous area around the town of La Alberca, various local customs, and the intense poverty of its occupants, who are so poor in land that bread is literally unknown. He says: "Though the Spaniards as a race are naturally given to song, never once did we hear anyone singing in these dreary streets. Occasionally we came across a wretched little stream, trickling through the village. In summer this is the only water available, and men and beasts make common use of it."[9]

I refer to *Land Without Bread* as the grandfather of the postrealist film because it scorns those DAWKI films so anxious to amplify in ourselves our investments in our self-centered viewer selves. Buñuel fractures and deflates that self-centered reception, that desire to travel to remote places and meet interesting people, by a series of puns and quips delivered with a straight ethnographic face for experience-hungry viewers.

These are the Hurdanos, Buñuel tells us in a voice-over. "One eats goat meat only when one of the animals is killed accidentally. This happens sometimes when the hills are steep and there are loose stones on the footpath."[10] We watch Buñuel's perfectly constructed, three-shot sequence of a mountain goat slipping off a high ledge and plunging to his death (figures 2.6–2.8). The improbably dramatic second shot is directly above the animal falling to the rocks below, and the third a wide shot of the goat in helpless flight to its doom.

It's obvious to the audience that the goat was pushed off the ledge by the film crew, perhaps so that the villagers would have a rare meal of meat that evening, but more likely so that Buñuel could

FIGURES 2.6–2.8 *Las Hurdes (Land Without Bread)*, Luis Buñuel, 1933

produce his absurdly improbable sequence . . . intentionally giving his hand away. Besides a potential meal, the displays of the Hurdanos impoverishment—for instance, their dependence on the "accidents" of falling animals—is etched in unacknowledged irony.

Occasionally, the Catholic Church and the town's feudal history are noted, but even these are suggested as strange and curious cultural details. Buñuel tells us that only one priest and one toad live nearby in an otherwise abandoned monastery, a monastery with eighteen chapels. We watch young children in school (Catholic, of course) learn the lesson of ownership. From an illustration of an aristocratic colonial lady pasted up on the blackboard, the children copy into their notebooks, "Respect the property of others," an absurd command to the impoverished children who live in a *Land Without Bread*.

> There are shots where the realism is intentionally given a touch of the tragic, romantic and melodious music, and a commentary terser than a chemistry lecture. This aesthetic approach lends the whole reportage an air of fantasy.[11]
> —FREDDY BAUCHE

The key here is the tension between this "air of fantasy touched with a touch of the tragic" and the terse, straight facts of the Hurdanos's miserable circumstances. The film's touristic distance from the Hurdanos makes our classic empathetic relationship to the impoverished inaccessible. In *Land Without Bread*, Buñuel practices the aesthetic of *denial*. He withholds from the audience everything it has learned to expect from documentary cinema—the thrill of leaving one's body and going elsewhere to see and understand, without self-consciousness, how things work there. In conventional documentaries, everything is delivered clearly and simply to the eye, the ear, and the brain, and there is no work to be done. The classic ethnographic cinema of poverty, and our practiced empathic relationship to it, has been cartooned and drastically lampooned as well.

We do not recognize ourselves in the face of this film. His arch *Ripley's Believe It or Not* style of narration seems vaguely condescending to the Hurdanos, almost as if they are a big sad joke, a surrealist comedy. We'd like to separate from our guide, but we can't. Buñuel keeps thrusting us forward, and we have to follow in his steps.

The critic Dominique Russell calls it

> a documentary that posits the impossibility of the documentary, placing the viewer in the uneasy situation of complicity with a cruel camera probing the miseries of the Hurdanos for our benefit. These miseries are piled on in what Ado Kyrou termed a "yes but" structure that is desolate and grotesque ("When a viper bites them, the bite itself is rarely fatal, but in trying to cure it with herbs, they infect the wound and die.") The tension between image and sound is brilliantly exploited to undermine the very authority posited by the documentary genre.[12]

Buñuel has written: "The goal of surrealism is liberation . . . to shock you out of your bourgeois optimism."[13] Study *Land Without Bread* to see if eighty-six years later it still compels his audience to doubt the permanency of the prevailing order.

POETRY—A "BEST PRACTICE" FOR THE NONFICTION FILMMAKER

Something should happen to you when you watch a nonfiction film. Something should change . . . your capacity for analysis and understanding should grow, and ideally, your capacity and desire for action. In his book *Attack of the Difficult Poems*, Charles Bernstein tells it like this: poetry's not about what it says but what it does.[14] With this in mind, think about what a film can do. Consider the following excerpt from the fifteenth-century Indian mystic poet/saint Kabir translated by Robert Bly. See what the poetry offers, what it does.

> The purpose of labor is to learn;
> when you know it, the labor is over.
> The apple blossom exists to create fruit; when that comes,
>   the petal falls.
> The musk is inside the deer, but the deer does not look for it:
> it wanders around looking for grass.[15]

In simple, quiet language, with examples from nature, it teaches us escape from compulsive activity, to let go of labor when it has been completed. It teaches us how to rest when our work is done, and then to wander around looking for food to nourish ourselves.

Good poetry can rewrite and rewire aspects of the human mind in an instant, and we should learn a few filmmaking things from it. As it's said, poetry makes nothing happen, instead it changes its reader and then something might happen. That's what the postrealist film can do . . . make nothing happen but change the viewer and her understanding of the vectors of her social and political world. Then something might happen.

The poem itself must, at all points, be a high energy-construct and, at all points, an energy-discharge. Poetry says what can't be said otherwise or what never could be said before. In doing so, it can awaken our mind to new understanding.

Consider this poem, a response to Eddie Adams's AP photo, *Saigon Execution*, of police chief Major General Nguyễn Ngọc Loan shooting a Viet Cong prisoner, Nguyen Van Lem, on a Saigon street, February 1, 1968 (figure 2.9).[16]

FIGURES 2.9 Eddie Adams for AP, *Saigon Execution*: police chief Major General Nguyễn Ngọc Loan shooting a Viet Cong prisoner, Nguyen Van Lem, on a Saigon street, February 1, 1968

Witness to Murder, Alden Nowlan

The cameraman must be running backwards
in front of the soldiers and their prisoner
who wears black shorts and a sportshirt
imprinted with sunflowers and daisies
and has sandals on his feet
and does not look as if he understands
that he is about to die.
But we know
he would not be there on the screen
unless something horrible
were in store for him.
And I hear myself talking
to his picture, as I haven't talked
to a picture since I was ten:
There's a chance you'll make it.
Grab for a gun, maybe you'll take
one of the bastards with you.
But he can't hear me.
He keeps on walking.[17]

The poet adopts the position of the photographer, walking backward in dread, anticipating the action, and talking to the man in the sportshirt and sandals. We get it. we've been there, helpless in the face of violence. We hear it in ourselves. But the photo is numb, static, and irreversible. We experience our desperation, our powerlessness. The poem is powerful, and we're stuck in it.

Like poetry, useful films can create a paradigm crisis so that we are temporarily unmoored or released from the social imaginaire, then reanimated with a refreshed, active, self-aware intelligence. A useful film gets us thinking, and without thinking there is no moral imagination. Thinking isn't about mastery, control, or rationalization. Thinking is a way of being, and that's what useful films try to achieve: an expanded way of being in the world, in dialogue with the world. Not film as politics, but politics as vision. It's the vision button that "Witness to Murder" starts to provoke, a poem where you experience walking backward with your mind, trying to refuse what you know will come.

We look at things all the time but often fail to really see them. Poetry can convey information in a way that makes the reader rethink and reimagine what we look upon. Our job as filmmakers is to make viewers see something they've never seen before . . . to understand something anew. Each poem makes up its own rules . . . you'll see how in the poems that follow here. Poetry is the most *anarchic* form of art—it's *self-governing* and *decentralizing*—and you will need skills just like these poets to make a postrealist film.

In the toolkit, there's an item called "Teach Yourself Poetry," where I encourage poetry writing as a tool to loosen your mind and help you think creatively about what's possible in the nonfiction film you may be contemplating. Start by writing poems about some of the films described in this book, then about the subject of your next film. Then plan your film.

Notice how your filmmaking could borrow from poetry's jousting with the rules of grammar and spelling—by its leaps—horizontal and vertical—by its repetitions, by its punctuation, and more. How useful poetry is for evading the traps of conventional documentary thinking. Poetry isn't the only tool for loosening up your nonfiction thinking. There are other liberating techniques as well: playing with images, making collages, or by attending to lyrics and their relation to the music that accompanies them. Try them all.

Here's one postrealist, poetic film technique, a very useful film "map"—Harun Farocki's twenty-two-minute *Inextinguishable Fire* (1969). The film outlines Dow Chemical's development and production of napalm B—an incendiary bomb and agent of terror dropped on Vietnamese villages to destroy their crops and drive rice farmers off their land and into the safekeeping of the U.S. military's "protective strategic hamlets." Napalm was designed to expose the Viet Cong insurgents left standing in an open field, visible and ripe for destruction. As commissioned by the Department of Defense for the Vietnam war, Dow Chemical developed and produced an improved napalm, napalm B, which is literally inextinguishable. It can't be rubbed or washed off skin, snuffed out, or extinguished. Dropped on humans, it burns through flesh down to the bone.

In Farocki's film about Dow Chemical's development of napalm B, there are no confrontations with Dow personnel in the company parking lot in Midland, Michigan. There is no footage of the catastrophic and lethal effects of napalm B on humans and vegetable life. Everything is a substitution. A dead lab rat, doused in kerosene, is set on fire in a high school chemistry lab. As the rat ignites, this voice-over: "Napalm burns at 3,000 degrees. The slightest drop burns half an hour. It sets free poisonous gases which attack human respiration and drive people from their shelters. Within 80 meters, survival is impossible."[18]

At Dow, no one but the CEO and the project director knew they were making napalm B, a better napalm. For instance, a new plastic substance, being developed for rubber soles of shoes, turned out to be the ingredient that would make napalm B stick to human skin. Another department figured out how to make the improved napalm float on water. The project director put all these building blocks together and created the "better" napalm. The building block concept offers a perfect analysis of modernism/industrialization, which, since the Enlightenment, is the way of "progress" without knowledge.

Farocki's film flattens out the development of napalm B at Dow with emphatically uninflected performances. He performs "weak" models of tests in high school chemistry labs and barely adequate representations of corporate conference rooms. These techniques reduce Dow Chemical's production process to its essential activities: meetings, tests and test results, and models of deployment.

Farocki's reconstructions—for instance, the dialogue between the project director and the CEO—are not presented as actual dialogue but rather as the essence of a kind of professional language designed to mask the actual lethal substances at hand.

> The DOW CEO to the Project Director:
> CEO DOAN: A new order from the State Department concerning fire producing weapons, re-bombs, and flame throwers.
> CEO reads from papers on desk: A scenario is included with descriptions of situations which require production of specific weapons for battle.

PROJECT DIRECTOR: Mr. Doan, you know I'm not in favor of the war in Vietnam, but I'll do anything I can to end it quickly.
CEO DOAN: The technology of our firm is at your disposal.
They stand and shake hands. The Project Director leaves.[19]

Farocki's performers (I call them "stand-ins") use flat, affectless speech. The stand-ins work the same way puppets do in a puppet theater. We, the audience, lean in and commit to the act of imagining the performance of the actual Dow staff and the fact-based language of the Dow factory.

At the beginning of the film, Farocki, on camera and seated at a small table, speaks to camera:

> How can we show you napalm in action? And how can we show you the damage caused by napalm? If we show you pictures of napalm damage, you'll close your eyes. First, you'll close your eyes to the pictures; then you'll close your eyes to the memory; then you'll close your eyes to the facts; then you'll close your eyes to the connections between them. If we show you a person with napalm burns, we'll hurt your feelings. If we hurt your feelings, you'll feel as if we've tried out napalm on you, at your expense. We can give you only a weak demonstration of how napalm works.[20]

The camera dollies in to Farocki's left hand, resting on the table. With his right hand, he reaches off-screen for a burning cigarette and then presses the cigarette into the back of his left arm, midway between the wrist and elbow. The critic Franziska Buch writes, "The heat which comes from napalm becomes representable, thus imaginable, through something much weaker, which the filmmaker abruptly and unexpectedly puts in front of the camera—a burning cigarette."[21]

VO NARRATOR: A cigarette burns at 400 degrees. Napalm burns at 3,000 degrees.

Suddenly there's a cut to a medium close-up of a dead laboratory rat. A Bunsen burner enters from frame left, a flame appears (figure 2.10); then, with a *poof*, the dead lab rat is engulfed in flames.[22]

46   Take Action—Make Useful Postrealist Films

FIGURE 2.10 *What Farocki Taught*, Jill Godmilow (1998), a replica of Harun Farocki's film *Inextinguishable Fire*, 1969

The dead lab rat clearly feels no pain, but the audience flinches. Again, a weak model stands in for the horror of famous photograph of the naked napalmed Vietnamese girl on the road—the one in our minds. The gap between the two is where the experience lies. Napalm is made actual, and, for once, we are given agency in the face of atrocity, and with that comes the ability to step away from the system that creates napalm and, by extension, killer drones, smart nuclear bombs, and the like. Farocki short-circuits empathy and emotional catharsis and compels objective, accurate observation of mundane routine evil. The film suggests what we need to know about how our labor can be organized by corporate institutional practices and also what products eventually might be extracted from it, perhaps without our knowledge.

Conventional docs hand you an answer key with your quiz. They tell you whom to hate, love, or mourn. Farocki isn't a such a lazy educator. He makes you, the viewer, consider how society might be so broken as to create such evil. The lack of "the actual" creates an essential space for connection and reflection. *Inextinguishable Fire* exposes our complicity as individuals participating in an economic and social community that scorches the earth and its people.

As Farocki tells it in the film, "Because of increased division of labor, many scientists and technicians are no longer aware that they're producing instruments of death. In view of crimes in Vietnam, they feel like observers."

Just as when we read a poem we are engaged with language that is being used most skillfully to express powerful ideas and possibly new unimaginable experience. Reading a poem is a creative act. Watching this Farocki's film is as well. We're expertly wound into that experience and somehow absorb, then become what we behold. Farocki's underrepresentations of corporate conversations and lab demonstrations produce a profound new understanding of how war is produced in a capitalist economy. His strategies might seem cold and purely informational, but it's the stringent stripping away of everything except that coldness that leaves one in a transformed state, aware of our unwitting participation in the war-making of the state. Farocki does this without finger pointing, without anger, and, most important, without the "pornography of the real."

Ultimately, the task of Farocki's films is didactic: his films are conceived and produced for an audience open to learning how see and understand images. They are, so to speak, a form of training the viewer's eye and mind in the lifecycles of images.

As Rosa Luxemburg said, "The most revolutionary thing one can do is always to proclaim loudly what is happening."[23] That's what Farocki's film does. It is the only film I know about the Vietnam War that speaks not about "what happened" but rather about "what was done."

I saw this 1969 film, *Inextinguishable Fire* in 1991. The filmmaker, Harun Farocki, was at the screening. I was stunned by it. I wanted to do something with it, make a film about it. I asked him if he would meet me for breakfast the next day. He came. I gave him a dollar, and he signed a piece of paper that said I could use some of his film in one of mine. Later, I had the idea to make a perfect replica of his film because I wanted everyone to see it but didn't want to become the American distributor. It took six years to find the funding. I made it with an all student crew at the University of Notre Dame, where I had gone to teach.

I made an exact replica of Farocki's film, in English and in color, twenty-nine years after his film first appeared in Germany and twenty-three years after the end of the Vietnam War. Why? At the time Farocki's films were unknown in the U.S., and I thought they should be because they proposed entirely new forms of nonfiction filmmaking. So, I replicated *Inextinguishable Fire*, in order to circulate it as a possible model for postrealist film. I called it *What Farocki Taught*. At the end of my replica, in a short on-camera interview, a student asks, "What do you call your film?" First, I joke. "Let's see. I could call it . . . a sequel . . . a remake . . . a reissue . . . an American adaptation . . . (then laughing) the Thirtieth Anniversary Special Edition." Then I say, truthfully, "We could call it maybe "agit-prop." It seeks to agitate, to stir things up, and then propagate . . . to plant some new seeds. I spell out A-G-I-T-P-R-O-P. "Well, agitprop in the way Lenin meant it—to keep stirring the pot, to keep the issues from going dead and then, yes, to renegotiate the terms of the discussion and redirect them toward the cold facts of hard reality."

What made me take such a radical action—replicating someone else's film? For starters, to recycle it, or you could say, to *redistribute* it. And

- to study it myself, to learn how to make films this way;
- to reiterate Farocki's analysis of who makes war and how to stop one;
- to not let "mourning" Vietnam go on and on and on—instead to look it in the eye, in the clear light of morning;
- to make a literal reinscription of a hidden page from recent film history and thus to make film history useful;
- to get film people to ask, "who is this Farocki and what did he teach," betting that the travesty of my replica would attract attention to his other films (I consider Farocki the most important nonfiction filmmaker in the twentieth century);
- just to see what would happen.

What was so radically new and important about Farocki's *Inextinguishable Fire*? In no particular order:

Farocki's film employs logic over morality, or empathy, or psychology. It's simply a useful explanation of how things happen, what happens to our labor, and what kind of language is used to rationalize it.

The film's international utopian address—the Germans were not responsible for our Vietnam tragedy of napalm, Agent Orange, and all the rest.

His refusal to subscribe to the myth of unintelligibility—napalm *can* be explained.

He offers no absolution. There's no place in the film to weep.

His discussion of state terror (a horrorshow) without the use of violence—avoidance of "pornography of the real. Here we cannot weep for the small girl walking down the road on fire with napalm.

His film is uncontaminated by identification systems. His refusal of the "us" and "them" construction. The Dow chemists are us and we are them.

His dirt-cheap filmmaking. His budget: 5,000 Euros . . . back then about $5,000.

His avoidance of ethical issues with social actors. These are the filmmaker's friends . . . stand-ins for the imaginary Dow chemists.

His address to self-conscious individuals, not communities.

I was also inspired by J. M. Coetzee's 1986 article, "Into the Dark Chamber: The Writer and the South African State." Coetzee speaks of novelists in South Africa being "drawn to the torture room" in search of "novelistic fantasy." He says,

> Yet there is something tawdry about following the state in this way, making its vile mysteries the occasion of fantasy. For the writer, the deeper problem is not to allow himself to be impaled on the dilemma proposed by the state, namely, either to ignore its obscenities or else to produce representations of them. The true challenge is: how not to play the game by the rules of the state, how to establish one's own authority, how to imagine torture and death on one's own terms.[24]

This is what *Inextinguishable Fire* does . . . it ignores the obscenities of the Department of Defense and Dow and establishes its own authority. What I learned from Farocki and Coetzee became foundational to my understanding of what the postrealist nonfiction film can do— literally, "to imagine torture and death on one's own terms."

Learn from Farocki. Divorce nonfiction cinema from realist representation. Do without the pedigree and the pornography of the real.

Do without a confrontation with the real Dow CEO, Mr. Doan, as he exits his car in Dow's parking lot. Do without those photographic "proofs," like the naked napalmed girl running down the road, on fire.

From an editorial on Farocki when he died in 2014, by Julieta Aranda, Brian Kuan Wood, and Anton Vidokle:

> Farocki's films lead us to think that the real brutality of power that uses advanced forms of technology, transmission, and mediation goes far beyond the application of physical violence on human bodies, and towards something much more delicate, much more refined. Its real violence arrives in something like boredom, in rendering the actual functioning of power as boring—uninteresting and technical on the surface, but eventually and ultimately authoritarian in its inaccessibility. It is from this point that Farocki's mastery begins by identifying cinema as a historical meeting point between technology and seduction. Cinema has always been the name of the machine for merging warfare and entertainment, propaganda and pornography.[25]

Enjoy and learn from this poem. In terms of method, the French poet Charles Baudelaire recommends:

Intoxication

One must be forever drunken: that is the sole question of importance. If you would not feel the horrible burden of Time that bruises your shoulders and bends you to the earth, you must be drunken without cease. But how? With wine, with poetry, with virtue, with what you please. But be drunken. And if sometimes, on the steps of a palace, on the green grass by a moat, or in the dull loneliness of your chamber, you should waken up, your intoxication already lessened or gone, ask of the wind, of the wave, of the star, of the bird, of the timepiece; ask of all that flees, all that sighs, all that revolves, all that sings, all that speaks, ask of these the hour; and wind and wave and star and bird and timepiece will answer you: It is the hour to be drunken! Lest you be the martyred slaves of Time, intoxicate yourselves, be drunken without cease! With wine, with poetry, with virtue, or with what you will."[26]

Now that you are drunk on Baudelaire, consider these first four stanzas of the poem "The Desert Survival Series," a part of the *Transborder Immigrant Tool,* a GPS cellphone safety-net app for crossing the Mexico-U.S. border, developed by Electronic Disturbance Theater/b.a.n.g. lab in 2007 by artists Micha Cárdenas, Amy Sara Carroll, Ricardo Dominguez, Elle Mehrmand and Brett Stalbaum. These four poems were written by Amy Sara Carroll.[27]

1

The desert is an ecosystem with a logic of sustainability, of orientation, unique unto itself. For example, if the barrel cactus—known otherwise as the compass cactus—stockpiles moisture, it also affords direction. As clear as an arrow or a constellation, it leans south. Orient yourself by this mainstay or by flowering plants that, growing toward the sun, face south in the Northern Hemisphere.

2

Climb or walk in the morning. Rest midday beneath creosote bush or mesquite, insulating yourself from the superheated ground. Remember—even the sidewinder hovercrafts, the bulk of its body above the scalding sand as it leaves its trademark J-shaped tracks across the desert dunes.

3

Just before sunrise, Bedouins turned over half-buried stones in the desert to catch the dew that the night's coolness had condensed on the stones' surfaces. Indigenous travelers in the Mexican-U.S. corridor searched the broad leaves of yucca and agave. Rainwater collected at each plant's base—the leaves' apex—remaining there up to a few days after a summer or winter shower. Proceed from the simple premise: The desert caches water in unlikely places that it resists divulging. Do not expend all your energies searching for its secret stashes, but likewise do not assume that its pockets of moisture are nonexistent. Restrict your water reconnaissance to early or late in the day when your liquid net-gain will outweigh the perspiration you expend. A thirst is seldom quenched; it morphs to reappear on the horizon. Meanwhile, the desert reflects the sun back like a mirror. You are caught in that pair's uneven, inconsummate exchange.

4

U.S. Marine Corps pilot Lieutenant Edwin Zolnier's plane crash-landed in the Sonoran Desert. Rescued five days later, Zolnier credited the barrel cactus with keeping him alive. Technically you can survive on moisture from select cacti, but you have to recognize the difference between the tenable and the untenable. Some cacti's sap and pulp are so toxic you will need to be hospitalized afterward if you drink or eat them. Other cacti won't kill you, but will leave you sick as a dog. Baseline rule: Only take the risk of eating or drinking cacti if the alternative you face is dying of thirst. Saguaro and organ poison. Punto. And, not all barrel cacti are created equal. To make matters worse, young saguaros easily could be mistaken for barrels. So, don't just look for squat, rounded cacti; differentiate, think fishhook. J-shaped, outer "fishhook" spines, literally used by the Seri Indians for fishing, mark and distinguish the true rescue cactus from its peers. When you've found the right plant, cut off its top with a knife or sharp rock but, don't expect to find a font of liquid. Center yourself, cut out a chunk of the whitish inner pulp from the cactus' correspondent center. Chew it. Let the juice run down your throat. Spit out the pulp when you've sucked it dry. Don't swallow the pithy fiber. Rest, digest. (Exertion after eating could cause you to forfeit the little you gained in the process.) If the taste of the juice makes you gag, place the pulp in literal or makeshift shade (e.g., shield it for a short time with your body). Cooler by even a few degrees, its liquid still will taste super-concentrated, more "vegetal" than most vegetables palatable to human beings, but it might be easier to choke down.

A UTOPIA is an imagined community or society that possesses highly desirable or near perfect qualities for its citizens. Alas, utopia is uninhabitable. As soon as we reach it, it ceases to be utopian. But utopia is a useful incentive. It gives us agency to act.

This is a useful poem, and I would argue that it is a *utopian* one in that it projects us back onto ourselves as probable agents of our own salvation. There is no fraudulent intimacy, no pornography, only precise, useful instruction in poetic form. Here is information for survival that stimulates an act of imagination and a projected sense of self. Pay attention, center yourself, and learn, it says. We are encouraged by this poem that could lead us out of trouble, this connection to our capacity and intelligence.

I have been tempted many times to try to make a film of this poem, but I still have two films in the works and this long letter to finish. Maybe you could/would make the film? How would you do it? Let me know and I'll help.

If you haven't encountered it yet, here is Zoe Leonard's 1992, exquisitely useful utopian poem-artwork *I want a president* (figure 2.11).[28] Leonard moves us forward with this song:

> I want a dyke for president. I want a person with aids for president and I want a fag for vice president and I want someone with no health insurance and I want someone who grew up in a place where the earth is so saturated with toxic waste that they didn't have a choice about getting leukemia. I want a president that had an abortion at sixteen and I want a candidate who isn't the lesser of two evils and I want a president who lost their last lover to aids, who still sees that in their eyes every time they lay down torest, who held their lover in their arms and knew they were dying. I want a president with no airconditioning, a president who has stood on line at the clinic, at the dmv, at the welfare office and has been unemployed and layed off and sexually harrassed and gaybashed and deported. I want someone who has spent the night in the tombs and had a cross burned on their lawn and survived rape. I want someone who has been in love and been hurt, who respects sex, who has made mistakes and learned from them. I want a Black woman for president. I want someone with bad teeth and an attitude, someone who has eaten that nasty hospital food, someone who crossdresses and has done drugs and been in therapy. I want someone who has committed civil disobedience. And I want to know why this isn't possible. I want to know why we started learning somewhere down the line that a president is always a clown: always a john and never a hooker. Always a boss and never a worker, always a liar, always a thief and never caught.

FIGURE 2.11 Zoe Leonard, *I want a president*, 1992, typewritten text on paper; copyright © Zoe Leonard, courtesy of the artist, Galerie Gisela Capitain, Cologne and Hauser & Wirth

This poem shocks the social imaginaire out of its dormant condition by proposing who an experienced candidate for president of the United States might actually be—perhaps someone "who has made mistakes and learned from them" or "who lost their last lover to aids" or perhaps, simply, who is "not a clown." It stokes our ability to envision exactly what kind of experience would be useful if they wanted to govern all the people of this richest, most powerful, most severely divided country. Our electoral system is put to shame as we work to imagine and enjoy Leonard's unthinkable. As a poetry reader does with a poem, to have the viewer work with the filmmaker in the construction of the film—that is what's most important.

This poem engages not just our imagination but also our hope. This world suppresses hope, but it always flickers, like a candle flame, looking for more oxygen, or food. This is a good reason for your film to communicate, in any of a thousand ways, in whatever way you can, *we're not dead yet*. As Leonard's poem does, your film could articulate that which does not yet exist. Make a doc of the possible and keep intelligence and insight alive and open the door to hope. The critic and Marxist theorist Raymond Williams says, "to be truly radical is to make hope possible, rather than despair convincing."

> ART IS AN ACTION THAT TRANSFORMS OUR THOUGHTS. It is a process that turns nothing into something. As Confucius says in the analects, "Thought without action is laziness: action without thought is labor lost." One the one hand, if we merely think but take no action, there would be no progress. On the other hand, acting on thoughtless impulse is doomed to failure. The relationship between thought and action is the most important source of wisdom and joy. With both, the process of turning art into reality is the path to happiness. It's like a game. Only through this process can we understand who we are. So the game will continue.[29]
> —AI WEI WEI, filmmaker, poet, painter

To make a useful film, you will have to find a unique way to ask your questions and point to new answers; you will have to arouse commitment. To do this kind of work you must sing a gutsy, plucky, audacious, intrepid song, one that the documentaries on public television never sing. Postrealist films should be and can be the poetry of the nonfiction world.

In 1983, the feminist Andrea Dworkin gave a speech, a performed poem of sorts, at a Midwest Regional Conference of the National Organization for Changing Men titled "I Want a Twenty-Four-Hour-Truce During Which There Is No Rape."[30]

Just twenty-four hours? Not good enough, you think? Me too. My labor organizer friend, who told me about Dworkin's performance, wrote, "It's a manifesto; it's an essay; it's a demand that at first seems absurd. But then the absurdity crumbles and the paradigm crisis sets in."[31] You're radically unmoored from your social imaginaire. You think that's actually not a lot to ask. That is something that could happen, that needs to happen, that needs to happen all the time. Imagine our Congress passing a ban on rape for a measly twenty-four hours. What would happen? Ten thousand arrests in a day? What else is possible in a measly twenty-four hours? Just today, September 16, 2019, the news reports:

> A new study reveals that the first sexual experience for one out of every 16 women and girls in the U.S. is rape. Almost half of those surveyed said they were physically forced into the act, and over half said they were verbally pressured into sex against their will. The average age of the assaulted is 15. In the following years, the affected women had poorer mental and reproductive health outcomes, including more unwanted pregnancies and abortions."[32]

As poetry and performance can do, as Dworkin does, can the nonfiction film intervene in our *hegemonic* culture? Can it upend our dominant narrative, a triumphant story of American exceptionalism in which the actions of individual people matter less than the inexorable wave of human progress that has swept the country forward from the Declaration of Independence until now? Can the nonfiction film produce oppositional values? Basically, that's our job as filmmakers—to intervene in the hegemonic culture, to move our audiences out of the habit of hegemonic thinking. Ultimately, to spark our moral imagination.

> HEGEMONY: Capitalism maintains control not just through violence and political and economic coercion but also ideologically through a hegemonic culture in which the values of the bourgeoisie became the "common sense" values of all. Thus a consensus culture develops in which working-class people identify their own good with the good of the bourgeoisie, and help to maintain the status quo, rather than revolting. The state maintains hegemony in civil society by manufacturing consent. Consent is not the spontaneous outcome of free choice but must be manufactured. The power to manufacture consent isn't distributed equally— there is not a level playing field.[33]
> —ANTONIO GRAMSCI

3
Forty Postrealist Strategies to Learn from and Borrow

RESIST—AN ESSENTIAL POSTREALIST STANCE

The word *resist* comes from the Latin root *resistere*. It means to stand. My friends and fellow filmmakers Ernie Larsen and Sherry Millner offer this useful understanding of acts of resistance:

> In the English language, the term resistance is commonly used to describe the concerted acts of people who take a stand, often against great odds, against the powers that be.... Such acts of opposing power, as the root word confirms, do not initially imply active violence. To the contrary, it is clear that this (resistant) motion of standing up together does no more than block the continuation of force (such as the legitimated violence of the state, at whatever level). There is always an alternative to resistance: not standing up—staying supine, a suppliant, a doormat.[1]

JG: It would be wise to heed the words of a late science-fiction visionary, "We live in capitalism. Its power seems inescapable. So did the divine right of kings. Nay, human power can be resisted and changed by human beings. Resistance and change often begin in art, and very often in our art, the art of words."[2]
—Ursula K. Le Guin

Postrealist films are the cinema's resistance; they can block a forward flow or create an imaginative rupture wherein new intelligence can be received. They can create a cinema that breathes. Focus on the idea of play, which implies looseness, experimentation, chance, and a suspension of judgment in favor of open-ended curiosity. As Emily Dickinson wrote, "It's easy to work when the soul is at play."[3]

I'll lay out here many examples of useful films to study. You can devise your own way to upend classical systems of representation and replace them with your own designs. You will find your film when you abandon realism and remember that you are an ethical artist first.

Our corporate culture has offered us the language they want us to use, the DAWKI language we already know. You have to refuse it because it tells you your film must play by certain rules. The conventional documentary is subject to just as large a matrix of obligations as the commercial fiction film: to produce fascination with its materials, to entertain its audience, to achieve closure, to satisfy. But to make a useful film, we must refuse all that. How to begin? How do we make a useful film—*with fingernails* or *with claws?*

Make it like jazz: loosen it up, like Charlie Parker loosens up a ballad. Don't be wasting our time producing inauthentic memories of something, somewhere—memories that most likely could not be ours.

A prime example of what *not* to do is the Burns/Novick eighteen-hour PBS series, *The Vietnam War* (2017), which fabricates an inauthentic memory of that war that endangers any memory we might have of it, individually or collectively.

The series doesn't attempt to produce a sincere or *just memory*. Instead of investigating the lies and mistakes this tragic history could reveal, the series organizes the war into a tale, offering resolution and redemption through that most comfortable form of memory—a narrative. From the final voice-over, "The Vietnam War was a tragedy, immeasurable and irredeemable. But meaning can be found in the individual stories of those who lived through it: stories of courage and comradeship, and perseverance, of understanding and forgiveness and, ultimately, reconciliation."[4]

DOCUMENTARIES ARE MEMORIALS—ways of burning/burnishing people and problems: The memorial process is for the living rather than the dead. The monument not only commemorates but blocks the return of the dead—the stone is set over the grave to impede the corpse's resurrection.[5]
—ANNETTE MICHELSON

Burns/Novick speak of reconciliation, which is exactly what we don't need. What's required is not a conciliatory tale, but rather an examination of the ten years of black lies government leaders told us and themselves, which most U.S. citizens accepted for a very long time. The voice-over tells us that "meaning can be found in the individual stories." Perhaps, but not useful meaning. Instead, they are a distraction, offering us the pleasures of the narrative instead of an accounting of the scope of the destruction in Vietnam, Cambodia, and Laos. And, there is no adequate account of how this terrible debacle was finally stopped—by active-duty soldiers, by antiwar newspapers, by GI coffeehouses near military bases, and by years of protest, on college campuses and in massive mobilizations in every major city, and in smaller cities and towns across the U.S. and in England, France, Germany, Sweden, and in Vietnam itself.

You must make your film on your own terms. You must be impassioned by your strategy to provoke your audience to ask, who am I next to this? Who am I next to the Vietnam War? That's how you can offer *transformative* experience.

JG: AN EDITOR ASKED ME WHY I USE THE WORD *TRANSFORMATIVE* SPECIFICALLY in relation to film. Certainly there are books, poems, and other print and visual media that offer transformative experience, but cinema, a motion picture medium, produces concentrated experience, in time, with the audience present just then, in attention and open to the movement of ideas delivered by images and sound—an audience mind that is not released until the credits roll. A book is read over hours, a poem in just minutes, but nowhere is the audience's mind (the Buddhist say the mind is the sixth sense) captured, changed, and remembered as intensely as in the cinema and theater.

Defamiliarize the criminal, illegal, immoral Vietnam War. Don't normalize it; rather, make the familiar strange so that we can see it better—in stark relief. Put what you know in the now-time of a postrealist film. Give us a fresh perspective on things that matter, even small things, which often implicate big ones. (In the toolkit, there's an article, "A Brief Review of 2017 Burns/Novick PBS Series The Vietnam War" for a longer discussion of the film.)

Warning: so far there are no good distribution systems for these renegade, artist-in-exile postrealist films. Few people even know where to look for them, though there are resources like Canyon Cinema, Video Data Bank, and a few others where they can be found.

Swedish filmmaker Ingmar Bergman said, "I've thought a lot about when those feelings of fear and terror, nakedness and powerlessness come from, and I think it's because one perceives one's own work as incomplete and unprotected until it's surrounded by the consciousness of the audience."[6]

This filmmaker agrees. Who of you out there could produce a website where yours and others' useful films could regularly appear and be discussed? If that interests anyone out there, get in touch with me. Perhaps heartlessly, I recommend that these films stay out of "the private art gallery" where they often appear. Why should only art buyers and art browsers see your film? Get it into circulation for everybody to consider. The postrealist website awaits.

As I wrote earlier, there are thousands of escape hatches to get you out of the conventional documentary and as many doors to go through to make a useful film. Design your own hatch and walk through it. Unless you're hoping for a spot on of PBS's POV series, climb aboard.

Can the postrealist films be categorized/cataloged? Not really, but here are some of the things you can say about how any postrealist film breathes.

LOOSEN IT UP—UNSTICK IT. Think of Marcel Duchamp's urinal, titled "Fountain," submitted for an exhibition of the Society of Independent Artists under the name R. Mutt in 1917. "Whether Mr. Mutt with his own hands made the urinal has no importance. He took an ordinary article of life, placed it so that its useful

significance disappeared under the new title and point of view, and created a new thought for that object (figure 3.1).[7]
—Lewis Hyde

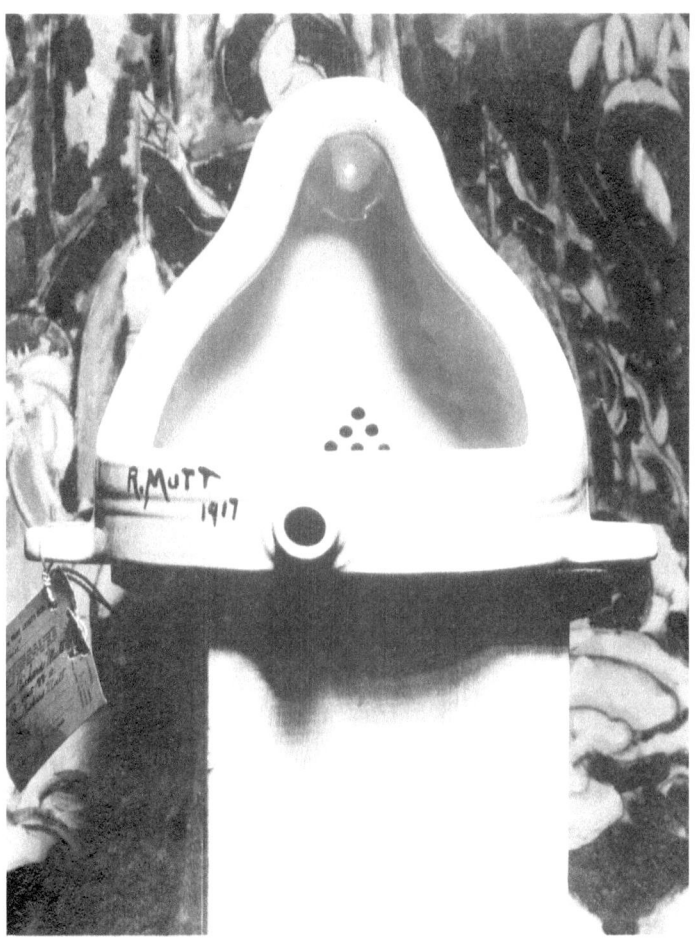

FIGURE 3.1 Marcel Duchamp's ready-made sculpture *Fountain*, photographed by Alfred Stieglitz at 291 Art Gallery following the 1917 Society of Independent Artists exhibit

THE AUTHOR OF THE FILM IS ALWAYS PRESENT, ONE WAY OR ANOTHER

Postrealist films always announce that they are written and designed by the filmmaker, that the ideas and insights are the filmmaker's and no one else's. Sometimes the artist addresses the audience directly in the film, on or off camera, or presents texts, as in Farocki's *Inextinguishable Fire*. Often the form or structure of the film tells us that it is authored.

Nothing happens in a postrealist film that is not imagined first. That's the filmmaker's job—to imagine something new and then try to open it up. How? One way is to identify and then try to solve an impossible problem.

DEFAMILIARIZE BY MAKING SUBSTITUTIONS—TRY RATS

Speaking of an impossible problem, watch Joyce Wieland's 1968 *Rat Life and Diet in North America*, a hilarious, acerbic observation of the dire and bewildered condition of U.S. draftees hoping to escape service in the Vietnam War. Speaking of candor, the film begins with the title card THIS FILM IS AGAINST THE CORPORATE MILITARY INDUSTRIAL STRUCTURE OF THE GLOBAL VILLAGE—an assertive, seemingly naive pronouncement, but ultimately a trustworthy one. The film recounts a hilarious, live-action saga of a group of wild rats (actually gerbils), frantic, childish, disorganized, and hungry, standing in for the young draftees scurrying for the Canadian border to escape the terror of conscription.

At first the rats are caged and hysterical, being terrorized and tormented by their prowling cat guards. Then another intertitle appears: THEY PLEAD FOR THEIR FREEDOM. More terror ensues and then another title card: AFTER TOO MUCH SUFFERING THEY DECIDE TO ESCAPE (figures 3.2–3.6).

Somehow, they do escape, and slip slowly northward toward refuge in Canada, eating everything they come across along the way.

The trip is nightmarish, the music mixed with silly scratching sounds and rat squeaks. But in Canada they find some flowers to eat

Forty Postrealist Strategies to Learn from and Borrow   63

FIGURES 3.2–3.6 *Rat Life and Diet*, Joyce Wieland, 1968

and some cherries, which they nibble furiously. Midway through their feast comes the intertitle SOME OF THE BRAVEST ARE LOST FOREVER.

Suddenly, the comedy of rodents standing in for teen-age boys collapses toward tragedy. Suddenly the stakes are profound. The desperate escape attempt, once trivialized, gains human depth, and the possibility of death or being captured and locked in a stockade for years is palpable. After gorging themselves at a banquet table in upstate New York, the rats are soon scurrying northward again. Now we are urgently hoping they make it across the border.

Another intertitle appears: THEY ESCAPE TO CANADA AND TAKE UP ORGANIC GARDENING, and they do. (Estimates are that sixty thousand to one hundred thousand drafted or draft-age young men left the U.S. during the war years, mainly for Canada or Sweden.) But Weiland, a Canadian, warns us: 72 PERCENT OF CANADA IS OWNED BY THE U.S. INDUSTRIAL COMPLEX. The Canadian National Anthem plays as we learn that the rats RAISE MORE GRASS THAN THEY CAN POSSIBLY USE. The rats then attend a Cherry Festival where they nibble away at a couple of dark red ones, followed by a Flower Ceremony in which the rats gobble up all the flowers. An intertitle appears: NO D.D.T. USED, and their journey continues.

As wacko as it might sound in my description, this is sincere and astute political filmmaking, a stunning dramatization of the desperate attempts of young men to avoid death or maiming in a strange jungle eight thousand miles from home. And as people who were around then may recall, organic gardening was part and parcel of the sixties dream of a peace-loving, antiwar countercultural life. Its mention in the film calls up the yearning for what arrival in Canada might bring—not just safety, but a new way of life.

Defamiliarizing the terrible stories of being an eighteen-year-old draftee in 1968, the contrast between the silly manic rats and the real escape fantasies of the draftees produces a profound awareness of the terrible costs of war. As the film draws to a close, this appears: AT THE MOMENT THE C.I.A. READS IN NEWSWEEK THAT CANADA IS 3 PERCENT COMMUNIST, and then the last title: THEY INVADE CANADA. Absurdly, the battle against the CIA is marked by just the sound effects of punches, grunts, howls, and body blows, and then the copyright title appears.

This film is part of you now. You've done all the work of imagining the terror and the draftees' desire for safety without footage of U.S. planes dropping five-hundred-pound bombs full of napalm on Vietnamese villages.

I don't think there's a more important film about the Vietnam War, or any war, for that matter. Watch it, maybe write a poem about it, then dream up your own postrealist strategies for your next film. Use cats? Kangaroos? Fish? Postrealist strategies and ethics—that's how you get a useful film.

DECONTEXTUALIZE

Postrealist films can take up old motion picture materials and show them in a new context or *map* them, so that we can see our prior investment in them from a distance. In 1976, the filmmaker Bruce Conner reassembled government footage of the first underwater atomic bomb test, conducted on Bikini Atoll on July 25, 1946. In *Crossroads*, he used twenty-three recorded documentations of the Bikini explosion at different distances and heights from air, sea, and land and added a complex, mesmerizing score by Patrick Gleeson and Terry Riley to produce the nuclear explosion as a kind of cosmic sublime. Each shot captures the moment the mushroom cloud erupts from the ocean, varying between a few seconds and about eight minutes in length. Is it gorgeous? Yes. Is it seductive? Yes. Can we understand the devotion of the scientific, political, and military communities to maintaining our nuclear arsenal through this sublime display? We are both stunned by the beauty of the explosion and aghast at what it portends.

Crossroads is a visionary utopian film. The mind is working all the time, our awareness shifts up and back from magnificent radiance to radiation death. *Crossroads* refuses the idea that war is utterly *abject*—so horrible and wretched—that it must be forgotten. Rather, it asks us to look at its beauty as well as its destruction and allows the viewer to comprehend the *rush* of the men who had their fingers on those triggers.

Understanding that sensation allows viewers to realize that the rush is the enemy. That's why many people would run from it or claim not to understand it. *Crossroads* and other utopian films are the liveliest and most useful. *Crossroads* will be playing on screens in a hundred years—if we are still around. This film was made in 1976, just fourteen years after President John F. Kennedy and Premier Nikita Khrushchev came close to igniting a nuclear war during the Cuban Missile Crisis, the nearest we've come to total world destruction. If Kennedy hadn't already developed a relationship with Khrushchev over the Berlin Wall Crisis, and if the two men had not trusted each other, I wouldn't be writing you this letter, and you wouldn't be reading it.

Some background: as of 2018, there have been more than one hundred nuclear close calls, fifty-seven of which occurred since the 1986 Chernobyl disaster in Ukraine. While Chernobyl is the most well-known, about 60 percent of all nuclear-related accidents have occurred in the U.S. Now, nuclear weapons have been institutionalized. They're part of the annual U.S. budget, rationalized under the rubric of "deterrence." The *Bulletin of Atomic Scientists* says that the U.S., Russia, and other nuclear states (France, China, the United Kingdom, and more) have brought us to one hundred seconds before midnight on the Doomsday Clock—that is, one hundred seconds until midnight and the destruction of the Earth and all living things by nuclear war. The question is posed.

Indulge me if I slide sideways to a contemporary irony. As Motoko Rich wrote on June 1, 2018, in the *New York Times*:

> The Americans and South Koreans want to persuade the North that continuing to funnel most of the country's resources into its military and nuclear programs shortchanges its citizens' economic well-being. At the time, the U.S. had just embarked on a trillion-dollar-plus upgrade of its already massive nuclear arsenal. Our government doesn't understand why the North Koreans are funneling money into their nuclear arsenal when their citizens are hungry, but multiple congresses and presidents have allocated at least a trillion dollars annually to the national security state and nuclear deterrence, even as our infrastructure sags and crumbles.[8]

In Lewis Carroll's *Through the Looking Glass*, to Alice's assertion that "one can't believe impossible things," the White Queen replies, "I daresay you haven't had much practice. When I was your age, I always did it for half an hour a day. Why, sometimes I've believed as many as six impossible things before breakfast."[9]

Daniel Ellsberg calls his 2017 book on our nuclear situation, *The Doomsday Machine: Confessions of a Nuclear War Planner*, a "chronicle of human madness." I sent him a copy of Conner's *Crossroads*. At only thirty-six minutes, this film should be required viewing for every U.S. administration and all its diplomats—that is, if they have a little time for cinema.

"PREPOSTURIZE" (THAT'S NOT A REAL WORD—I KNOW)

To *preposterize* is to take a preposterous position and play it to its limit, to its preposterous end. Along the way, expose the societal flaws that make a perfectly sensible act illogical, even preposterous. Then see what is possible.

Želimir Žilnik's *Black Film* (1971) is what I could call a *preposterized* documentary. We watch as Žilnik *preposterizes* the problem of "how to house the homeless" by outrageously inviting ten homeless men to bed down for the night in his own small apartment in Novi Sad, Serbia (figure 3.7). His wife and son accommodate the men as best they can, dragging mattresses around, etc., as the men offer comedic anecdotes about their homeless adventures: "I'm only staying two or three days, then I'll die like a dog." "It's boring. There are suicides. Guys hang themselves." "It's easy—take three prunes and put one in your hand, one in your mouth, one in your ass. Turn around . . ."

After the men have settled in, Žilnik takes his camera out into the streets to ask shopkeepers, workers, and average citizens how the homeless should be housed. One guy: "Notify the police, they should help find a place in prison." An official: "We have no jurisdiction." Another guy: "Find a hotel, or a youth center . . ." Another: "The fish market, where fruit sellers hang out?" No productive answers are forthcoming.

The problem—whatever can we do with these homeless people, a question people often ask with solemn headshaking but never really earnestly consider—is propelled into the absurd. *Black Film* has no answers, but by "preposterizing" the problem into his own living room,

FIGURE 3.7 *Black Film*, Želimir Žilnik, 1971

it asks us the questions about homelessness that everyone avoids—an issue we face only out on the street, but forget when we enter the safety of our cozy homes. Does one have to study the economic policies that produce homelessness to approach this problem? Why not just give the homeless a home in your home? An absurd but provocative proposition? Or is it common sense?

In 1987 Joel Bellman wrote in the *Los Angeles Herald-Examiner* about the skid row district in Los Angeles:

> Los Angeles, for all its purported affluence, glamor and sophistication, is becoming a city that is not unable, but unwilling, to care for itself. . . . On every street I drive, bag people are sleeping on benches, slumped in doorways, or huddled on the sidewalk. . . . On the radio, their voices plead for shelter and jobs. . . . I read about them being shuffled from the City Hall lawn to abandoned public buildings to vacant-lot—"camps." A county supervisor proposes to ship them out to a rusty hulk anchored in the LA harbor. One councilmember wants to truck them out to a military base, another would send them to Terminal Island.[10]

As *Black Film* does, the postrealist film can *preposterize* in order to despectacularize its subject as spectacle. It can debunk the shared assumptions of the hegemonic state and, at the same time, refresh our social imaginaire by helping us to see beyond what we have accepted and believed to what actually is—and to reimagine what could be.

TRY CAMP—THERE ARE MANY ROUTES TO USEFUL EXPERIENCE

Andy Warhol's single-shot, silent film *Mario Banana* (1964), will serve here. In exotic drag and in seductive medium close-up, Mario Montez slowly and seductively peels then licks a banana (figures 3.8–3.9). His performance for the camera splits our trust in two: is he lost in pleasure, or is he having his way with us, suggesting that we've always wanted to see how gay men entertain themselves with other men's bodies? Mario teaches us how to be gay (at least how to suck cock, sort of)

FIGURES 3.8–3.9 *Mario Banana*, Andy Warhol, 1964

but is also using his forbidden banana pleasure to taunt and dick around with us. In Warhol's film, Mario is instructing us on survival and cocksucking his way to immortality, with panache.

Camp almost always cuts both ways, producing a crisis of knowingness/knowledge for the viewer. Susan Sontag writes, "Camp sees everything in quotation marks. It's not a lamp, but a 'lamp'; not a woman, but a 'woman.'"[11] It's not a dick, but a "dick," or perhaps it's not a banana, but a "banana," which is what produces the paradigm crisis. Why are we watching a man licking a "banana?" After all, women suck dick too.

DEMOLISH IT, BURN IT DOWN

Ant Farm's *Media Burn* (1975) records a short event they produced and recorded on Independence Day, July 4, 1975, in a large parking lot at the Cow Palace in San Francisco. Ant Farm was an avant-garde architecture, graphic arts, and environmental design group, a self-described art agency "that promotes ideas that have no commercial potential, but which we think are important vehicles of cultural introspection."[12]

The event begins when an actor, a sort of look-alike/sound-alike JFK, makes a short speech to a milling crowd: "Who can deny that we are a nation addicted to television and the constant flow of media? And not a few of us are frustrated by this addiction. My fellow Americans, haven't you ever wanted to put your foot through your television screen?"[13] He climbs into a shiny black Cadillac El Dorado, converted into a tail-finned, jazzed-up futuristic Phantom Dream Car. A media circus of reporters, cameramen, and curious bystanders assembles. At the end of a short runway sit forty or fifty old television sets, stacked high to form a giant pyramid and doused with kerosene. The Phantom Dream Car, piloted by two men dressed as astronauts (referred to as "artist dummies"), guided only by a video monitor between their bucket seats, takes off and smashes through the pyramid of TVs at 55 mph, setting everything ablaze. *Media Burn* is the ultimate send-up media event, simultaneously ridiculing and ridiculous. Remember, power is fearful, but laughter is triumphant. Let's celebrate it.

SYNCOPATE IT, UNWRAP IT

How do we undo the spectacle of the circus, our delight with daredevil feats on the high wire, our fascination with the scantily clad women here as masters of elephants and horses, and goofy self-destructing clowns? Watch Jonas Mekas's *Notes on the Circus* (1966). With his Bolex camera, Mekas shot the same circus three nights in a row. The second time, he rolled back the first night's footage and superimposed the second night's over it—same elephants, same clowns, same acrobats but now thickened into a dense porridge of absurd thrills. The next night a third performance was superimposed over the first two. We watch it right out of his camera, a triple set of glamorous performing beauties, wild, madcap feats of balance and strength, animals trained to prance, hold still, and prance again. He is punning for sure, matching the three-ring circus with his triple recording and thus producing a visual fugue, delivering the wildest minutes of beauty, silliness, horror, and syncopated silliness in cinema.

Kicking the footage further into insane high gear, Mekas adds a musical soundtrack, the zany *Storybook Ball* by Jim Kweskin's Jug Band, which recounts a Mother Goose tale of a storybook heaven with animals running amok. Sing along . . .

> Smartie smartie says I think we'll have a party
> And he called on the old woman in the shoe

Forty Postrealist Strategies to Learn from and Borrow 71

> Now the cat he brought his fiddle
> And he played Hey diddle diddle,
> And what happened then I'd going to tell to you—

You might never go again to a circus, but if you do, you'll remember this stinging take on human concoctions of dominance and pleasure.

The filmmaker/exhibitor, Jonas Mekas, after being arrested for a public screening of Jack Smith's sensational, banned film *Flaming Creatures*, wrote,

> Art is concerned with the spirit of man, with the sub-conscious of man, with the aesthetic needs of man, with the entire past and future of man's soul. Like any other art, like painting, music or poetry, our art cannot be licensed or censored. There is no one among us to judge it. We have not only the Constitutional right but more important, the moral right, to communicate our work to 'other people. . . . The duty of the citizen and artist is not to let the police and the law abuse the rights of the people, both the Constitutional rights and the unwritten, moral rights.[14]

DWINDLE, DIMINISH, CHOP IT TO DUST

How could you debunk the absurd pretensions of a "caring" nation at war? Watch John Greyson's *14.3 Seconds* (2009), a morbidly wicked film about the terrible destructive power of war and the impossibility of restoration and redemption.

Remember the U.S. invasion of Iraq in March 2003, under the false premise that Iraq possessed "weapons of mass destruction" that Iraq did not possess? Remember the stories of the looting of the Iraq National Library and Archive in Baghdad? Saad Eskander, the current director of the Iraqi archive, estimates that, because of damage from theft and fire, 60 percent or more of the collections were stolen, burned, or otherwise destroyed: "Within the space of three days, the Iraq National Library and Archive . . . lost hundreds of thousands of archival documents, historical records, and rare books . . . a large portion of historical memory."[15] Remember how the U.S. promised to help restore the collection as best it could?

Watch Greyson's *14.3 Seconds* (2009) a haunting speculative fiction about less than two feet of film that might have survived after an accidental U.S. bombing of the Iraqi Film Archive in Baghdad.

Using text on screen, Greyson points out that when the U.S. bombed the National Film Archive, "A century of Arab cinema was reduced to melting scraps of celluloid." He shows us the scraps that were left, all 14.3 seconds of them—just seven shots. He writes, "In 2004, ICARP, The Iraq Coalition Archives Project, announced that it would use these scraps to painstakingly reconstruct what was once considered the greatest collection of Arab cinema in the world." Greyson demonstrates how the National Film Archive is now being restored from these seven fragments of film. One after another, his reconstructions of actual films (the card catalog was saved, he notes) become more and more absurd, ludicrous, and devastating in their preposterous claims. Sometimes Greyson's insane fabrications are even instructive about film editing: without a blink, he borrows close-ups of horses from a scrap of historical film about the battle of Qadisiya, 636 A.D., for the reconstruction of a contemporary film requiring a horse.

My favorite is when an on-screen text tells us that a guy (a man looking out the window of a plane) looks into a mirror. Greyson cuts to the same close-up but flipped left to right (figures 3.10–3.11). The illusion of the perfect mirror image delights in its wonderful absurdity.

Dissonant is too soft a description of the film, especially as more and more words in the text are blacked out as censorship proceeds apace and sequences are destabilized by an increasingly dubious array

FIGURE 3.10–3.11 *14.3 Seconds*, John Greyson, 2009

of explanations. These absurd constructions are violent. They perform, ironically, as revolutionary poems against a violent U.S. nation. Perhaps they must be violent, even wicked, to shake up our self-willed fantasy that we have nothing to do with the destruction of others' lives. Or perhaps that what the U.S. has destroyed it cannot make whole again.

The Iraq War has resulted in some 200,000 civilian deaths and more than 100,000 combatant deaths at a cost of $2.4 trillion (through 2017). Despite a formal withdrawal of troops in 2011, this U.S.-led military operation was renewed in 2014 as Operation Inherent Resolve and continues in Iraq to this day.

Thinking about the defiant absurdity of Greyson's *14.3 Seconds*, I recall Deborah Brown's series of large glass mosaics, *Platform Diving*, at the Houston Street stop on the #1 southbound subway line in New York City. A series of seven large panels portray fish, whales, dolphins, and the like serenely going about their business in their underwater subway tube. In one, a Beluga whale peeks over the shoulder of a man on a bench reading a newspaper, under water of course (figure 3.12).

FIGURE 3.12 *Platform Diving*, Deborah Brown's series of large glass mosaics at the Houston Street stop on the no. 1 southbound line in New York City

Forty Postrealist Strategies to Learn from and Borrow

The Beluga is curious—why is that guy focused on that paper with lines and lines of black marks? Check out these provocative mosaics. You will wonder who we are in this watery underground subway tunnel and who we are in this world.

DECOMPRESS GENDER RELATIONSHIPS

Take a look at Chick Strand's *Fake Fruit Factory* (1986). In a quiet pastoral space, under a tree somewhere in Mexico, women workers expertly mold and paint papier-mâché fruits and vegetables for the tourist market, delivered in ravishing close-ups of faces and hands in wet paste and paint. Soon enough the women are casually talking about whether the boss is sexy or not. Here is women's talk—unrepressed, intimate, and seductive. Out comes a soft critique of patriarchy and capitalism: "Patti is pregnant. The boss did it."

How women talk—what they know—how revealing, how frank, and sometimes amusing, it is (figures 3.13–3.15). "He eats very hygienically, not a lot of calories. They (white men bosses) are good at it because they don't do anything else. Because of this they are very strong for sex. They have nothing else on their minds."

Later the women eat lunch while Mexican love songs play. Finishing up, they paint black seeds on the watermelon slices, then stamp each fruit and flower *Made in Mexico*. They calculate their income and get paid in cash. Jimmy, the white boss, tells them, "I want to get rich and get out."

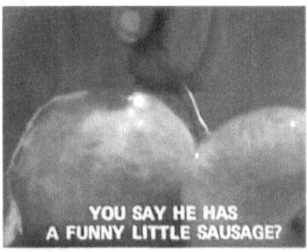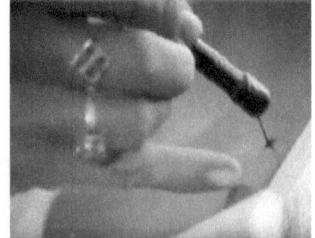

FIGURE 3.13–3.15 *Fake Fruit Factory*, Chick Strand, 1986

CREATE RADICAL NEW SPACE; PERFORM THE UNTHINKABLE THERE

In *Ausfegen* (aka *Sweeping Up,* 1972), filmmakers Joseph Beuys and Jurgen Boch take the notion of "civic duty" literally. We're in West Berlin, after a May Day parade by several political groups in the extraparliamentary opposition (as an alternative to the official May Day celebrations sponsored by trade unions in Karl Marx Platz). Boch shoots while Beuys and two art students, an African and a Japanese from the Dusseldorf Art Academy where Beuys teaches, are sweeping up every piece of trash, every cigarette butt, every political flyer littering the streets after the parade. Wielding a broom with red bristles, in this otherwise black-and-white film with a filter for reds and yellows, only the brooms red bristles, the yellow scraps of flyers and flags appear in color.

The deliberate sweeping action was a demonstration of dissonance, pointing to the unseen working class's labor to keep the streets clean after the labor unions' parade. The film reiterates Beuys's contention that each of us, every day, has opportunities to produce useful antiauthoritarian visions of class solidarity—beyond didactic political argument and petitions, even with humble brooms.

The film commands our patience and commitment as we watch patiently, yet not without pleasure, as the bits of trash disappear into the plastic bags of our common good.

> I've come to the conclusion that there is no single possibility to do something for people that does not come from the realm of art. And so I need a pedagogcal conception, and I need an epistemological conception, and I have to bargain ... the pedagogical conception is based on the idea that man is a creative being, and to make him conscious of this, that's very important. First of all, to create a consciousness that as a creative being, he is also a free being, and because of this, his behavior must necessarily be anti-authoritarian.[16]
> —Joseph Beuys

76   Forty Postrealist Strategies to Learn from and Borrow

It's a performance of right action—art as careful and humble as right action can be. In a voice-over, Beuys says, "I wanted to make it clear that the demonstrators' ideological orientation needs to be swept up as well, namely what is proclaimed on the banners as the dictatorship of the proletariat."[17] Beuys—sculptor, performer, theoretician, pedagogue, and shaman—takes every opportunity to criticize forms of political ideologizing. You can perform an unimaginable action of your own, shoot it, and make it stick in our hearts and minds.

SUCK OUT THE PORNOGRAPHIC—INTERROGATE THE APPARATUS

In Harun Farocki's *An Image* (1983), we are granted access behind the scenes to a *Playboy* centerfold shoot in Munich, Germany (figures 3.16–3.18). The painstakingly slow activity, the hundred close adjustments

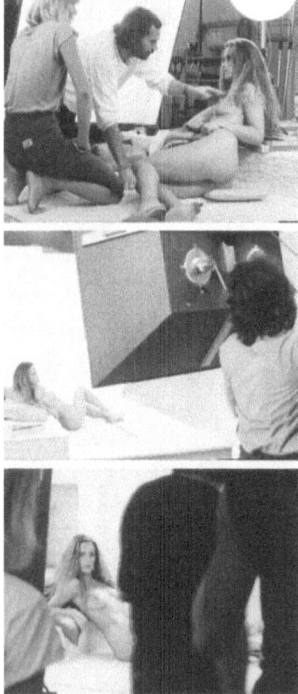

FIGURES 3.16–3.18
An Image, Harun Farocki, 1983

Forty Postrealist Strategies to Learn from and Borrow 77

to the naked female model, the set, the lighting, and the studious self-importance of the director and his assistants—all these recorded by Farocki—eventually do desire in. Farocki sucks the air out of the images and renders it dull, tedious, mundane . . . even antierotic.

Voyeurism evaporates. Desire drips, then collapses. The assertion of cool, remote rationality—distancing over visual engagement—is central to the structure of this and all Farocki's work.

He writes, "One must work with existing images in such a way that they become new. There are many ways to do this. Mine is to look for buried meanings and to clear away the debris lying on top of the pictures."[18] One of you, perhaps inspired by Farocki, should undo other images that keep us desiring useless things.

RECALIBRATE A HISTORY

Consider Isao Hashimoto's *A Time Lapse Map of Every Nuclear Explosion Since 1945* (2012). Through this tensely mapped enactment of every nuclear bomb and test exploded in the world so far, we get to see our nuclear weapons "progress" evolve in a unique and shocking way. Each test produces a flash on a map of the world and adds to the tallies at the top of the screen. It begins with U.S. tests in the Pacific, then with U.S. bombs dropped on Hiroshima and Nagasaki in 1945, then continues, on and on. By 1966, sparks are flying and colored lights are flashing and beeping with each new nuclear event. The U.S., Russia, Britain, and France dominate the sequence. It concludes with Pakistan's nuclear tests in May of 1998. It is a stark, ugly picture.

There is no death portrayed, no radiation contamination described, no horror at all; rather, it's a simple, accurate moving map that becomes a sober and devastating way to watch the nuclear dangers piling up in our world. It methodically tallies up which parts of the world test the most bombs, as well as which countries are most likely to suffer destruction—these being the nuclear-bomb nations, of course.

Again, we are waiting patiently through cinema time to the present, wondering when there will be more tests and more bombs. In this remapping of our world's explosive nuclear history, the dread of total annihilation is palpable.

PERFORM WHAT COULD HAVE/SHOULD HAVE BEEN

Watch Chen Chieh-Jen's *The Route* (2006). Here is a black-and-white silent film about forty or so Taiwanese dockworkers who break into an empty warehouse in the port of Kaohsiung and secretly stage a performance of a strike that never took place. For whom? For themselves, for the Taiwanese people, and for the camera—that is, for us. In 1995, Prime Minister Margaret Thatcher's neoliberal regime busted the dockworkers' union in Liverpool, replacing union workers with scabs who loaded up, among others, a small freighter under Singapore sail, the *Neptune Jade*. An international dockworkers strike was called, and when the *Neptune Jade* arrived at its first destination in Oakland, California, the International Longshore and Warehouse Union workers set up a picket line and refused to cross it to unload the ship. Dockers in Canada and Japan followed suit. The international strike lasted until 1998, but when the *Neptune Jade* arrived in Taiwan, the dockworkers were unaware of the strike and unloaded the ship. The dockworkers there would have struck if they had known of the international longshoremen's action and appeal, but they hadn't heard of it. In deep regret, in 2002, they staged the action they would have taken if they had known (figures 3.19–3.21).

The Route is a solemn silent film, unhurried, deliberate, meticulously filmed, and profound in its dedication to international solidarity. Dubbed a collective "film action," it was a collaboration between the filmmaker and the dockworkers who agreed to produce this cinema record of what could and should have been. We watch the dockers carrying strike signs into the warehouse: "The World Is Our Picket Line," "Solidarity Has No Borders," "Change the Outcome: Reclaim the Future," "Dockers Will Never Walk Alone." We watch them viewing newsreel of the dockers' protest in Liverpool. We watch as they arrange themselves, side by side, in a long line that stretches across the width of the warehouse yard.

> As soon as one is engaged in a productive process, total pessimism becomes improbable. This has nothing to do with the dignity of labour or any other such

crap; it has to do with the nature of physical and psychic human energy. . . . Work, because it is productive, produces in man a productive hope.[19]
—John Berger

There is nobody watching this performance. It's a performance for themselves. Its double purpose, besides acknowledging the Taiwan dockworkers' solidarity with the international strike, it is to make a record for future generations. The film attempts to get at the invisible—how years of neoliberalism have erased Taiwan's history and disabled Taiwanese society's ability to fully reflect on its present situation. It insists on what has been repressed . . . the experience, intelligence, and

FIGURES 3.19–3.21 *The Route*, Chen Chieh-Jen, 2006

will of the Taiwanese working class. By this solemn enactment of a strike, the dockers have shown us how to resist the loss of memory. *The Route* declares that resistance is possible in Taiwan and, for that matter, everywhere. I can think of hundreds of situations from our own histories that are prime candidates for this could-have-been performance strategy.

The filmmaker has this to say:

> Taiwan has become a "fast-forgetting" consumer society that has abandoned its right to "self-narration" and this has spurred me to resist the tendency to forget. One of my methods of resistance is to view each film I make as an act of connection, linking together the history of people who have been excluded from the dominant discourse, the real-life situations of areas that are being ignored, and "others" who are being isolated. In this way, I resist the state of amnesia in consumer society.[20]

Consider enacting something that never happened but could have and should have. Think about producing a memory—not for the history books but for people to know what is possible, whether it has happened yet or not. One example: with asylum seekers and refugees from Mexico, Honduras, Haiti, El Salvador, and other countries, who are separated from their children are never reunited, never allowed to apply for refugee status, you could make a film about the children being returned to their parents after getting their sought-after immigrant status and settling in to their new homes. Enacting the possible—what could have and should have been and someday maybe will be.

PROMOTE CRIMINAL BEHAVIOR WITH A STRAIGHT FACE

The French political philosopher and anarchist P. J. Proudhon is well-known for his assertion that "property is theft." And so, with a straight face, Sherry Millner fashioned *Shoplifting: It's a Crime?* (1979). Her film is a cross between a humorous (perhaps useful) demonstrations of shoplifting techniques and a dramatized essay about stealing as a rare, cheerful moment in the otherwise grim social injustice of poverty. These tips are simple and useful: "Always plan your escape route." Then, "Remove all telltale signs (for instance, labels)." Next, "Wear loose clothing and have plenty of pockets." On it goes. The advice continues, and, as it does, the figure of the shoplifter is freed from the zone of the bourgeois, then resituated within an anarchistic alternative economy. And for a moment viewers implausibly do the unthinkable and shed their bourgeois perspectives on who has the right to someone else's property.

The arthritic conventions of the educational documentary—how to drive a car, how to brush your teeth, how to duck and cover—are bent way out of shape. Proudhon lives! Pity the Stop & Shops, the 7-Elevens, and the QuikTrips, for they are vulnerable to these instructions.

RECAST THE TERMS . . . THE POETRY

Borrow strategies from David Fourier's *Majorettes in Space* (1996), a uniquely useful film most tender in its juxtapositions of hetero- and homosexuality and life and death. It's a fairytale of sorts, beginning with a voice-over: "Of all living beings, only man knows he's going to die. Of all living beings, only man is capable of humor and poetry." In the spirit of wild incongruity, the director places side-by-side images of a rubber tree, shoes made from cowhide, boys playing soccer, a bottle of vodka ("a clear drink, invented by man to forget he's going to die"), Pope John Paul II's long white dress and clerical idea of heaven (where there is no homosexual sex), and a man with AIDS at a gay pride parade who knows for sure he's going to die. Fourier points out the parallels—for instance, that Vincent, the young man with AIDS, and the old "don't use condoms" puritanical pope both soon will die.

It's a choreographed hallucination and a poetic protest against the idea that certain things are unrelated: even a "fat cow," which a vodka-inebriated man calls his wife, produces both leather for soccer balls and the tasseled white boots that young majorettes adore. This sweet and useful film offers up visual and poetic pleasure while gently unraveling the skein of sexism and pervasive denial of death.

PIRATE FROM FILMS AND TEXTS TO EXAMINE AND REMAP THEM

In 1974, a radical leftist group, the Symbionese Liberation Army, kidnapped nineteen-year-old heiress Patty Hearst, demanding enough ransom money from her wealthy family to feed the poor of Oakland, California (at $70 worth of food for every needy Californian, the operation would have cost an estimated $400 million). Kidnapped Patty was supposed to convince her father, the American publishing magnate Randolph Hearst, to pay the ransom and teach him how to distribute the food.

Years later, four of Patty's audio letters to her father were made public. In an art gallery with a few friends and supporters, performance artist Sharon Hayes, in a severe close-up, records *Symbionese Liberation Army (SLA) Screed #16* (2003) from memory. In a monotone, she struggles to repeat, exactly, word for word, the audio letters Patty Hearst sent her father during the SLA crisis.

With Hayes's halting recitations of the letters, the occasional mistakes corrected by off-camera supporters, Patty's alternately cajoling and sometimes soothing language is unwrapped, and the Hearst family's helplessness exposed. It becomes impossible to separate the performer's occasional flubbed lines from the stress or coercion of a hostage: "I mean, I am fine. I mean I am, I mean. I am fine."

From Hayes's recitations, slowing the text down for acute examination, one reads Patty not as the foolish debutante the media made her out to be but as a savvy witness to her family's wealth and a supporter of the SLA's efforts to feed the poor of Oakland, perhaps if only in exchange for her release.

In making this kind of film, your strategic strength might come through, as here, the *anthropophagic*, the carnavalesque, the self-reflexive, the magical realist, the preposturized, the excessive extreme, or any other postrealist strategy described in this letter.

> ANTHROPOPHAGIC: originally the custom and practice of eating human flesh or cannibalism—here meaning to borrow texts and stories, to appropriate them or reperform them somehow.

Another *anthropophagic* film worth studying is Leslie Thornton's *Another Worldly* (1999). It's just now in distribution by the Film-Makers Coop (though at first it was mistakenly called *Another World*). Hunt it down.

Leslie Thornton built *Another Worldly* out of a reel of old "soundies" she happened upon at a flea market. Soundie films were produced between 1940 to 1946 for self-contained, coin-operated 16 mm rear projection machines called PanOrams, installed in nightclubs, restaurants, but mostly in saloons, and thus of particular interest to men. Some were specifically intended to attract wartime military personnel on leave.

Soundie reels often included cheesecake segments—nightclub routines with groups of women in skimpy costumes, high heels, and fishnet stockings, all moving together to music in perfect synchronicity and always, like the Rockettes, smiling to the camera as if unaware that the camera was pointing directly up their tiny skirts (or as chaste Wikipedia notes, at the groin or the lower ventral area). Soundies slipped by industry censors who didn't consider them "movies," so they were allowed to operate uncensored, at ten cents a play. The dance routines invite viewers to focus on the high kicks and fantasize over what's at the far end of those long legs.

Thornton strung a bunch of these "entertaining" Soundies together, then stripped out the original night club band music and replaced it with German techno music with powerful beats. The techno music penetrates and interrogates the once pornographic, now impenetrable dance routines. Without the original music to rationalize the choreography, what's left is a thickened new "show"—a series of visual slashes that build an analysis of cinema as an essentially pornographic medium. Without the artifice of dance "entertainment" to distract us, what is revealed is our relentless gaze and ourselves as obsessive consumers of all things photographic.

Another Worldy is a severe and sober film about cinema, laying bare America's uncensored dream life, suggesting that all cinema is pornographic—seeking the thing that excites under the pretense of science, education, knowledge, democracy, or, in this case, simply casual, innocuous pleasure (figure 3.22).

The titillating films that gained legitimacy in nightclub locations cannot support the weight of Thornton's musical revisions, which drain the pornography from the originals and collapse them onto themselves,

FIGURE 3.22 *Another Worldy,* Leslie Thornton, 1999

becoming visually absurd. Thornton's film is everything and its opposite: innocent/perverse, legitimate/illegitimate, here/there, educational/commercial. The male gaze, robbed of pleasure, cannot be sustained (figure 3.23).

To further extend the anthropophagic dilemma, Leslie occasionally inserts sequences of men "dancing": soldiers in uniform goose-stepping in a military parade, up and then back, optically produced; three long, tall young white men in fussy colonial attire daintily performing a tap dance; a tall man in blackface and Uncle Sam costume bumping brilliantly for two white showgirls in what could be called early breakdancing while they feed coins into his mouth . . . a parking meter or a bank? These shots complicate the "show" of orderly performance produced by synchronous matched female bodies. Discovery and rediscovery of meaning is reached through the cannibalization of these familiar "entertainment" texts.

What is the content of *Another Worldy?* Here's my best shot, in just two long sentences: because men will pay money to watch perfectly matched sets of talented young women in high heels and revealing costumes (as long as they don't look like their wives or daughters) dancing in perfect unison in perfectly matched dancelike configurations, and because, under patriarchy, women can be paid to dress up in high

Forty Postrealist Strategies to Learn from and Borrow 85

FIGURE 3.23 *Another Worldy,* Leslie Thornton, 1999

heels and short, cute costumes and perform dance routines that coyly reveal the location of their hidden genitalia as they largely pretend they are not being observed, while at the same time the women's occasional glances at the camera signal that they are aware of being peeked at, because that is the most titillating thing of all. And in this way, the cinema was born.

JIGGLE AND JUGGLE IT AROUND

Tami Gold's *Juggling Gender: Politics, Sex and Identity* (1992) is the most seductive nonfiction film I know. It features Jennifer Miller, a naturally bearded, articulate lesbian circus performer who juggles in her own Circus Amok! I'm guessing Jennifer seduced the filmmaker—and now the filmmaker wants Jennifer—tough, coy, vulnerable, flirtatious, and independent, to seduce us (figures 3.24–3.26). And so she does.

Watching the film, we soon forget to be visually staggered by Jennifer's beard, by her naked juggling-jiggling breasts, and her gender freedom. We understand how boxed in we are by our "normalcy," our plucked, hairless chins, our shapewear girdles, and our blown-dry hair. In the film, Jennifer has no more secrets—but we do. She is saner than

86 Forty Postrealist Strategies to Learn from and Borrow

FIGURES 3.24–3.26 *Juggling Gender,* Tami Gold, 1992

we are, and we know it. It's hard not to feel inferior, but that's not what the film is promoting. Rather, it is promoting gender freedom.

Along with other films distributed by Women Make Movies, *Juggling Gender* was circulated through the halls of Congress by right-wing Republicans in an attempt to defund the National Endowment for the Arts, which supported *Juggling Gender*. It almost worked, until the Ford Foundation, also a funder, interceded. However, there are far fewer federal grants to independent filmmakers today. From a recent study by the Ford Foundation:

Artists are now increasingly responsible for being their own producers, and the vast majority must now manage the range of production, marketing, distribution, and fundraising functions once handled by agents, managers, and marketers. Technology and social media may reduce financial costs, but they require substantial time to learn and utilize effectively, and artists may face an opportunity cost if they do not participate in the new online systems with skill.[21]

There used to be film distributors, now there is just you.

LIST EVERYTHING THAT PERTAINS—REVEAL THE ESSENCE OF ALL

Harun Farocki's *How to Live in the Federal Republic of Germany* (1990) is a film about the social behavior of the German middle-class, where life is rehearsed and skill-tested every day. In scene after scene—just a list of sequences in no particular order—we watch German middle-class folks learn how to practice for job interviews, how to correctly get out of an overturned car, how to wash an infant, how to express pain in group therapy sessions, and many more.

Through it all, the incessant effort to be prepared for emergencies—and whatever life throws at them—can be observed. Cops learn how to calm abusive husbands. Bank clients practice complaining to bank tellers. Old people learn how to call the police in an emergency, and on and on.

Here is a country in which happiness as well as misery is disciplined by means of social techniques and freed from any measure of unpredictability. The big picture grows slowly as we recognize the essential terms of these lives; the Germans, and likely we in the middle class everywhere, can hold our uncomplaining central place in the economic and social spectrum. Here is a superb depiction of late twentieth-century capitalism and its production of us, we ourselves.

You could make a film from a list of guns available on the U.S. market and short explanations of their special features. You could make a film from a list of . . . ? Well, you can figure this one out. The possibilities are endless.

RECORD SOCIAL RITUALS, WHAT THEY OFFER, WHOM THEY IGNORE

Perhaps you are too young to know the jingle that little girls used to sing as we jumped rope: "First comes love, then comes marriage, then comes baby in the baby carriage." Study Su Friedrich's *First Comes Love* (1993). In this black-and-white film, we see footage of four traditional weddings in process much as a passerby might observe them on any spring day from the sidewalks of New York City. The four wedding parties, intercut with one another, proceed along parallel lines. In each, the first guests arrive and greet the bride and groom. Hugs and kisses all around. Then come the bridesmaids in their matching gowns, then the best men in tuxes. Then more limousines, flower girls, ring boys, and so forth, all eventually mounting the stairs into the church.

In *First Comes Love*, there is no synchronized sound—nothing that stitches the audience into the time and place of these rituals on the church steps. Rather, Friedrich covers the sequences with short chunks of the best of sixties and seventies passionate love songs: Aretha Franklin, Smokey Robinson, Stevie Wonder, Janis Joplin, Marvin Gaye, Tina Turner, and others. We remember them well—they're *our* songs. "I was made to love you, made to adore you," sings Stevie Wonder for a few phrases, then the song cuts abruptly to the next, then the next. For a few seconds, the music seems to organize time, memory, and feelings, but then the comfort of the music fails as each romantic song is abandoned and the next one cuts in. The film instructs us to remember these wonderful moments when music accompanied our dreams of love and longing. For Friedrich, the music clips are just some facts of our social dream, enumerated in no order, explaining nothing, just cultural facts. The arrangement of the songs is antiorganizational—producing a simple list of pleasures from our past. For a while you don't understand why, but soon . . .

Sometimes I think filmmakers' radical stubbornness is the best tool they have for crashing through the DAWKI's dilapidated techniques. Friedrich wields her stubbornness here to great effect.

Soon all the wedding parties have mounted the church steps and we are inside, watching a bride and groom move toward the altar, accompanied by Mendelssohn's traditional wedding music. As they walk, we're confronted by a superimposed text: "If two men or two women wanted to legalize their commitment to each other, for any reason, they would be denied that privilege in the following countries." Alert, we watch a slow upward crawl of the alphabetized names of 172 countries—every country in the world but one, but we don't know which. It takes a long time, and we try to guess, but soon our best bets—the Netherlands? Norway? crawl off with the Ns and we abandon hope. Somewhere around South Africa the Mendelssohn wedding march fades out. We watch the rest of the countries in naked silence. The last, the United Kingdom, rolls up and off the screen, and most of us still haven't figured this puzzle out.

Then, back on the church steps, the four wedding parties emerge, and the old love songs start up again. The photographers get busy. Everyone on screen is smiling, but we in our cinema seats are not. We are waiting for the name of the missing country, not sure it will ever be offered. This is the stark transactional experience of the film—the whole ritual, the dress-up, the ring boys and flower girls, the kit-and-kaboodle of the entire wedding celebration—in 1993, these are denied all gay persons everywhere except in one small country.

Willie Nelson finishes "You Were Always on My Mind" as the limos carry off the married couples. The wedding parties are all gone, and young boys appear to start sweeping up the rice. Four nuns walk up the empty church steps. We are running out of time, we know, but then a final title appears: "In 1990, Denmark became the first country in the world to legalize homosexual marriage." This is what we have wished to know for a long time, but now that we do it's unsatisfying. The brutally truncated love songs and the dilemma posed by the crawling text have made the operations of the state too disturbing.

Why four weddings? To see that the rituals of the marriage are proscribed—that they are socially "necessary" and basically all the same. There is no tension about what will happen next, no narrative and nothing at stake except the rights of same-sex couples to marry—that's all. Remember: just as the belly's hunger gives no clue to the complexities of human cuisine, the sexual organs don't determine appropriate sexual conduct or what kind of love should be celebrated, sanctified, and legalized. *First Comes Love,* to be sure, but what comes next? In 1993, it wasn't marriage, not for everyone, not until the Supreme Court Decision twenty-two years later, in 2015.

POSTREALIST FILM AS A KOAN

What is a koan? Wikipedia says "a koan is a story, dialogue, question, or statement, the meaning of which cannot be understood by rational thinking but may be accessible through intuition or lateral thinking."

> JG: AS YOU PROBABLY CAN TELL, I OFTEN CONSULT WIKIPEDIA. Some days, three times or more, I go there to look up a date when something was published or the correct spelling of a name. We need to respect and be grateful for stuff that is easy to use and free and smart and built by many hands and minds.

A Buddhist master/mistress might offer a koan to a pupil to shock him or her into some new consciousness, to ask for a different kind of attention. Here's a koan I just read in a short story by Haruki Murakami: "What is the nature of a circle with many centers and no circumference?" Your high school algebra won't help you here—your mind has to go somewhere else, somewhere more invigorating, more unthinkable.

Nonfiction film could work as a koan does. It could present a story, dialogue, question, performance, or statement, "the meaning of which cannot be understood by rational thinking but may be accessible through intuition or lateral thinking." Here is what I would call a film koan: a postrealist one. *The Eternal Frame* (1975), by the collective Ant Farm and T. R. Uthco, is a recording of a very carefully made, near exact reenactment of the November 22, 1963, assassination of President John F. Kennedy, the thirty-fifth president of the United States, at Dealey Plaza, Dallas, Texas. It's staged exactly where the president was assassinated twelve years before. The "JFK" and "Jackie" look-alikes appear in the presidential limousine driving slowly down the street. When shots ring out, secret service men leap onto the tail of the car. While dumbfounded onlookers watch this strange ritual reenactment, what emerges is not a question of accuracy but a chance to meditate on the power of these iconic images, the first televised U.S. tragedy. (The name *The Eternal Frame* plays on the "eternal flame" at Kennedy's gravesite.)

Almost all of us older folks can say where we were when we heard the news, or when we watched the footage on TV, but somehow this reenactment cannot reinvigorate our sentimentality, cannot reproduce our solemn recall of that memory. And it shouldn't. In the face of the reenactment, our thinking must move laterally. We must begin to consider what might actually have happened: Who wanted JFK dead and why? Why the immediate assassination of the shooting suspect? Why the confusing cover-up? All these unanswered questions were suppressed. Our nostalgia for that historical moment, when we all grieved together, is dislodged.

The Eternal Frame compels objective, accurate observation of mundane, routine evil. Somehow, our democratic exceptionalism has survived this catastrophe, unmarked by the violence it portended. Once we have witnessed it again, can we discard our cherished old memories to comprehend something new about our country and its ability to distract and defeat us. But what is the meaning of this murder? Why do we remember it with affection? Contemplate the koan.

MAKE MAPS SO THE LAY OF THE LAND CAN BE GRASPED

A very useful map—think of it as an outline or a model—is *Videograms of a Revolution* (1994) by Harun Farocki and Andrei Ujică, a Romanian media philosopher. For about three years, Ujică and Farocki collected material of all sorts around the fall of Nicolae Ceaușescu's regime in 1989 and with it built this compilation film of "found footage" from myriad sources: from the Romanian state TV broadcasts as the Communist leader's regime stumbles, from citizen-produced camcorder footage in their streets and homes, from excerpts from the Bucharest TV studio overtaken by demonstrators during the 1989 revolution. (Sony released the first camcorder, the Betacam system, in 1983; by 1989, it had traveled widely.)

Videograms of a Revolution presents us with a list, in order, of what was recorded over three days during the December 1989 Romanian

Revolution. At the start, a female narrator, in uninflected tones, tells us, "In order to assert his endangered power, Ceaușescu addressed a mass rally like so many others he had ordered to be held during the prior twenty-five years. TV transmits live." We are watching this speech at a central square in Bucharest on the state TV channel. Suddenly there is a disturbance in the crowd. Under Ceaușescu's orders, if there is even a ripple of discontent, the TV cameras have been instructed to pan up to the sky. Citizens watching the broadcast on television begin moving out of their homes and pushing toward the square. Soon there is camcorder footage taken by individuals in the streets; there is self-recorded footage of the newly democratic politicians negotiating and improvising the platforms they would offer the citizens of Romania; there is TV footage of the dead bodies of Ceausescu and his wife being brought back to Bucharest after their attempted escape by helicopter; there is footage taken by families of themselves in their homes, watching the two dead bodies being unloaded from a tank on their TVs. There is also a humorous citizen's recording of a BBC reporter hunkered down in a subway entrance, waiting for the shelling to cease so he can begin his "eye-witness" report.

The film asks us to consider the structure of reality. What map does the film offer? *Videograms* demonstrates that if it hasn't been recorded and shown on the TV it never happened. When there is a crisis of identity, only the TV can resolve it. That's the structure of reality, not just in Romania, but everywhere. Farocki and Ujică demonstrate how important is the way in which footage is recorded, captured, and, above all, consumed, how important for active players/politicians to make sure their participation is recorded and broadcast. The film's thesis is that there is no history—no revolution or counterrevolution, no war, no deposed dictators—that goes untelevised. If it's not on your TV, it never happened.

When President Reagan was shot in 1981, the three major U.S. TV networks started to perform as Romanian TV had, to reassure the citizens that everything was under control. But suddenly then Secretary of State Alexander Haig called a press conference, invited in the networks, and made as if he would have to take over the government, "I am in control here," he asserted. It was scary. Everyone knew that if Reagan didn't recover, the vice president was supposed to take over, then the speaker of the House, then the president pro tempore of the Senate. We had learned this in eighth-grade civics class.

The TV faltered. The state faltered. Confusion reigned. Soon Haig was whisked off the air and not heard from again for a long while. The Haig footage was erased from all the networks, demonstrating that the government was still in control.

REJECT PESSIMISM—COLLABORATE WITH OTHER FILMMAKERS

How in the worst of times, confronting national tragedies and extraordinary discord, can film keep hope alive? *Germany in Autumn* (1978) provides a variety of meditations on the distracted situation of the Federal Republic of Germany in the wake of terrorism, assassinations, and state repression. It's an omnibus film made by eleven German filmmakers. Rainer Werner Fassbinder, Volker Schlöndorff, Alexander Kluge, Edgar Reitz, and seven others each contributed a sequence to mark the dire atmosphere in the Federal Republic of Germany after the abduction and killing of German business executive and former SS member Hans Martin Schleyer by the radical Red Army Faction and the (doubtful) 1978 suicides of the accused terrorists in the high-security Stammheim prison.

Germany's democracy was at risk of collapsing. There was fear of fascism returning. There was resentment among young people that many important positions in German society—in the police, the media, universities, etc.—were occupied by former Nazis. Young activists had become disenchanted with USSR communism and had begun a romance with Maoism. Radical students designated the consumer state as the enemy of the people. Many feared the reunification and subsequent rearmament of Germany.

The filmmakers decided to join together to produce a television program that would represent all parties and air all the issues. The result, *Germany in Autumn,* mixes media forms. Some segments are self-performed—Fassbinder, at the kitchen table, brutally educating his mother about the deplorable state of democracy in the FRG. Others depict two funerals: the state funeral of Schleyer and the collective funeral for members of the Red Army Faction who died in alleged suicides. Some segments are dramatized. In one, TV executives who have commissioned a teleplay of Sophocles' *Antigone* argue about whether to broadcast it or not, worried that the story involving "terroristic women" and a refusal of burial could be misinterpreted as a political statement. "Irony is one thing we can do without right now," they conclude. They decide neither to broadcast the film nor to scrap it, but rather to "put it on ice until quieter times."

Though grim, the film is never pessimistic. It asks, where we are now, in this terrible mess—how can we go forward? The collaboration of Germany's most important filmmakers itself demonstrates a way forward through the cinema. The Reverend Dr. Martin Luther King Jr. said, "We will be remembered with hope because hopelessness is the enemy of justice."[22] In its own way, in the late seventies, the national broadcast of *Germany in Autumn* helped to keep hope alive in those troubled times. You can find other filmmakers to collaborate with. Make *The U.S. in Autumn*. Keep hope alive.

REJECT THE WESTERNCENTRIC GAMES ANTHROPOLOGISTS CAN PLAY

The filmmaker, writer, and theorist Trinh T. Minh-ha calls ethnography *a conversation of Western men talking among themselves*. In her film *Reassemblage* (1982), her cinematic take on three rural villages in Senegal, she speaks of the usual "awe, wonder, and celebration" that circulate in ethnographic film.

> Films (unlike written reports) use images drawn directly from the "away" culture. These images make it seem as if the "away" culture were speaking for itself. But of course, camera angles, methods of shooting, focus, and editing all reflect the world of the filmmaker. If the filmmaker is from the "away" culture, the point of view may be more from the inside—but maybe not: technology enforces its own logic.[23]
> —Richard Schechner

Trinh T. Minh-ha is determined *not* to produce a knowable, underdeveloped, inferior Senegal for our consumption, swathed in Western constructions of us/them, primitive/developed, rich/poor, gender liberated/enslaved. "I had the urge to make a film to demystify or alleviate the authority of that kind of language. I wanted to show that you can approach a culture without accumulating all this "knowledge" or accumulating all these "pompous profundities." She tells us that, as the filmmaker, she is just "speaking nearby," not naming, not inspecting, not defining—just watching and recording.

In *Reassemblage*, it's not possible to feel you are there with the Senegalese portrayed in the film. You cannot feel yourself in their space. Rather—you see pictures that Trinh took and you hear sounds that she recorded, sometimes more than once. She wants to put these sounds and images in relief. In the final sequence, surrounded by a group of young Senegalese women, she puts her finger on the most significant ethnographic object around—herself: *What I see is life looking at me*. In her later book, *Women/Native/Other*, she writes, "Seeking to perforate meaning by forcing my entry or breaking it open to dissipate what is thought to be its secrets seems to me as crippled an act as verifying the sex of an unborn child by ripping open its mother's womb. It is typical of a mentality that proves incapable of touching a living thing without crushing its delicateness."[24]

Trinh deconstructs claims to authenticity, holding them to be the product of patriarchal and colonial epistemologies. She insists on dislodging the illusory purity of documentary's inherited categories to make way for the hybrid and the in between. "Reality is delicate," she tells us. If there is only one idea to take away from her film and book, as well as from this book, here it is: reality is delicate.

REJECT THE CLICHÉS OF JOURNALISM

Raoul Ruiz, a Chilean filmmaker, moved to France in 1973, forced into exile after the U.S.-sponsored coup and assassination of President Salvador Allende. In 1978, Ruiz was asked by French TV to make a "personal documentary" about the upcoming national elections in his Parisian arrondissement . . . perhaps "personal" meant not representing the TV network's position. Contrary to the network's expectation, the left lost the election and Ruiz seized on this anticlimax to make a documentary about nothing except itself—a film whose central subject became the very film he was making.

> Ruiz drolly exaggerates every hare-brained convention of TV reportage, from shot/reverse shot "suture" and talking-head experts to establishing shots and vox pops (narrator's note to himself: "Include street interviews ad absurdum"). Every fragment of reality (e.g., polling booths on voting day) comes through the lens as a prefabricated televisual cliché.... When an actual TV news clip is included—a crazily kitsch extract from the election coverage, complete with tacky graphics and the countdown to a computed poll results—the effect is devastatingly hilarious.[25]
> —ADRIAN MARTIN

Speaking about his film, *Of Great Events and Ordinary People,* Ruiz said, "I must be an exile in television land, to see the TV as a Martian would, to stand outside its 'shared assumptions,' but to see it and accept it for what it is—as a sign of the culture." In so doing, he challenged the ancestry of the documentary and its implicit links with imperialism and a false political unanimity. "When 80 percent of potential interviewees refuse to say anything to the camera, how are the 20 percent who respond supposed to be taken as representative of the population? When one bar does not allow filming, is the second-best location good enough, or is there something hidden in the other that merits looking into?"[26] An excellent question. *Of Great Events and Ordinary People* is perhaps the best film about documentary filmmaking I know. Take a good look.

DODGE THE PRIVILEGED GAZE

Anthropophagy figures here, but in a slightly different iteration. Instead of actual film cannibalism, the word can be used more gently to describe the practice of collecting together the work of others into a film of your own.

From Gulf to Gulf to Gulf (2013), by Shaina Anand and Ashok Sukumaran of the Mumbai-based collective CAMP, is composed of cellphone footage shot by a group of sailors carrying cargo from Sharjah in the United Arab Emirates to Somalia. Constructed entirely of extended selfie films shot by the sailors on their long voyages, often accompanied by songs that they Bluetooth each other, it's the result of four years of dialogue, friendship, and exchange between the CAMP collective and the sailors, splintering our standard mode of documentary perception, *the privileged gaze*.

The film is about men working together, building boats, fishing, cooking, sharing love songs, and trading links that unite people in control of their own labor. In this way, an economic activity with previously invisible actors is revealed. The sailors' travels and those of co-seafarers from Pakistan and southern Iran show us a world cut into many pieces. The common documentary categories of "subject," "sovereign," "money," and "labor" are emptied. This film doesn't pretend to give others a voice as many documentaries do. Rather, it is built around the wild and inspired selfies of the sailors. I have never seen a film that offers such a picture of confident cooperation and collaborative play among men. Bravo!

EXCESSIFY IT—I MEAN BLOW IT UP BIG AND LET US PONDER IT

I recommend that you study and enjoy Bruce Conner's *A Movie* (1958). Here Conner collects up anything and everything that's exciting in the cinema, every film thrill we can remember—bombs exploding, exotic animals, exotic diseases, feats of daring, sports mishaps, celebrities, motorbike races, porn stars—everything we come to the movies for. Conner takes short bits and pieces from news footage, science and ethnographic films—from anywhere and everywhere in the cinema—and jams them into impossibly close proximity, as if they belong together. These hundred or so shots tell no tale, argue no platitudes, make no sense. Once, perhaps these bits and pieces thrilled, amazed, or tickled us, but here they make us aware of our enormous appetite for the extreme and bizarre in the motion picture. It's a film poem not unlike the violent footage shown to the murderous hoodlum Alex in Stanley Kubrick's *Clockwork Orange*, meant to cure him of his addiction to violence. It purges. We gorge until we can gorge no more.

A Movie is a kind of pornography of the real, but Conner puts the act of watching pornography on display. No film has spoken so profoundly about our attachment to the cinematic medium. Technically, yes, one might call *A Movie* a compilation film—a documentary film compiled of existing documents—but actually it's an extraordinary document of us watching his movie. That's what makes it postrealist: the subject of a postrealist film is always "us," not "them."

Conner says he was inspired to make *A Movie* by the Marx Brothers. About sixty-seven minutes into their 1933 film *Duck Soup*, Groucho, as Rufus T. Firefly, savior of Freedonia in its battle with neighboring Sylvania, gets on the telephone and calls for help. An insane stock footage sequence follows—fire trucks, motorcycle cops, marathon runners, rowers, swimmers, baboons, elephants, dolphins, and more, all come racing in to save Freedonia. It's a testament to the early comedies, which, burdened only with the necessity of producing pleasure, were free to invent extraordinary sequences that could never appear in any other kind of cinema. The comedies had no rules to break—nor do the antidocs like *A Movie* and so many others. (See first Groucho's *Duck Soup*, then Conner's *A Movie*, and then Godard's *The Image Book*—one after another, if you dare!)

> Human beings forget they created images in order to orient themselves in the world. Since they are no longer able to decode them, their lives have become a function of their own images: imagination has turned into hallucination.[27]
> —Vilém Flusser

Defamiliarize, recontextualize, excessify! Use your film to extricate us from our visual stupor. Undo the ties that bind. Expose them, undercut them, or overplay them as *A Movie* does, taunting us with endless pieces of cinema horror and pleasure, hurled at the viewer at a million miles an hour! As the comic books say, SPLAT! BLAM! POW!

ANIMATION ANYONE?

Consider *Waltz with Bashir* (2008) by the Israeli writer/director Ari Folman. As a nineteen-year-old infantry soldier in the 1982 Israeli war with Lebanon, Folman witnessed the Phalanges' massacres of Palestinians in the Sabra and Shatila refugee camps. The Phalanges were a predominantly Christian Lebanese right-wing party, allies to the Israeli Defense Forces, who were ordered to clear Sabra and Shatila of Palestine Liberation Organization fighters. The celebrated and seasoned reporter Robert Fisk, one of the first to enter the camps after the killings, said he found an estimated two thousand civilians "butchered." (Some later estimates climbed far higher.) "I'd never seen so many bodies," he later told the British *Observer* newspaper.

Traumatized by the horror of the massacres, Folman lost all memory of the events. In 2006, he sought out other Israeli soldiers who had served with him in Beirut to discuss their memories—and to stimulate his own. The soldiers' memories, reenacted entirely in animation, give the film a disturbingly surrealistic and dreamlike quality. It is a tale of horror that we can witness with pain and with care

*Waltz with Bashi*r pushes hard and successfully against the boundaries of documentary filmmaking. It distances us from realistic horror so we can see that which, without animation, could not be told or shown.

MIX INDIGENOUS HUMOR WITH COLONIAL NIGHTMARE—BLEND CAREFULLY

Take a look at Kidlat Tahimik's wise *Perfumed Nightmare* (1977). With infectious, exuberant energy, this narrated, seriocomic film takes account of Tahimik's childhood in his native Philippines, its folktales, its revolutionary history, and its devastating relationship with U.S. popular culture. His "perfumed nightmare" refers to his existence in the lotusland of American cultural colonialism. (Kidlat rejected his given Spanish name for its colonial taint and adopted his new name, which means "silent lightening" in Tagalog.)

It's an amazing performance of self-decolonialization and self-ethnography, undoing, for instance, the childish bonds of his membership in the Werner Von Braun Fan Club. It was Von Braun who helped to develop the V-2 rocket for the Nazis during World War II. Later he was secretly moved to the United States, where he became a popular and celebrated figure who helped develop the U.S. intermediate-range ballistic missile program and the rockets that launched the first space satellite, Explorer. Everywhere, in the U.S., and it seems in the Philippines as well, Werner Von Braun Fan Clubs bubbled up. Kidlat was the president of his chapter in the tiny village of Balian and here restages the riotous discussions among members trying to decide whether girls should be allowed to join the club.

He elaborates the tragedy of the Philippine-American War at the turn of the century and the rabid behavior of the U.S. troops that killed tens of thousands of Filipino combatants "as dogs," the containment policies that shuffled the populace into concentration camps where roughly one-sixth (some five hundred thousand) of the civilian population died of famine and disease. He unearths the story of his father's death fighting in the anticolonial revolution, as well as the death of a couple hundred thousand civilians, mostly from a cholera epidemic.

Kidlat offers a profound undoing of ethnographic film clichés and an intense penetration into village life in this U.S. territory. Film curator Murtaza Vali writes, "Here, for once, the ethnographic subject shares the truth about U.S. colonialism. . . . For Kidlat Tahimik, indigeneity is not a cultural formation arrested in the past but a vital set of beliefs and practices—a way forward."[28] Made for $10,000 and shot on expired stock, the film is a model of resourcefulness. He filmed with a simple Bolex camera without synchronous sound, produced false eye-line matches (a water buffalo watches the statue of St. Marcos go by), dream sequences, dubbed voices, ridiculous/wonderful sound effects and tricks of scale, shaking the camera to produce a typhoon, and more. He calls his method "Cups of Gas Filmmaking," as opposed to "Full Tank Cum Credit Card Filmmaking." His film is more like an essay on postcolonial ethnography, Philippine culture, globalization, and disillusionment (isn't that what perfumed nightmares are made of?), delivered with a comical and eccentric flair. Steal from Kidlat if you can.

COLLABORATE INTENSELY WITH YOUR SOCIAL ACTORS

It has commonly been white, first-world filmmakers who go in search of people who are in trouble, need help of some kind, or who are ethnographically interesting. In this process, the personhood of the people being filmed is often lost, and the values and aesthetics of their culture are compressed, but rarely expressed, by the filmmaking itself. What is the antidote?

To make useful films about others, I recommend that you *collaborate* fully with your participants or "social actors." Make them your filmmaking partners. Make every decision and solve every problem together. Usually your partners know more about the situation and issues than you do. Make a film with them, not about them. Invent adequate techniques to represent their aesthetics and yours. Your filmmaking will be transformed, and so will you.

Take the case of the film *Two Laws* (1981), an episodic history of the struggle for land rights by Aboriginal people in Australia. *Two Laws* produced a new kind of ethnographic cinema, where people reperform their own history—not a description of it as you would see in the conventional documentary. The Aboriginal people of Borroloola have a traumatic history of massacres, institutionalization, and dispossession of their lands. People of the four language groups near the outpost of Borroloola in the Northern Territory invited two white Australian filmmakers, Carolyn Strachan and Alessandro Cavadini, to come help them make this film. Why a film? The Aboriginal people have no written language, so of course a film. *Two Laws* is a reperformance of Borroloola history by its people—an accounting of how difficult and frustrating it is for the Borroloola to live simultaneously under their own Aboriginal laws and the Australian laws that claim their land.

Two Laws is many things at once: a collaborative work of advocacy filmmaking in the political tradition of film collectives like Frontier Films, the Dziga Vertov Group, or Ogawa Productions; an experiment in reflexive anthropology inspired by recent theoretical developments in the academic world; a legal document, designed to enter and influence the formal spaces of what the film's subjects called "white" or "European" law; a work of radical theater with roots in Brecht and other European modernists; an inscription of collective memory, meant not only to provide its subjects with an opportunity to perform sacred rites but to provide a lasting image of these rites as well, one that could also remind others in a similar struggle with the state to stake a claim to their ancestral lands. This history is a touchstone, the Borroloola people's basis for action and for the consolidation and definition of their goals. The integrity, beauty, and functionality of *Two Laws* results from the community's complete trust and collaboration with the Australian filmmakers (figure 3.27). It's an excellent model for any filmmaker proposing to take up the struggles of others. Strachan says:

> *Two Laws* was a work of nine months with 100% collaboration of the four language groups from the Borroloola area; all film decisions were made within the framework of Aboriginal Law. There were about three hundred people, scattered over hundreds of miles and living in separate little camps. Before shooting began, the filmmakers spent two months traveling from one camp to another, showing and discussing a variety of ethnographic films—many of them about Aboriginal peoples.
>
> The people rejected many conventions of Western filmmaking, especially documentary cinema: the close-up, continuity cutting, the seamless projection of history.... The reenactments of historical events involve a wholehearted commitment by the participants to their own performances, which are not seen as just for the camera, but as performances that reactivate their own history and remember it for their own community.[29]

Two Laws addresses three main audiences: the Borroloola community, their children and descendants, and the Australian authorities. The film was conceived of as a tool for establishing a basis to their claims for the land, operating as a historical record and legal document. Yet *Two Laws* is also addressed to us, interested onlookers who want to witness the Booroloola decision-making practices and learn their history. In all the community meetings, the people sit on the ground and discuss current issues. These meetings are shot from the ground, and in this way the film offers us awareness of where *we* sit and who *we* are as we watch and, in turn, where we are when we walk out of the cinema and who we are as we arrive home. This awareness is an amazing gift.

Forty Postrealist Strategies to Learn from and Borrow 103

FIGURE 3.27 *Two Laws*, Carolyn Strachan and Alessandro Cavadini, 1981

Empowering ordinary people through direct participation in production is a way to demonstrate that social change is created not only through counterhegemonic discourses imposed by the filmmaker but also by altering the process of production itself. *Two Laws* violates Western viewers' expectations, particularly about time. I would argue that the film's strength comes from the Aboriginal people's sense of time and dedication to their community, as well as the patience we must bring as viewers. Their time is what we might call democratic time, the time it takes in their community meetings to agree on what is to be told, how, and by whom. This is what creates the cinematic time of the film. (How can we know a people without engaging in their sense of time?) We agree to surrender, to watch a truly collective process of decision-making: what should be told; how it will be told; how are roles assigned, the props and costumes gathered and tested; the rehearsal action tested until it is satisfactory for all involved and ready for the camera. Then it is performed in a kind of deliberate, semiformal enactment. There is a scene in "Part One: Police Times" that recounts the story of the brutal beating and eventual killing of Dolly, one of a group of Aboriginal people who were being marched off their land. Dolly was ostensibly being punished for some unstated crime. This sequence is staged this way: one by one, the persons who will be playing in the scene say their name and who they will be playing. Crew members hand out costumes. Somebody, on camera, sets the scene: "December 15th, 1933. Constable Stott brought us to Borroloola, taken there for no good reason. Our people never understood anything."

The reenactment begins. Constable Stott, the white man in charge, says to a man, "Did you kill that bullock?" Then to a deputy, "Go get the nulla-nulla" (a long wooden rod). Stott performs a brutal beating of a man with the nulla-nulla, never actually touching him. "Come on. Get going. Move. Donovan, get these men up."

The men get up. The players engage in discussion of the beating, getting the details straight. "That policeman was too cruel for one dead bullock." A man demonstrates the beating, using the nulla-nulla against a tree.

Stott continues, "Tell me straight, did you kill that bullock? Yes, I ate the whole thing." Laughter breaks out as people enjoy the joke (a bullock is a noncastrated bull). Stepping out of his role, the white man playing Stott tells what he's learned: that the local white guys used to kill bullocks but the Aboriginal people were too afraid to do so; that Aboriginal people were used for slave labor, cutting down trees, etc. He tells us that the white colonials wanted to get all the Blacks off the land.

Then a discussion among the Aboriginal women takes place. "They took six women to Robinson Crossing. They made a camp. Stott started hitting everyone, my sister Dolly, then Flora and us. Then back to Dolly, again and again. They put salt in the fresh water and made her drink. Then Stott had Dolly tied up. They hit her all one day and all one night. They hit all the men and women along the road."

Reenactment: A small campfire. The women are sitting nearby, waiting. Guards bring in Dolly and sit her down, but she falls over and just lies there. Stott orders two women over to her. They bring grass and herbs and press them into Dolly's body. Announcement on camera, "She died. She died. On the sixth of February Dolly died." Then a discussion takes place. An old man takes the group to the exact location where Dolly died. "I was lying next to her. Dolly was dead. Stott said she had been sick. He lied. He made the prisoners bury her that night (pointing), over there." They all walk over to that place. "The next morning, we packed up and left."

> When Western, even progressive ideologies talk about decolonization, it remains problematic for me, both in theory and practice. I'm still expected to discuss my culture and explore my imagination through their language in terms of the traditional versus the contemporary, where "native" is still inscribed by outsiders' fixed values and practices.... Should we not seek a scholarship of our own, articulated not simply by placing us as new participants in their discourses on art, but instead placing us on a path that moves on its own course, sometimes in their same direction, but just as often, according to its own flux and flow?[30]
> —LORETTA TODD

One way to see the film is as a gesture of decolonization, using white man's film sophisticated technology to reassert local and traditional values and to replace hundreds of years of racist myths and historical falsehoods with an encouraging record of Indigenous people's resistance to disinheritance and domination. This is not a process for all ethnographic films, but it is a provocation for what is possible with collaboration.

In the toolkit at the end of this letter, I discuss five superb films, all feature-length, all written and performed with the collaboration of their subjects. For lack of a better word, I call these films *hybrids*: Marin Karmitz's 1972 *Coup Pour Coup*, Kent MacKenzie's 1961 *The Exiles*, Abbas Kiarostami's 1990 *Close-Up*, Lizzie Borden's 1983 *Born in Flames*, and Rolf de Heer and Peter Djigirr's 2006 *Ten Canoes*. Watch and borrow from these outrageously successful collaborative films.

MAKE US STARE AT IT—MAKE US COUNT THE TIME

Sometimes, all you have to do is show something and not talk about it at all. Stan Brakhage's *The Act of Seeing with One's Own Eyes* is a film he shot in a Pittsburgh morgue in 1971 (figures 3.28–3.30). The title is

106   Forty Postrealist Strategies to Learn from and Borrow

based on a literal translation of the term *autopsy*, which is what the film offers our eyes—the dismemberment of a human body for medical research or, perhaps, to certify the cause of death.

In this silent film, unguided by narration or any visual text, we stare as a forensic pathologist opens a human corpse's cavities (the skull, the chest, etc.), breaking bones and removing organs of all kinds.

We gaze intently at all sorts of human organs, which, unless we are medical students, we cannot do in any way but in film. We study death, imagine our own, and, perhaps, through our fascination with these

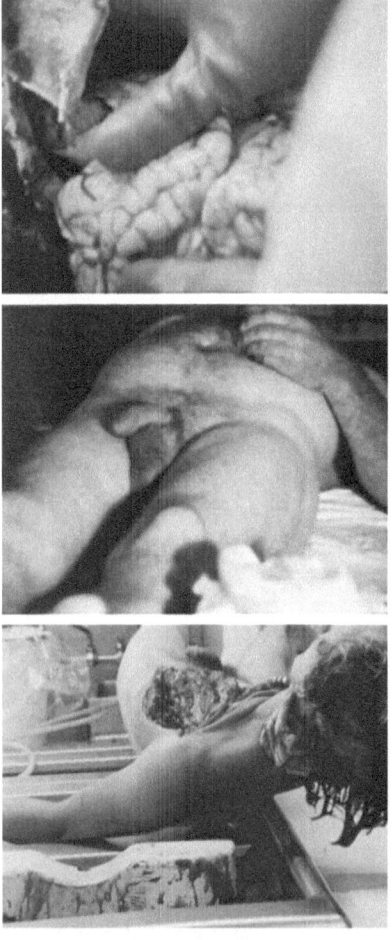

FIGURES 3.28–3.30 *The Act of Seeing With One's Own Eyes,* Stan Brakhage, 1971

exposed and manipulated organs, begin to accept these realities of our own bodies.

Like all postrealist films, *The Act of Seeing with One's Own Eyes* is about each of us—not "us" plural but singularly, and certainly not "them," those whose histories aren't told yet whose organs we explore. Brakage's film is a profound meditation on living and dying. What other unimaginable things, taken literally, can film show us? Viewers will stare if you invite us in.

Kyle Kibbe's *100 N.Y., N.Y. 1989* is another. In 1989, Kibbe went into the streets of New York City and photographed one hundred homeless people for exactly seven seconds each. All had agreed to stand for a portrait, holding small cards numbered from 1 to 100. It takes sixteen minutes to meet all one hundred. No speech is offered: no prehistories, no tales of homeless woe. There's just background street noise from the location and, periodically, the briefest of Kibbe's ruminations on this homeless person or that one, projected in voice-over as if in imaginary dialogue with them: "Looking backwards, things were better, and you were someplace else. Your letters have not arrived. No keys to fit in doors. No buzzers to repair. Just this life passing."

Questions spring into our minds: Who was that man or woman before they were homeless? How did he lose his home? Doesn't she have any friends, parents, children? Are there more men than women living on the streets? Why?

Just stare, the film says, as the numbers grow, 67 . . . 82 . . . 99 . . . 100 . . . followed by a fade out. Just one hundred out of the many we walk past every day. In 2013, there were a reported 48,471 individuals living in homeless shelters in New York City. Who knows how many more, uncounted, were living on the streets and in subway stations where we do everything possible to avoid their gaze, to ignore our complicity in their homeless condition? In the film, we look directly at their faces one by one, knowing nothing, but perhaps speculating. We can't help it.

We watch ourselves agreeing to see it through, fascinated, yet waiting for the hundredth person, counting cinema time. Again, not documentary-as-we-know-it, not DAWKI, but audience collaboration with the film artist. Ask us to stare. Ask us to count the time.

MISADDRESS AN AUDIENCE; PRODUCE A NEW UNINHIBITED ONE

A seminal postrealist performance film which everyone should see is Martha Rosler's *Semiotics of the Kitchen* (1975). Like a sober Prussian housewife in an apron, Martha herself stands in her kitchen performing a mock cooking show. In alphabetical order, she barks out the names of a series of kitchen utensils while more and more aggressively mimicking their use: apron, bowl, chopper, dish, eggbeater, fork, hamburger press, icepick, grater, and so on. As her gestures begin to veer in an unexpected and possibly alarming direction, the character eventually dispenses with the tools and uses her body as a kind of semaphore system.

> JG: As I was growing up, I watched my mother produce three meals a day for our family and then wait for compliments at the dinner table. As a girl, I knew I was supposed to participate in food prep but frequently found ways to wander away. Each time I was called back by my mother's warning, "Someday you'll have to do the cooking for your family. You better watch carefully." This prospect terrified me and guaranteed that there would be no family for me. At age seventy-seven, I can cook only seven items for my own consumption. The first time I saw *Semiotics of the Kitchen* I rejoiced.

We seem to be misaddressed. Of course, we recognize each item well before her fierce naming and primitive demonstrations. We know the names of kitchen tools and their uses, but perhaps we have not yet acknowledged the female prison of food preparation itself. At first, we're amused by Martha's furious performance, but then less so, as her demonstrations grow more violent and her symbolic resistance to the role of the woman in the kitchen grows more vehement. In her own published words, she "replaces the domesticated 'meaning' of tools with a lexicon of rage and frustration." The process is one of unharnessing the woman from the sign—the sign of our kitchen. And it's terrifying.

SHOAH, AN EDUCATION IN IMPOSSIBLE FILMMAKING

How could you make a film that struggles to depict exactly what happened: when, where, and how more than four million European Jews, stripped of their clothes and property and shorn of their hair, stepped inside the fake showers of the Auschwitz-Birkenau, Treblinka, Chelmno, and Sobibor camps where they were gassed to death with Zyklon B? There are no photographs or films of the actual deaths, yet millions died this way, suffocated in two or three minutes, then incinerated to ash in ovens and buried. An impossible film, you say.

As Claude Lanzmann has done in *Shoah* (1985; Hebrew for catastrophe, also known as a Holocaust) you could make a very long, impossible film built out of interviews with those who were *near* the places where the actual killings occurred. You could talk with the surviving Sonderkommandos, work units composed of prisoners, usually Jews, who were forced on threat of death to aid with the disposal of the gas chamber victims. You could ask some of the Nazi officials who ran the camps how they kept them running to full capacity. You could go to these now barren locations and study the landscapes, the ruins, the ashes, and the old trains that brought the Jews to the gates of the camps. Perhaps you could watch a train slowly pull up to the Birkenau camp, maybe six or seven times. You might get some clues.

By its long duration, a runtime of nine hours and forty-three minutes, its repetitions, and its determination to get as close as possible to these eradications, Claude Lanzmann's *Shoah* is asking for a kind of attention and endurance that is worthy of the scope of its subject. Lanzmann questions Polish people who watched the trains roll through their villages. He meets the people who moved into the once Jewish-owned homes. He studies the fields of ashes now grown over with grass. The achronological order of events, the fullness of some things (the testimony of the Sonderkommandos and their unspoken but palpable survivor guilt) and the thin evidence of others, all these provoke the desire to understand more and more clearly. The lack of graphic images of the murders themselves means that the film constitutes not so much a history of what happened in the past, but rather documents the horror of recalling it—producing a strange sort of poetry to be grasped as we see and hear fragments of experience in the here and now.

Shoah is exhaustive yet incomplete. It is inadequate, and Lanzmann knows it. How could it not be? He asks us to keep watching because it's crucial to try to understand the imponderable enormity of what happened in these places. *Shoah* has rendered the limits of representability.

> Lanzmann's ten-hour film is one of the few on the Shoah that include, as part of their content, the process of finding a form for representing the unrepresentable nature of the event.[31]
> —Jeff Skoller

The film works within the incomprehensible and the unrepresentable. It avoids closure because the *Shoah* experience cannot close. Can we understand the murder of six million Jews, and the homosexuals, the Polish resistance fighters, the Soviet prisoners of war, the Jehovah's Witnesses, the Roma, and countless others who died there? We cannot, but through the film's efforts, we experience trying to take hold of it. It was Lanzmann's underlying principal to refuse any "understanding" that would put his audience "in the know" and thereby shut this history down. Lanzmann wrote: "There is an absolute obscenity in the very project of understanding. Not to understand was my iron law during all eleven years of the production of Shoah."[32]

Shoah is the exact and necessary counterpoint to films like Steven Spielberg's *Schindler's List*. Spielberg's evil is an evil we can live with, that can be defeated with skill and perseverance, willpower and determination—that is, with heroics. In his book, *Murder in Our Midst*, Omar Bartov says that "Schindler's List tells an authentic story that almost never happened."[33] Before his suicide, the Auschwitz survivor Primo Levi said that "stories told by the saved distort the past, not because they are inauthentic, but because they exclude the stories of the majority who 'drowned,' not for lack of will to survive, but due to a combination of circumstances in which individual will and skills rarely played a role, and chance was paramount."[34]

To make a postrealist film, Lanzmann's "not understanding" is perhaps the most useful strategy of all. To not finish it off, not complete or explain it. To search through the evidence but to refuse resolution. Leaving questions unanswered is fundamental for our thinking further on. To say more with less, to let the viewer enter with his or her own imagination, that is key.

Now compare *Shoah* to the Burns/Novick's eighteen-hour *The Vietnam War*, which attempts to write the complete encyclopedia of that war and to actively close its chapters down, one by one, so as to reconcile us to our miserable history. Which of these is the useful film? You decide.

WANT MORE? STUDY THIS SUPERB POSTREALIST FILM

Nothing happens that is not imagined first. That's the filmmaker's job—to imagine something new or to reimagine something old and then open it up. One way is to identify and then try to solve an impossible problem.

As Lanzmann did with *Shoah*, find a way to tell something that can't be told any other way and tell it in the present tense, not the past. How can the Cambodian genocide be understood and how can the perpetrators and victims be imagined? And how can their repressed memories be released? Consider reenactment, as Rithy Panh has done in his extraordinary film *S-21: The Khmer Rouge Killing Machine* (2003).

Between 1975 to 1979, the Khmer Rouge, the ultra-Communist party supported by Mao Zedong's Communist Party of China, killed approximately 21 percent of Cambodia's population, that is, about 2,000,000 people. For four years, under the Khmer Rouge, schools were shuttered, currency abolished, and religions banned. Forced labor camps were established, and terror, torture, and executions were routine. Tuol Sleng, a former high school turned into a prison and renamed *S-21*, was just one of at least 150 prisons and execution centers operated by the regime. Over two years, in Tuol Sleng, 14,000 were imprisoned, interrogated, tortured, and killed during the Cambodian genocide. Only seven adults survived. Today *S-21* is a museum of the genocide.

Panh set out to formally expose and decipher the system there. It took him three years to locate and persuade a handful of former guards

112 Forty Postrealist Strategies to Learn from and Borrow

to participate in the collaborative project. Many of them were barely teenagers at the time and had been coerced into service and indoctrinated through fear. Reenacting their service at *S-21*, the former guards, now middle aged, walk the corridors of the prison, showing how they banged their batons on the cell bars, blared out punishing orders, took prisoners out for interrogation, and took some out to be killed (figure 3.31). Instructions about torture were given to the guards: "Never use it to relieve your anger."

Through this collaborative film practice, the guards were able to recover their repressed memories and become accountable for their actions.

Two of the surviving prisoners of *S-21* also agreed to participate (figures 3.32, 3.33). Vann Nath was a painter who survived because he had painted an iconic portrait of the Khmer Rouge leader Pol Pot, and other officers wanted their portraits done as well.

Chum Moy was an engineer who survived because he could repair broken equipment and was thus deemed useful to the deputy head of prison security. The two worked with the filmmaker, the former guards,

FIGURES 3.31 *S-21: The Khmer Rouge Killing Machine*, Rithy Panh, 2003

Forty Postrealist Strategies to Learn from and Borrow   113

 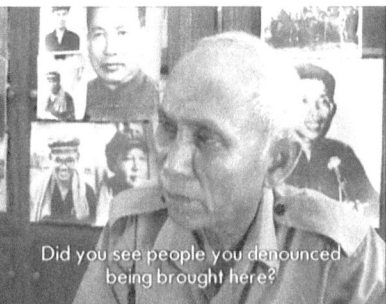

FIGURES 3.32–3.33 *S-21: The Khmer Rouge Killing Machine*, Rithy Panh, 2003

and other officers to recover the details of what had happened there. In those now empty cells, we imagine Vann Nath, Chum Mey, and other prisoners listening to the screams of tortured prisoners in the night, each wondering if this was his moment for interrogation, humiliation, torture, and probably death if he failed to confess to "crimes against the Kampuchea people."

In both *Shoah* and in *S-21*, the murders themselves were not documented, and, if they had been, footage of those *horrorshows* is unrecoverable. Panh felt an imperative to speak about the history of the Cambodian genocide without this imaginary footage. Equally important, he wanted to reverse memory loss and numbness in the psychic aftermath of this unspeakable event, not just for the young guards but also for prisoners who had, necessarily, concocted false confessions to save their lives and who still live with distorted psyches and moral injuries.[35]

> HORRORSHOW, A WORD I'VE BORROWED from Anthony Burgess's 1962 dystopian novel, *Clockwork Orange*, is based on a Russian-influenced argot he invented called "Nadsat." In Russian, the word *khorosho* (хорошо) means "fine" or "good." Burgess uses it to represent the opposite, a horrorshow.

These stories can be told, and events in the prison can be referenced and approximately reenacted. Viewers have to do the work of being nearby as witnesses while the evidence rolls out, and do so without the benefit of photographic proofs. We listen and watch intensely. We pay close attention to the film's reenactment strategies, to the reading aloud of old Khmer Rouge lists of who will be interrogated, and on which mat, in which cell, and how. (My friend, scholar Deirdre Boyle, who first brought the *S-21* film to my attention and who has written extensively of Panh's work, tells me that he abhors violent images and spectacles that commonly receive gut-wrenching responses. Thus, he avoids them.)

Both *Shoah* and *S-21* tell horrendous, almost incomprehensible stories. Both are devoted to accuracy so these accounts of what happened then can make the organization of terror and death for the victims comprehensible now. But in neither film are we there/then—neither in the death camps of 1945 nor in *S-21* of 1976. There is no pornography here—and its absence is productive.

> Imagine, suddenly, the substantial material world (tomatoes, rain, birds, stones, melons, fish, eels, termites, mothers, dogs, mildew, salt water) in revolt against the endless stream of images which tell lies about them and in which they are imprisoned! Imagine them, as a reaction, claiming their freedom from all grammatical, digital, pictorial manipulation, imagine an uprising of the represented.[36]
> —JOHN BERGER

We are witnesses to the struggle—not to relive the past—but to learn where the capacity to cooperate in genocide resides . . . what we humans are capable of when we lose heart, hope, love, and grace. Poetry is everywhere in these films. The human is everywhere, in both the perpetrators and the victims.

Don't turn your viewers into voyeurs. Instead of opportunities for empathy, jolt your audience into a different kind of experience, as Andrei Tarkovsky recommends here.

> It is obvious that art cannot teach anyone anything, since in four thousand years humanity has learnt nothing at all. We should long ago have become angels had we been capable of paying attention to the

experience of art, and allowing ourselves to be changed in accordance with the ideals it expresses. Art only has the capacity, through shock and catharsis, to make the human soul receptive to good. It's ridiculous to imagine that people can be taught to be good . . . art can only give food—a jolt—the occasion for psychical experience.[37]

TEN THOUSAND MORE STRATEGIES: HERE'S A GOOD ONE

There are many strategies to produce this kind of artist-in-exile work. Here's a fine and very different model. Watch *Too Early, Too Late* (1982). The filmmakers Jean-Marie Straub and Danièle Huillet employed rigorous staging strategies to present a sequence of tranquil shots of rural French landscapes accompanied by readings of political texts about the struggles of poor farmers there. Texts include part of a letter by Friedrich Engels describing the impoverished state of French peasants; excerpts from the *Notebooks of Grievances,* compiled in 1789 by the village mayors of those same locales in response to plans for further taxation; later, a more recent Marxist text by Mahmoud Hussein about Egyptian peasants' resistance to English occupation prior to the "petit-bourgeois" revolution of Neguib in 1952. The film is accompanied by Beethoven's late quartets, and their slow rhythms are central to the experience it yields.

During a full retrospective of Straub/Huillet films at MoMA in New York in 2016, Gilberto Perez, writing in *Film Comment,* put it this way:

> They always start with a given text, something already fashioned, written or painted or composed, and handed down from the past. They stage it and have it performed in a way that keeps it at a distance, at a remove from the present, because they want us to recognize it as a document of its time, just as they want us to recognize its cinematic staging and performance as a document of a later time, and just as they want us to recognize our own situation as spectators at a still later time.[38]

Straub and Huillet's films always achieved this important effect: audience recognition of our own confounded situation as spectators. By refusing an invitation to project ourselves into the time/space of the landscape as concerned citizens, we are left to consider these old texts and their intelligence and try them on today, in those spaces. To experience and interrogate ourselves, our own position and its contradictions, to consider it all in our own terms—that is a task for postrealist film.

Speaking of Straub/Huillet's films, I'm reminded of Adrienne Rich's redemptive vision of poetry: "the act of clearing away the mythical accretions, the inherited narratives, that prevent analysis and understanding and liberation: the wreck and not the story of the wreck/the thing itself and not the myth."[39]

Let me also offer a charming note from the novelist Mary Renault to a young writer, quoted by Daniel Mendelsohn in "The American Boy:"

> Your nice letter came this morning. Something tells me you're going to have a future as a writer. Keep at it: very few people get published at 16 or even 20, but don't worry. There is only one way to learn to write and that is by reading. Don't read for duty, try all the good stuff though, sample it, and then devour what stimulates and enriches you. This will seep into your own work, which may be derivative at first but this does not matter. Your own style will develop later.[40]

WHEN YOU'RE FORBIDDEN TO MAKE A FILM, GET STARTED MAKING IT

Consider *This Is Not a Film* (2011) by the Iranian director Jafar Panahi. Yes, this is not a film, and it isn't, but certainly it is. In the months following Iran's fraudulent 2009 presidential election, Jafar Panahi (*The White Balloon, The Circle, Offside*) was among the notable figures who sided with the Iranian people and the Green movement. Panahi, charged with propaganda against the Iranian government, was arrested in March in 2010 along with his wife, daughter, and fifteen of his friends. Despite widely publicized support from international filmmakers, film organizations, and human rights organizations around the world, Panahi was eventually sentenced to six years in prison and a twenty-year ban on directing movies, writing screenplays, giving interviews with Iranian or foreign media, or leaving the country except for medical treatment or making the Hajj pilgrimage.

Forty Postrealist Strategies to Learn from and Borrow 117

While awaiting the result of an appeal, he invited a friend and director, Mojtaba Mirtahmasb, over to help him make what later turned out to be *This Is Not a Film*, a sort of video diary, shot entirely in his apartment in Tehran, from which he was forbidden to leave. First, Panahi sets up his cellphone and records himself making tea, then making phone calls to his lawyers about his court case. Mirtahmasb arrives and starts shooting Panahi watching TV news stories, interacting with his neighbors, talking about his past films and describing scenes from the film that he had begun shooting when he was arrested. He mentions that many of his films have been banned in Iran and that people often ask him why he continues. He explains that if a film of his can't be shown in Iran, it will be shown somewhere, someday. "If I have done my job right, the films will still be meaningful then. I feel like I am reporting to history."

Initially Panahi was placed under house arrest, but he has since been allowed to move a bit more freely, though he's still forbidden to make a film or travel outside Iran. His "not a film" was smuggled out of Iran on a flash drive hidden inside a birthday cake and shown at the 2011 Cannes Film Festival.

Here are some helpful lessons in filmmaking. Panahi demonstrates using masking tape to mark out floor plans for this scene and that and discusses why the shots should be this way or that. The film he's describing, seized by the authorities after thirty days of shooting, was based on a Chekhov short story, "A Girls' Notes," where the girl, having been locked in her room by her parents, tries to commit suicide and fails. But, soon frustrated, he gives up. "If I can tell a film, then why make a film." He describes two other films he was forbidden to make. Mirtahmasb takes off from the apartment, but, on the dining room table, leaves his camera, which continues to record. Panahi goes to the balcony, waters the plants, lights a cigarette, and watches a huge crane swing up and back, this way and that. He tries to locate a scene from one of his earlier films, *Crimson Gold*, to demonstrate the instinctive genius of one of his nonprofessional actors.

A young man rings the doorbell and asks for the trash to take down to the basement. Panahi, recording with his cell, films the interaction. They chat a bit, then Panahi rides down with the young man and the trash in the elevator. Soon enough, they're outside on the courtyard, looking through an ornate metal gate at a huge display of fireworks on the street. It's Noruz, the Iranian New Year, the day of the vernal equinox that marks the beginning of spring in the Northern Hemisphere. Tempted, Panahi makes a move to go out through the gate, but the young man cautions him, "Mr. Panahi, please don't come outside. They'll see you with the camera." Panahi keeps shooting but stays inside. Fade to black.

This film is not a prank. It is not surrealism, as in Magritte's "This is not a pipe" caption of his painting of a pipe. It's a not-a-film that demonstrates Panahi's sangfroid in respecting the letter of the law, exposing its preposterousness as well as the meanness of its spirit. The film is a statement of creative resistance, an announcement of the condition of the intelligentsia in Iran, and an absurd demonstration of his obedience to the terms of his confinement. It is a political speech act, though he never mentions the political situation in the film. It also illustrates Panahi's is successful struggle to stay alive creatively.

Like the new Iranian cinema as a whole, he combines documentary and narrative (yes—there is a dramatic ending), moral intelligence and poetry. There is even a pet iguana he has been commissioned to care for by his daughter, who, with her mother, is staying with friends for the holidays. Like all superb films, it is a film about filmmaking and what I would call *a necessary film*.

Since 2011, Panahi has made three more "illegal" films, *Closed Curtain* (2013), *Taxi* (2015), and *Three Faces (2018)*. To me, he's a heroic figure, for defying the authorities, for figuring out how to keep making films, and for producing, one after another, superb cinema. See them all and borrow from this courageous filmmaker. But please remember, "this is not a film."

EXPLOIT SOUND AND ITS ABSENCE

Here is a disastrous episode of history and two extraordinary films that came from it. In June 1942, on orders from Adolf Hitler and Heinrich Himmler, SS troops accomplished the complete destruction of the village of Lidice, a village of miners in the Protectorate of Bohemia and Moravia in what is now the Czech Republic. The action was in retaliation for the assassination of Reich Protector Reinhard Heydrich. The village of Lidice was suspected of harboring the men who killed him. All 173 males from the village who were over 15 years of age were executed, as well as a further 11 men from the village who were not present at the time but later arrested and executed, along with several others who were already under arrest. One hundred and eighty-four women and 88 children were deported to concentration camps. A few children who were considered racially suitable for Germanization were handed over to SS families, and the rest were sent to the Chelmno extermination camp where they were gassed. Then the physical village of Lidice was obliterated, after which it was literally buried.

One year later, in 1943, a British documentary filmmaker, Humphrey Jennings, made the seminal thirty-six-minute docudrama *The Silent Village*, featuring coal miners and their families from the village of Cwmgiedd in Wales, collectively reenacting the Nazi annihilation of the village of Lidice and its people. The film opens before the storm troopers arrive, as a large car traverses the village's roads sporting a huge loudspeaker, announcing that anyone violating or suspected of violating laws will have their property confiscated and will be arrested and killed. The loudspeaker broadcasts the message: "Irrefutable evidence has been established that you have aided the circle of suspects in question. The incriminating evidence has been established without your assistance. You will produce the assassins." Jennings's excellent film, *The Silent Village*, filmed under wartime conditions in Wales, was a supreme gesture of solidarity with the Lidice families and all those living under Nazi occupation.

Filmmaker Deborah Stratman has borrowed about three minutes of *The Silent Village* for her very sober seven-minute film *Village, silenced* (2012). She repeats the sequence of shots of the large car with loudspeaker three times, the first time with the original soundtrack, *Irrefutable evidence have been established . . .* In the second iteration, the car travels the same route through the village but with gunfire in the distance and multiple sirens wailing nearby. The third time, the car travels the same route in the same sequence of shots but in complete silence. It's stunning to watch that footage again in silence. Certainly, Stratman's film is an homage to Jennings's lucid commemoration of Lidice's fate, but, more than that, in the silence of the third iteration it's a mediation on those moments *before* occupation begins and perhaps a rehearsal of our refusal to anticipate what threatens our coming loss of freedom. A brilliant, courageous, anthropophagic warning of danger.

CAN YOU DANCE A NONFICTION FILM? CAN YOU DRUM A USEFUL TALE?

Watch *La Bouche* (2017) from Guinea, by the Colombian filmmaker Camillo Restrepo. It's a kind of self-ethnography, the materialization of a folktale or parable, chanted, drummed, and danced by superb musicians and singers. *La Bouche* (the mouth) enacts the tale of an old man who has learned that his daughter has been brutally murdered by her husband. Time stands still as the father, paralyzed, oscillates between the need for solace and his urge for revenge. He sits alone in his hut. He can't move. Two singers call out "the mouth, the mouth," "wake up, Father," "your daughter is dead." But the old man, Guinean master percussionist Mohamed Bangoura, is silent, immobilized. (The story is loosely based on Bangoura's own story.)

Three drummers pick up the pace. The singers fiercely chant "We know who killed her." "You can catch him." "Why don't speak?" "Wake up, Father. Wake up." "Spit out your rage and your pain." "Only you can make this end." We watch the father smashing crockery with his feet. The two singers begin to dance ferociously. The son, one of the drummers, goes to the father's hut and convinces him to begin to move. The two walk slowly through the woods, then rest on a huge log. The son says, "See, it feels better already."

The father, back in his hut, sits over his jenbe. (It looks like a conga drum.) He strokes and strokes it for a long while. Then slowly he begins to drum, and drum. Slowly his face loosens, his eyes begin to see, his mouth begins to move. He becomes beautiful. The drumming is exhilarating.

How is this nonfiction you ask? I answer, not only is it a fierce depiction of paralyzing moral injury and the role of community in its energetic care and wisdom, it's also an account of despair and rejuvenation, told in song and dance, far from realism. We learn from the remote village without learning *about* that village—its name, specific location, judicial system, etc.—because of the film's formal elements, and, if I may invent a word, *unrealism*. That allows us to focus on how we navigate grief in common ways, aided by the universal reach of music in a nonfiction song. There is insight into a remote village culture with much to teach us about caring for ourselves and those in our community. The film is not fiction. Rather, it is a song itself.

Learn from the best and use it well.

Watch as many of the postrealist films that I have recommended as possible. (See my list in the toolkit called "Where to Find All the Postrealist Films I've Mentioned Though Sometimes They Disappear.") Take a break, then watch a few more—ten, or even more. Then come back here.

WHAT IS THE POLITICAL USEFULNESS OF THE POSTREALIST FILM?

Recently I read a poem by Ron Padgett called *Ladies and Gentlemen in Outer Space*. It begins:

> Here is my philosophy:
> Everything changes (the word "everything"
> has just changed as the
> word "change" has: it now
> means "no change.) so
> quickly that it literally surpasses my belief,
> charges right past it . . .[41]

We're told we now live in a post-truth society where all assertions about the way things are now contradicted by other, contrary assertions. To engage in a battle of truths in nonfiction cinema is a fruitless game. Postrealist films engage us differently, without inviting us into a contest of facts, but rather asking us to consider useful ideas offered by unique experience. Želimir Žilnik's *Black Film* doesn't argue about the causes and numbers of the homeless. Instead, it invites us, provocatively, to consider giving the homeless a home in our homes, a seemingly preposterous proposition, but Žilnik shows us how. Chen Chieh-Jen's *The Route*, a meticulous enactment of a shipyard strike that never happened, asks us to puzzle over the value of performing, remembering, and honoring our will to resist oppression. Raul Ruiz's *Of Great Events and Ordinary People* performs the absurdity of standard documentary tropes. Soon enough the useless documentary "evidence" dissolves into farce.

In his nine-hour film *Shoah*, Claude Lanzmann doesn't try to understand the eradication of six million Jews and others in Nazi concentration camps. He omits a number of key elements of cinematic artifice that might enable us to distance ourselves from his subject. There's no narration to tie large swaths of footage together with grand statements, no reenactments to goose audiences with conventional drama, and no music to cue Pavlovian emotional responses. In this nine-hour film, the Holocaust is unaccountable and unexplainable, but the film's reckoning of how the speedy annihilation of masses of people was organized poses questions for our individual roles in the next racial oppression—and anticipates our resistance. There is time to ponder what *you* might have done then or are doing now about our current wars, occupations, and genocides. Through the film's efforts, we experience trying to take hold of it, but, as mentioned earlier, it was Lanzmann's underlying principle to refuse any understanding that would put his audience "in the know" and thereby shut this history down. It's an invaluable refutation of more conventional works that seek to contain the atrocities of the Holocaust with reassuring implications of its singularity. But it could happen again; it *has* happened again—in Cambodia, Rwanda, and Bosnia, among other places.

What exactly is the usefulness of the postrealist film—especially the political usefulness? The forty or so postrealist films I discuss employ a variety of strategies, but they all produce useful experience and even, perhaps, enlightenment.

I know it's an old-fashioned word, but I lean toward it. What's possible with the postrealist film *is* enlightenment, an awakening through an excavation of a situation and its roots in our neoliberal, hegemonic thinking and language. As Franju invites us to witness in *Blood of the Beasts*, we're asked to look at the mechanical precision of the slaughter and dismemberment of meat-producing animals and their transformation into the foods we desire. How does that slaughter reflect on us, on our willingness to "kill without anger"? As Farocki demonstrated in his 1969 film *Inextinguishable Fire*, to stop the war in Vietnam you have to stop the war in factories where the war materials are produced. We must think about how our labor, at a chemical plant, a tech company, or even in the classroom, can be corralled into something destructive such as facial recognition systems or a better napalm. As Buñuel has insisted in *Land Without Bread*, we need to watch ourselves, fascinated with the details of dire poverty yet resisting the unpleasant truths of whoever ignores the peasants' plight. We observe both our horror and our prurient pleasure, as well as our refusal to take responsibility for it. It is unforgettable.

There are many people who don't deny poverty, but they don't want to know much about it because it's all so terrible, and what can you do? Postrealist films offer paths through these weeds . . . a chance to go beyond these prevarications and evasions. What is possible in a postrealist film are opportunities for viewers to see through the language configurations that keep us passively watching the world literally burn up . . . to see beyond the persistence of oppressive hierarchies of gender and race, to watch exactly how our forever wars go on apace. Postrealist films offer opportunities to surpass passivity.

How? Postrealist films are addressed to an active mind, and our minds respond in kind, especially when, for instance, undoing depictions of who-is-not-us. In Trinh-T Min-ha's *Reassemblage* about three small villages in Senegal, she refuses to speak *about* the villagers. As she puts it, she is just *speaking* nearby, and so we have to adjust to listening and watching *nearby.* Joseph Beuys and Jurgen Boch's *Ausfegen* offers us an unusual opportunity to interact with the filmmakers' radical propositions about creative citizenship and to watch it performed in minute detail. Kyle Kibbe's *100 N.Y., N.Y. 1989* demands close observation and endurance while we count the one hundred unidentified homeless in the streets of New York City. Carolyn Strachan and Alessandro Cavadini's *Two Laws* offers models of useful cooperation with the Australian Aboriginals' struggle for their land. Chick Strand's *Fake Fruit Factory* offers access to private gendered spaces where we can learn about what women know and don't tell. Women, but also men, can learn a lot in Martha Rosler's kitchen about the repetitive gendered roles we have been modeled, or maybe baked, into. John Greyson's *14.3 Seconds* decimates the government's preposterous fantasy of the successful reconstruction of war damage in Iraq and elsewhere—and maybe everywhere. Think about that before you agree to invade . . . well anywhere.

These films are not designed to inspire a movement or get people to sign petitions. They are discrete opportunities for radical, useful knowledge and often for pleasure of various kinds. These films are educational in what I consider the most essential sense . . . in the development of our political minds, questioning our inherited values and understandings, deconstructing and then refreshing our social imaginaire.

You could call them "a vibration of sense used as energy"—as the French critic Jean Davie once wrote about Paul Celan's post-Auschwitz poetry.[42] The writer Ruth Franklin calls it "a phenomenon that surpasses mere comprehension."

FINALLY, SOME USEFUL NOTES FROM THE POETS

Sylvia Plath has written, "Art is theft. Art is armed robbery. Art is not pleasing your mother."[43]

The Argentine Jorge Luis Borges said: "A writer, or any man, must believe that whatever happens to him is an instrument; everything has been given for an end. This is even stronger in the case of an artist. Everything that happens, including humiliations, embarrassments, misfortunes, all has been given like clay, like material for one's art. One must accept it. . . . Those things are given to us to transform, so that we may make from the miserable circumstances of our lives things that are eternal, or aspire to be so."[44]

The novelist Toni Morrison said in her acceptance of the Nobel Prize in 1993, "Say more with less. Let the reader enter with his or her own imagination. . . . Dead language actively thwarts the intellect, stalls conscience, suppresses human potential. Unreceptive to interrogation, it cannot form or tolerate new ideas, shape other thoughts, tell another story, fill baffling silences. Official language smitheryed to sanction ignorance and preserve privilege is a suit of armor polished to shocking glitter, a husk from which the knight departed long ago. Yet there it is: dumb, predatory, sentimental. Exciting reverence in schoolchildren, providing shelter for despots, summoning false memories of stability, harmony among the public.[45]

As Aldous Huxley, author of *Brave New World*, wrote, "The most shocking fact about war is that its victims and its instruments are individual human beings, and that these individual beings are condemned by the monstrous conventions of politics to murder or be murdered in quarrels not their own."

And Béla Tarr has written, "Who says there is a correct length of a movie? . . . After the credits roll, are you stronger or are you weaker? If you are stronger after seeing my movie, I am happy. If you are weaker, then I must say that I'm sorry."[46]

And, from the chorus of Leonard Cohen's song *Anthem*:

> There is a crack in everything.
> That's how the light gets in.[47]

Live like you are free. Find those cracks in everything and make your film there.

AFTERWORD

This book used to be called *Useful Film—How to Make One*. Names change as these things go. Recently, at a museum exhibition in Poland, I found this definition of a *useful film* from 1932 and took a lousy picture of it, so I've typed it out here:

> A useful film is one that draws on all the achievements of a film language to provoke the intended emotion or impose specific ideas. It is a film whose creators are in harmony with their social conscience (and they possess such a conscience). It is a film that does not falsify reality, but captures it in an artistically ordered form.
> —The Polish Film in the Wilderness. Between the Order of Profitability and the Order of Art. Cooperative Production as the Road to Artistic Film, *Glos Stolicy*, 1932

4
The Toolkit

CONTENTS

The Questionnaire: For Doing a Close Reading of a
    Documentary Film
Definitions of the Documentary Over the Years
The Unspoken Pleasures of the Documentary-as-We-Know-It
The Documentary Writ Broad in Just Five Sentences
Where to Find All the Postrealist Films I've Mentioned
    (Though Some, at Times, Tend to Disappear)
Teach Yourself Poetry . . . Just the Basics
Five Superb Hybrid Feature Films to Study
A Brief Review of the 2017 Burns/Novick PBS Series
    The Vietnam War
"Kill the Documentary as We Know It," Jill Godmilow, 2001
What Happened to Jill in Poland and How Postrealism Entered
    Her Life
I Want to Be Useful
144 Feature Films You Should See Before You Croak
Filmography

THE QUESTIONNAIRE: FOR DOING A CLOSE READING OF A DOCUMENTARY FILM

When I was teaching in a university, I used to require students in all my documentary film courses to apply this questionnaire for five of the fifteen or so nonfiction films we watched over the course of the semester . . . to produce what's called a "close reading" of the film.

For each assignment, answer ten of the following twenty questions, including these mandatory six: 1. Organization, 3. Address, 10. Us/Them, 13. Title, 19. Argument, and 20. Thrust. Pick four other questions that stimulate your fullest, most critically penetrating analysis. Don't answer any questions that do not lead you to insight and try not to repeat the same answers. Answer all parts of each question.

The Questionnaire—to Do a Close Reading of a Documentary Film

1. Organization
    a. What are the basic elements/materials of the film? interviews? expert testimony? charts? demonstrations?
    b. How are the materials organized, i.e., how is information ordered, arranged, and presented so that the film's argument can be made? Is it in narrative form? expository? mosaic? formal/experiential/postrealist? none of the above? some combination of forms? Explain.
    c. Speculate about why the filmmaker chose to structure the materials this way?
2. Participation of social actors: why do you think the people who were filmed agreed to participate—to perform themselves as *social actors* in this film? Or didn't they? Speculate about the contract (spoken, unspoken, conscious, unconscious, legal, illegal, monetary, uncompensated) between the filmmaker and the filmed?
3. Address: who is the ideal audience to receive this film's message—to whom is the filmmaker speaking? That is, to whom is it addressed? Is it men? women? young? old? rich? middle class? poor? white? nonwhite? hip? college educated? ignorant? sophisticated? leftist? liberal? conservative? religious people? a mass audience (everybody)?

In other words, who is the you that the film addresses? Remember that the address is something invisible, but something built into every aspect and every choice in the filmmaking process. You aren't supposed to notice how you're being addressed (conned, charmed, engaged, made guilty, repaired, resolved) and you're not supposed to notice (consciously) what values the film ascribes to you.

4. Identification: did you identify with any character(s) in the film? Who? With whom did the director want you to identify, and why? Did you feel inferior or superior to anybody in the film? Explain how the film made you feel that way.
5. Fears and/or hopes: what fears and hopes did the film call up in you as you watched? Analyze the director's motives for constructing characters and story events to call up these feelings. Why are they necessary for the film's positioning of its audience?
6. Privilege/repress: What information or types of information about its subject did the film seem to *privilege* (make significant, stress, underline, repeat) and what information did the film seem to *repress* (avoid, deemphasize, disguise, obscure), and, in each case, why?
7. Values: what values does the film inscribe, underline, promote: fairness? freedom? simplicity? hard work? hipness? modesty? responsibility? devotion? peace? courage? compassion? self-determination? benevolence? perfection? progress? Does the director assume you share those values?
8. Shooting and editing style: exactly how did the director's shooting style, lighting, and editing/pacing support his/her purposes? Discuss two typical scenes as examples.
9. Music: explain the function of music in two scenes in this film. Then, generalize about the use of music in the film. For instance, is a particular sequence associated with one character? Does it call attention to itself and is it supposed to, or is it just background, perhaps to provide a rhythm to the sequence? Does it comment on the scenes, and, if it does, how? Is it there only to underscore (pump up) certain emotional sequences?
10. Us vs. them generalizations: what does the film say about *them* (race, nationality, ethnicity, class, or period of history) portrayed in the film? That is, what does it say about *us* . . . "our society" as opposed

to "theirs"? Derive five large generalizations about "us" (what is said implicitly and presented as normal or natural) and "them" (how they are represented as different or other).
11. Psychology: what, if any, psychological explanations are made for character behavior? Is this "cheap" psychology, or a profound analysis, or somewhere in between? (Don't answer this question if the film doesn't suggest psychological explanations of behavior.)
12. How was it made: did the film say anything, implicitly or explicitly, about *how* it was made? (Every documentary film speaks, in one way or another, about why it was made the way it was: its crudeness or slickness; why it stops where it does; what its limits are; why certain materials are included, etc.) Are there any moments in the film that are self-reflexive—that inscribe evidence into the film's text of the processes of production and/or the fact of authoring—insisting, thereby, on the subject's awareness of the author and the author's intentions? If so, why do you think they are there?
13. Title
    1. Exactly why was this title (and not something else) chosen for the film? What does it promise (as an advertisement for the film) and how is it useful for spreading positive word-of-mouth by viewers after the film has been seen? (Titles are almost always decided on after a film is finished and are designed to address both of these problems.) How does it attempt to intrigue the viewer? What question(s) does it raise, and does it actually answer those questions? Why, in some cases, does it only vaguely suggest what the subject of the film is? What cultural references does it make?
    2. How does it function as language/sound—does it feel good in the mouth? Do you like saying it (i.e., is it "sexy" or hip or exciting to say, in a literary or poetic way)? Does it have a certain rhythm?
    3. Give the film another name—an accurate one that actually describes the film. (If the title had no job to do except accurately name the film, what would that title be?)
14. Flip ethnicity: if the main character's ethnicity were changed (to African American, Latino/a/x, LGBT, trans, impoverished, wealthy, single parent, handicapped or any other identity group), could the film make the same argument? Try it before you answer.

15. Flip gender: if the main character's gender were otherwise, could the film make the same argument? Why, or why not? Try it before you answer.
16. Elevation: did the film try to elevate you? To elevate the audience is to make viewers feel they are better people for having watched this film, more sophisticated in their understanding of the world, or a morally or spiritually deeper.
17. Sleep: why didn't you fall asleep—assuming you've been getting enough? What kept you awake? Beside the fact that you are required to screen films for the class, what kept you interested in continuing to watch? This question is specifically about structure and movement. For instance, what, if anything, was withheld until the end? How did the filmmaker keep you fascinated? With what strategies? At what point did you know what the rest of the film would say or what would happen in the end? How did you know?
18. Your film: could you make a different film out of the same material . . . one that argues the opposite of what this film proposes? How?
19. Argument: in five precise, declarative, progressing sentences, express the film's central ideological argument about its subject and how it manages our relationship to what is offered. This may be explicitly expressed by the film or hidden within the film's text. Make sure that these assertions include the entire rhetorical thrust of the film and all the insight you've had about the film from your close reading. If you've made an argument, it should lead to a "thus" or "therefore" type final sentence . . . often the moral of the story . . . that helps the film to achieve closure—a sense of completeness and, finally, an ending. In your writing, try to characterize the tone of the film's argument—the force, the style, the kind of rhetoric used. This should sum up your understanding of the film and how it operates (see the following *Hoop Dreams* argument).
20. Thrust: in one sentence, describe the film's essential thrust. What did the film advocate? For instance, did it tell you what to do now? How to live in the world? Did it tell you to change something about yourself? Did it suggest that you've been missing something important in life? Did it warn you about something? Complete one of the

following sentences or a similar sentence: It asked me to
_____. It pleaded that _____. It appealed for
_____. It cautioned me to _____. It
condemned _____. It celebrated
_____. It warned me that _____.

Did the film actually tell you something you needed to know? Did the film tell you what you should know about this? Make sure you've got the most essential thrust of the text. Check your argument first, then defend your choice with the answer to this last question.

A Sample Argument: *Hoop Dreams*

Watch *Hoop Dreams*, then run it through the questionnaire process for yourself. Penetrate the ideology of that film, its address to the viewer, what it privileges and what it represses, its use of music, choice of the title, and much more. The last question—*what the film's argument is in five progressive sentences*—should be a summation of exactly how the film constructs or figures or defines you, the viewer, and makes its case. Don't worry about writing exceedingly bloated sentences if that's what it takes, as mine often do, to get it all in. It's perfectly acceptable. Here's my best shot on *Hoop Dreams*:

1. Our inner-city Black citizens are stuck in poverty and we don't know what to do about it.
2. For them, the one and only way out of the cyclical and endless failures of ghetto life—the only road to success—is education, and the only way to get an education for inner-city Black youth is through sports. But this is a tough road, and only the very best can achieve it.
3. Sometimes—in spite of the absent fathers, the drug pressures in the neighborhood, the violence, the terrible schools and irrelevant education, the irrational and punitive welfare policies and practices—some heroic and steadfast Black mothers (who share our middle class values and who have faith in God) are somehow able to sacrifice

enough to keep their families together and love and support their sports-talented Black sons, thereby giving them a chance to escape the destructive pressures on the Black underclass and helping them get into top basketball colleges from which they can have a shot at the NBA, which could provide them money, fame, and in every way make life worth living—if everything goes well.
4. These mothers deserve our respect and our compassion, and we should pray for the success of their sons.
5. However, finding the focus and determination to stay in school and keep your mind on both the game and your grades (and not on girls and clothes and drugs) is hard for African American kids, and when it doesn't work out for these sweet sons (especially within the exploitative system of professionalized amateur athletics), the least we can know and feel is that they tried, and we can continue to hope that someday, miraculously, just maybe one (or even two) of these deserving African American sons, those who have gotten a bit more education than they would have without basketball skills, might be able to avoid the pitfalls of the Black inner-city life that brought their fathers and their brothers down so low and finally climb out of the underclass to comfort and security. Someday.

DEFINITIONS OF THE DOCUMENTARY OVER THE YEARS

August Lumière: he said he was "documenting actualities."[1]
John Grierson: "the creative treatment of Actuality."[2]
Pare Lorentz: "a factual film which is dramatic."[3]
World Union for Documentary formulated the following definition in 1947: "Any film which, by rational or emotional means and with shots of actual phenomena or the authentic and valid reconstruction of these, has the express intention of enhancing human knowledge and setting out problems and their solutions from an economic, social and cultural point of view."[4]
William Stott: "The essence of documentary is the communication, not of imagined things, but of real things only."[5]
R. Spottiswoode: "The documentary film is in subject and approach a dramatized presentation of man's relationship to his

institutional life, whether industrial, social or political; and in technique, a subordination of form to content."⁶

Jeanne Allen: "The function or justification of the documentary, the characteristic which sets it apart as a separate genre, is its replication of reality, not primarily for the purpose of entertainment, but for evidence and argument."⁷

Marita Sturken: "The camera image constitutes a significant technology of memory."⁸

Trinh T. Minh-ha: "Reality organized into an explanation of itself." Also, "the documentary is the instrument of mastery over all of the unknown as I gather all that into the fold of the known."⁹

Charlotte Brunsdon: "Documentary films are films which, through aspects of their presentation and the use of particular conventions, give the impression that the events and characters seen on screen had an independent existence apart from the film. The idea is that the film simply records or reveals something that already exists . . . thus a documentary film is a film which indicates that this is what it is doing."¹⁰

Paula Rabinowitz: "A film that produces a theoretical audience of agents, and imputes to them a desire to act, to remake history, to become, in Walter Benjamin's phrase "Angels of History" (as opposed to the drama that produces an audience with a desire to desire)."¹¹

Alexander Kluge: "A documentary film is shot with three cameras: 1) the camera in the technical sense; 2) the filmmaker's mind; and 3) the generic patterns of the documentary film, which are founded on the expectations of the audience that patronizes it. For this reason one cannot simply say that the documentary film portrays facts. It photographs isolated facts and assembles from them a coherent set of facts according to three divergent cameras. All remaining possible facts and factual contexts are excluded. The naive treatment of documentation therefore provides a unique opportunity to concoct fables. In and of itself, the documentary is no more realistic than the feature film."¹²

Somebody: "A documentary is any motion picture that is susceptible to the question: 'Might it be lying?' "

THE UNSPOKEN PLEASURES OF THE DOCUMENTARY-AS-WE-KNOW-IT

1. identity: a comfortable definition/version of a unique "who I am," which is not "he," "she," or "them"
2. epistomophilia: knowledge of a knowable world; the well-received address to ourselves as rational animals; the joy of "seeing for ourselves" (corollary: the world is "knowable"); as Elizabeth Cowie writes in "The Spectacle of Reality in Documentary Film":

We believe the evidence of our own eyes, including the visual evidence of photography and cinematography, even though we know that our eyes are easily deceived and that, as Hine also notes, while "photographs may not lie, liars may photograph." Nevertheless there is an "attraction" in seeing for ourselves which sustains our belief over and above any knowledge of the falsity of our seeing. Or, to put it in its properly confusing way, seeing is more real than knowing. What arises here as well is, I suggest, the desire for the evidence of our own eyes.[13]

3. scopophilia: identification with the apparatus, the machine as an instrument of looking/seeing, (our TV is our privatized electronic grotto—our miniature sound and light show)
4. the proffered sense of community: by means of the address, the recognition of your presence and membership in a community (a synthetic group) through the production of the audience as a "unified spectator"

Godard: We are grateful to the world (and to the image machine) for recognizing us and permitting us to recognize ourselves . . ."[14]

5. the splaying of viewer out into and over the world with tremendous technical command, as in aerials, tracking shots, etc.
6. comfort: reconnection to the all-knowing mother . . . a state of regression into the comfort of a controllable, organized, simulated reality in which separation between one's body and external world, between ego and non-ego, is not clearly defined: a seemingly simpler, "real-er" existence than real existence

7. sometimes a kind of intellectual stimulation as in crossword puzzles, possibly; see *Spellbound*
8. voyeurism: a legitimatized opportunity to sit in the dark and peek at monsters, misfits, the abject, the "primitive," the unfree, the poverty-stricken, the ravaged, as well as the famous, talented, and perhaps extremely wealthy, etc.
9. art pleasures: such as narrative gratification (sometimes), elegance, order— and entertainment; an antidepressant (in that it allows for the flow of feelings)
10. pornographic pleasures: the capacity to watch rather than engage with someone else—which results in not having to deal with the possibly threatening "other" as a full subject
11. consolation—for uncomfortable self-consciousness about class status, educational level, etc.
12. physical experience that transcends physical reality—to zoom in and out; to cruise over a city; to see in slow motion or in high speed, or to traverse the moon, or to enter through the walls of a cell.

THE DOCUMENTARY WRIT BROAD IN JUST FIVE SENTENCES

1. Historically, the traditional documentary has been understood as the lesser stepchild of the dramatic fiction film. To carve a special space for itself—to gain and hold its audience—it had to position itself as uniquely different from narrative fiction film, primarily by its claims to represent factual truths: here is the real world, and you can know all about it if you watch.
2. The traditional documentary is also the most enduring vestige of cultural imperialism and the most significant way by which we define ourselves in relation to *them* . . . the *others*, exactly because the others can be constructed as *not us*.
3. Documentaries are the most efficient conveyors of ideology, which, through the use of what is called photographic realism, appears transparent and unmediated.
4. Documentaries present themselves in the interstices of culture as helpful, edifying, necessary experience. Documentaries always say,

"here is something you should know!" (This is what Bill Nichols usefully calls the "stance" of all documentaries.)

5. All films, including documentaries, are texts. There's nothing "natural" about them. Next to advertising texts, docs are perhaps the most carefully worked texts in the world. Some facts are stressed, some are repressed. Images are foregrounded or disappear into the shadows. Materials are ordered this way or that. And finally, the audience is addressed as this audience or that, but most often as a caring community of good citizens who would want to know about the world and bring respect, understanding, and happiness to all people.

But artists-in-exile might use what we consider nonfiction materials to do otherwise: to shake us out of the slumber of our selfness, out of our us/them binary; to clear the old furniture out of the attic of the mind. For instance, a postrealist doc could ask us to consider the question: "Do you think women should be permitted to smoke in public?" And offer a reasonable response: "Permitted by whom?"

WHERE TO FIND ALL THE POSTREALIST FILMS I'VE MENTIONED (THOUGH SOME, AT TIMES, TEND TO DISAPPEAR)

100 N.Y., N.Y. 1989 https://www.youtube.com/watch?v=z30aulednri.

14.3 SECONDS https://yorkspace.library.yorku.ca/xmlui/handle/10315/4214, https://letterboxd.com/film/143-seconds/, *Disruptive Film*, vol. 1, from Facets Multimedia, https://www.facetsdvd.com/Disruptive-Film-Vol-1-p/dv102386.htm.

ANOTHER WORLDLY https://vimeo.com/194599843, password "twiceremoved," or, to buy it, go to https://film-makerscoop.com/catalogue/leslie-thornton-another-worldly.

ACT OF SEEING WITH ONE'S OWN EYES in *Brakhage: An Anthology*, vol. 1 (Criterion Collection); also https://vimeo.com/160194525 with music track.

AUSFEGEN *Disruptive Film*, vol. 2, from Facets Multimedia, https://www.facetsdvd.com/Facets-Label-s/35.htm.

BLACK FILM https://www.zilnikzelimir.net/black-film, *Disruptive Film*, vol 2, from Facets Multimedia, https://www.facetsdvd.com/Facets-Label-s/35.htm.

BLOOD OF THE BEASTS included in the Criterion DVD of Franju's *Eyes Without a Face*; go to Amazon.

CROSSROADS go to the Museum of Modern Art and screen it there, https://www.moma.org/collection/works/200073?sov_referrer=artist&artist_id=1215&page=1, https://www.youtube.com/watch?v=xUm2rPejRrQ.

DR. STRANGELOVE Amazon Prime, rent for $3.99, https://www.amazon.com/Dr-Strangelove-Learned-Stop-Worrying/dp/B000P407K4.

THE ETERNAL FRAME you can buy or rent it at Electronic Arts Intermix: http://www.eai.org/title-search.

THE EXILES trailer https://www.youtube.com/watch?v=9VepP9Eyfp0; purchase from Milestone Films, https://www.milestonefilms.com/products/the-exiles.

FAKE FRUIT National Film Preservation Foundation, https://www.filmpreservation.org/preserved-films/screening-room/2011-nfr-fake-fruit-factory-1986#.

FIRST COMES LOVE https://vimeo.com/ondemand/damnedifyoudont/87371888. Scroll down to *First Comes Love*.

FROM GULF TO GULF TO GULF a three-minute excerpt at https://www.youtube.com/watch?v=kP6Ns8q5N2A.

GERMANY IN AUTUMN purchase at https://www.facetsdvd.com/Germany-in-Autumn-p/dv100625.htm or https://www.amazon.com/s?k=Germany+in+Autumn&i=movies-tv&ref=nb_sb_noss or watch twenty-six minutes at https://www.youtube.com/watch?v=LL14D9gmqMM.

HOW TO LIVE IN THE FEDERAL REPUBLIC of GERMANY purchase at Facets Multimedia: https://www.facets.org/images/constantcontact/farockicatalog2011.pdf.

AN IMAGE https://www.youtube.com/watch?v=0XgHMDWrAys, Facets Multimedia: https://www.facets.org/images/constantcontact/farockicatalog2011.pdf.

INEXTINGUISHABLE FIRE purchase from Video Data Bank, https://www.vdb.org/titles/inextinguishable-fire.

ISLE OF FLOWERS rent from Letterboxed https://letterboxd.com/film/isle-of-flowers/.

JUGGLING GENDER buy or rent: https://twn.org/catalog/pages/responsive/cpage.aspx?rec=1505&card=price#FilmPricing; also Jennifer's lecture in 2016 at https://www.youtube.com/watch?v=IN9LZgEtWZc

LA BOUCHE rent at https://vimeo.com/ondemand/labouchecamilorestrepo.

LAND WITHOUT BREAD https://www.youtube.com/watch?v=at-xnnNT8N8; rent or buy: https://www.amazon.co.uk/dp/B07WCHVF3T?tag=letterboxdod-21&linkCode=ogi&th=1&psc=1&language=en_GB.

MARJORETTES IN SPACE French with English subtitles: https://www.youtube.com/watch?v=EUN_6hsqt8s.

MARIO BANANA https://www.youtube.com/watch?v=1Ku9sGT2Ugg; rent/purchase from the Museum of Modern Art Film Library: https://www.moma.org/research-and-learning/circulating-film/, https://assets.moma.org/momaorg/shared/pdfs/docs/learn/Andy_Warhol_Complete_Price_List-US.pdf.

MEDIA BURN https://www.youtube.com/watch?v=FXY6ocvaZyE&t=383s ... not the original film but most of it + https://archive.org/details/mediaburn/mediaburn_256kb.mp4.

A MOVIE https://letterboxd.com/film/a-movie/ (you have to subscribe, but it's free).

NOTES ON THE CIRCUS rent on Amazon https://www.amazon.com/Notes-Circus-Jonas-Mekas/dp/B01M25VVXM/ref=sr_1_3?keywords=Notes+on+the+Circus&qid=1580246582&s=movies-tv&sr=1-3.

OF GREAT EVENTS AND ORDINARY PEOPLE https://letterboxd.com/film/of-great-events-and-ordinary-people/.

PERFUMED NIGHTMARE https://letterboxd.com/film/perfumed-nightmare/.

RAT LIFE & DIET IN NORTH AMERICA if you're an institution and you've got $100, go here: http://film-makerscoop.com/rental?source=3460; otherwise, try a public library with a decent film collection.

REASSEMBLAGE rent or purchase https://www.wmm.com/catalog/film/reassemblage/.

THE ROUTE purchase *Disruptive Film*, vol 1, from Facets Multimedia.

S-21: THE KHMER ROUGE KILLING MACHINE rent or purchase: https://www.amazon.com/S21-Khmer-Rouge-Killing-Machine/dp/B0007TKORS.

SCUM MANIFESTO, French w/English subtitles https://vimeo.com/72825633; in Polish with English subtitles: https://vimeo.com/198484997, password "scumm."

SEMIOTICS OF THE KITCHEN https://americanart.si.edu/artwork/semiotics-kitchen-77211.

SHOAH purchase: https://www.amazon.com/Shoah-Criterion-Collection-None/dp/B00BX49CME/ref=sr_1_2?dchild=1&hvadid=77721783083103&hvbmt=be&hvdev=c&hvqmt=e&keywords=shoah+claude+lanzmann&qid=1595728071&sr=8-2&tag=mhob-20.

SHOPLIFTING, IT'S A CRIME? purchase at *Disruptive Film*, vol. 1, from Facets Multimedia.

SYMBIONESE LIBERATION ARMY (SLA) SCREED #16 purchase: *Disruptive Film*, vol. 1, from Facets Multimedia.

TEN CANOES purchase https://www.amazon.com/Ten-Canoes-David-Gulpilil/dp/B000S8CLSS/ref=sr_1_3?crid=12VY27BHJT5AH&dchild=1&keywords=ten+canoes&qid=1595728179&s=movies-tv&sprefix=TEN+CANOES+%2Caps%2C152&sr=1-3.

THE SILENT VILLAGE https://www.amazon.com/Silent-Village-Humphrey-Jennings/dp/B09CKQF9LG/ref=sr_1_10?dchild=1&keywords=the+silent+village&qid=1633042220&s=movies-tv&sr=1-10.

THIS IS NOT A FILM purchase: https://www.amazon.com/This-Not-Film-Jafar-Panahi/dp/B008VR7U8O/ref=pd_bap_rp_1/136-2449334-4465225?_encoding=UTF8&pd_rd_i=B008VR7U8O&pd_rd_r

=d47891cf-5d1d-4330-8f58-9d651a763f6e&pd_rd_w=8APZA&pd_rd
_wg=6FovT&pf_rd_p=7669271c-2ef0-42ca-ad73-02617f1bf83b&pf.

A TIME LAPSE MAP OF EVERY NUCLEAR EXPLOSION SINCE 1945
https://www.youtube.com/watch?v=LLCF7vPanrY.

TOO EARLY TOO LATE https://www.youtube.com/watch
?v=zD2BcS9RZIw (click CC for English subtitles).

TWO LAWS purchase on Facets: https://www.facetsdvd.com/Two-Laws-p
/dv93421.htm.

VIDEOGRAMS OF A REVOLUTION purchase: https://www.facetsdvd
.com/Videograms-of-a-Revolution-p/dv88577.htm.

VILLAGE, silenced https://vimeo.com/54985133.

WHAT FAROCKI TAUGHT purchase: https://www.vdb.org/artists/jill
-godmilow; purchase: *Disruptive Film*, vol. 2, from Facets Multimedia:
https://www.facetsdvd.com/product-p/dv102418.htm.

WALTZ WITH BASHIR you can rent the full film for $3.99 or buy
https://www.youtube.com/watch?v=2B2-G3fvUec.

WINTER SOLDIER buy or rent from Milestone: https://milestone.vhx.tv
/videos/winter-soldier.

TEACH YOURSELF POETRY . . . JUST THE BASICS

There is no better preparation for liberation from the traditional documentary-as-we-know-it ways of thinking than to *read poetry* . . . Read it often. Read it aloud. Listen on-line to a poet reading his/her poetry. But even more important, *write a poem*. For starters, write about films that you admire, that have moved you or amazed you in special ways. Find good language to represent that film . . . to respect it, to devour it, to make it sing in language of your own. (Write about the any of the films I've recommended in this book. Try writing one film-poem every week.)

In the literature of every country, poetry comes first, before prose . . . it's closer to the origins of language. It predates reading and its rhythms help the listener remember it and keep it alive. It's more natural, more basic—a more total expression of the muscular, sensuous, emotional, rhythmical nature of the human mind.

Poetry, in ancient Greek, derives from the verb ποιεω (*poieo*), which means "to create" or "to make." By the way, the Greeks called the poet "the athlete of the word" . . . and poets can certainly be athletic.

The process, from the beginning to the end, is fostered and overseen by an organizing *mind*, acting with the common sense of everyday life, even when it is dealing with the uncommon sense of dreams or visions.

The poet is a seer, or *see-er*. And you must be a *see-er* in order to devise strategies to crash through the film language that has defined our social existence, as documentaries purport to do. I think filmmakers' radical stubbornness is the best tool we have for crashing through the documentary-as-we-know-it and its useless, petrified strategies.

In contrast, poetry is sensations, memory, and ideas, made of words that produce in us intense delight and insight: tears, sorrow, joy, anger, and more. Repetition, rhyme, and meter matter, especially as mnemonic devices . . . ways of making unique experience memorable and transferable and thus an early form of social media.

A poem makes *memorable* both the moment of the idea/impression/illumination expressed *and* the moment of thinking about the moment of the idea/impression/illumination . . . a double whammy, no?

I'm not a poet myself, but I write them from time to time . . . maybe twenty a year. Writing poetry is a useful way to get yourself out of prose writing and into some other part of your brain . . . the one on the other side of your brain wall, escaping the rules of grammar, punctuation, even the rules of spelling and the terrible obligations of explanation.

Here's one great poem about a film. Read it out loud . . . you'll appreciate it the best this way.

Enter Dark Stranger, William Trowbridge (b. 1941)

In *Shane*, when Jack Palance first appears,
a stray cur takes one look and slinks away
on tiptoes, able, we understand, to recognize

something truly dark. So it seems
when we appear, crunching through the woods.
A robin cocks her head, then hops off,
ready to fly like hell and leave us the worm.
A chipmunk, peering out from his hole
beneath a maple root, crash dives
when he hears our step. The alarm spreads in a skittering
of squirrels, finches, millipedes. Imagine
a snail picking up the hems of his shell
and hauling ass for cover. He's studied carnivores,
seen the menu, noticed the escargots.

But forget Palance, who would have murdered Alabama
just for fun. Think of Karloff's monster,
full of lonely love but too hideous
to bear; or Kong, bereft with Fay Wray
shrieking in his hand: the flies circle our heads
like angry biplanes, and the ants hoist pitchforks
to march on our ankles as we watch the burgher's daughter
bob downstream in a ring of daisies.[15]

This I love: "Imagine a snail picking up the hems of his shell / and hauling ass for cover. He's studied carnivores, / seen the menu, noticed the escargots."

Why Write Poetry About These Postrealist Films?

1. to sharpen your insights about these films by searching for adequate language to represent them
2. to appreciate their techniques and learn them well enough to steal from them
3. and simply, to help you remember them

Here's a fine prose poem from a student of mine, Bryant Davis, after watching George Franju's 1948 film *Blood of the Beasts*, two months after 9/11. Read it slowly, twice.

Blood of the Beasts

Sheep die their legs flailing. Others watch, wait, contemplate. I feel bad for them because my mother raised them and I used to play with them, but I am able to maintain my human hands. Adam Zagajewski said that, or described that, speaking of children born after the end of the Second World War and how it seemed impossible that they can be born the same as the children who came before. But I cannot quite relate to that. I can only relate that after there was that thing with the crashing planes, after twelve hours, I returned to playing video games. *Final Fantasy Seven.* I raced Chocobos which are brightly colored ostriches. Mine was fuchsia. I lost to one that was fluorescent blue. This time, after the sheep are dead and the cows are dead and the horse is dead, a reusable metal bullet through its forehead, I last only till dinner where, hungry for pasta, I eat three-cheese chicken tortellini. This is my magic power. I can forget mass murder like it were water.

Some Thoughts from the Poets

- Allen Ginsberg wrote, "The only thing that can save the world is the reclaiming of the awareness of the world. That's what poetry does.[16]
- Hafiz: The great religions are the ships . . . poets, the lifeboats. Every sane Jane person I know has jumped overboard.[17]
- In about 1800, Wordsworth wrote that poetry is the process of "fitting to material arrangement a selection of the real language of men in a state of wild sensation."[18]
- Samuel Taylor Coleridge said poetry is "the best words in the best order."[19]
- The British poet W. H. Auden, who got up very early and started to write, unwashed, on a rigorous schedule, treated writing "not as an inspirational mystery but as a real occupation like banking, or fucking, with all its attendant egotism, boredom, excitement and terror.[20]

PS—Poetry is not simply verse, or verse form (any singsong with rhythm and rhyme), like,

> Thirty days has September
> April, June, and November . . .

Though these lines could be *in* a poem—perhaps a poem about poetry or something else—but it ain't poetry, or it's just lousy poetry, only good for remembering or memorizing the lengths of months. Boring.

Read Aloud Some of These Fine Poems About Movies Past

Try this one, in dialogue form:

note, passed to Superman, Lucille Clifton

sweet jesus, superman.
if i had seen you
dressed in your blue suit
i would have known you.
maybe that choirboy clark
can stand around
listening to stories
but not you, not with
metropolis to save
and every crook in town
filthy with kryptonite.
lord, man of steel,
i understand the cape,
the legging, the whole
ball of wax.
you can trust me,
there is no planet stranger
than the one i'm from.[21]

Here's a lovely ode to the city of New York by eight-year-old Ben:

Manhattan

Oh Manhattan
How your rocky
ground is stuck
to the sea and how
you're able to hold us up for
all those years
without tipping us over
How you let us walk
on the ground without paying
you are the greatest thing
to me[22]

Even on a bad day you can experiment with words. Put a few down, maybe reorder them, find words that are more precise, reshape an arresting line, use it for the first line in a poem . . . later it may become the middle or the last. What might the poem's next sentence say?

It doesn't really matter *what* we write, or *how* (who's watching?). It only matters that these films teach us something unimaginable in any other way and that we can express what happened to us somehow in poetry.

Avoid Clichés

Clichés are stale familiar words and phrases and metaphors. *The language of poetry pays attention to itself as language.* By its nature, a cliché does not; it is language that is not listening to itself: "I think we are enjoying the backlash of the moral decline that peaked in Watergate." (Enjoy a backlash? Unlikely! There are no images here . . . nothing authentic from the speaker . . . no care taken.)

Experiment with Various Forms

1. A poem using allegorical animals:

   ### The Swan, Rainer Maria Rilke, translated by Robert Bly

   This clumsy living that moves lumbering
   as if in ropes through what is not done
   reminds us of the awkward way the swan walks.

   And to die, which is a letting go
   of the ground we stand on and cling to every day,
   is like the swan when he nervously lets himself down

   into the water, which receives him gaily
   and which flows joyfully under
   and after him, wave after wave,
   while the swan, unmoving and marvelously calm,
   is pleased to be carried, each minute more fully grown,
   more like a king, composed, farther and farther on.[23]

2. A Sufi ghazal: lyrical love songs to God, recited or sung by minstrels in the royal courts of pre-Islamic Iran. A ghazal has between five and fifteen lines, split into two equal parts (couplets). The final couplet contains the poets name. (Many today are set to music in Iran, Turkey, and India.)

   ### Look at This Beauty, Hafiz, translated by Thomas Rain Crowe

   The beauty of this poem is beyond words.
   Do you need a guide to experience the heat of the sun?

   Blessed is the brush of the painter who paints
   Such beautiful pictures for his virgin bride.

   Look at this beauty. There is no reason for what you see.
   Experience its grace. Even in nature there is nothing so fine.

   Either this poem is a miracle, or some sort of magic trick.
   Guided either by Gabriel or the Invisible Voice, inside.

> No one, not even Hafiz, can describe with words the Great
>   Mystery.
> No one knows in which shell the priceless pearl does hide.[24]

You could also write about a film: "The beauty of this *film* is beyond words."

3. A haiku is a Japanese poetic form, with three lines, seventeen syllables, usually arranged 5-7-5 (but you can vary this); an image or two of something particular in the natural world—a very particular moment of observation and insight; the juxtaposition of surprising images; and a flash of awareness or recognition (an important way of insight in Zen Buddhism).

> The temple bell stops—
> but the sound keeps coming
> out of the flowers.[25]
> —Bashō, translated by Robert Bly

> This line of black ants—
> maybe it goes all the way back
> to that white cloud![26]
> —Kobayashi Issa, translated by Robert Bly

> Eastern guard tower
> glints in sunset: convicts rest
> like lizards on rocks.[27]
> —Etheridge Knight (1933–1991)

4. Lyric—a Beatles song, or the Song of Songs from the Bible: directly explores emotions of its real or imagined speaker—usually brief and songlike.

Song of Songs (excerpt)

> Come, my beloved, let us go to the countryside,
>   let us spend the night in the villages.

Let us go early to the vineyards
    to see if the vines have budded,
    if their blossoms have opened,
And if the pomegranates are in bloom—
    There I will give you my love.

The mandrakes send out their fragrance,
    and at our door is every delicacy,
    both new and old, that I have.[28]

5. A limerick—five lines: 1, 2, and 5 must rhyme,; 3 and 4 must rhyme. This humorous limerick is titled "Relativity" and was written by professor of botany, A. H. Reginald Butler, appearing in an issue of the London humor magazine *Punch* in 1923, after Einstein published his "Theory of General Relativity" in 1915.

    There was a young woman named Bright
    Whose speed was far faster than light
        She set out one day
        In a relative way,
    And returned home the previous night.

6. The prose poem is a poem written in prose rather than verse, which makes it a weird hybrid, an anomalous genre. It avails itself of the elements of prose while foregrounding the devices of poetry. Prose poems work by the sentence rather than the line, the paragraph instead of the stanza, and yet they insistently define themselves as poems, which gives them an air of rebelliousness, a sense of breaking loose from old-fashioned strictures. These compulsively modern creatures may look like prose, but they think metaphorically, like poetry.

The Drink, Ron Padgett

I am always interested in the people in films who have just had a drink thrown in their faces. Sometimes they react with uncontrollable rage, but sometimes—my favorites—they do not change their expressions at all. Instead they raise a handkerchief or napkin and calmly dab at the offending liquid, as the hurler jumps to her feet and storms away. The other people at the table are understandably uncomfortable. A woman leans over and places her hand on the sleeve of the man's jacket and says, "David, you know she didn't mean it." David answers, "Yes," but in an ambiguous tone—the perfect adult response. But now the orchestra has resumed its amiable and lively dance music, and the room is set in motion as before. Out in the parking lot, however, Elizabeth is setting fire to David's car. Yes, this is a contemporary film.[29]

Here I offer you my favorite poem of all time, with a great punch in the last stanza.

Automatic Teller Machine, Ben Mirov

If you work at a steady rate
you may reach the river by nightfall
and if you have the will

a canoe will be waiting
by the ash factory
for you to take upstream

to the takoyaki shack
where you can eat delicious food
and drink as much beer as you like

until late into the night.
In other words you have
your whole life ahead of you

and no one can tell you
what to do or how to act
or what to say or anything

said the machine in the wall
before dispensing my receipt[30]

Here's an outrageous poem and great fun. *Oh let's just be hogs!*

A Performance at Hog Theater, Russell Edson

There was once a hog theater where hogs performed as
men, had men been hogs.
One hog said, I will be a hog in a field which has
found a mouse which is being eaten by the same hog
which is in the field and which has found the mouse,
which I am performing as my contribution to the
performer's art.
Oh let's just be hogs, cried an old hog.
And so the hogs streamed out of the theater crying,
only hogs, only hogs . . .[31]

Here are four more poems to inspire you. The first about a dying fish, the second about a child's coffin, the third about water, bread and art, the fourth about everybody Black.

Fishing, Dean Blehert

Take a bit of lowland, a basin, a small valley, a hole, fill it with water,
    even just a few feet,
and you get a mystery, this glossy flat surface from which you look
    back at yourself, broken, bent, puzzled, unable to see the
    bottom or walk there to talk to what may live there, through
    the looking glass, where your kind of life dies.
. . . . Fishing conquers the mystery, sitting
    under the old sun, dropping a barbed hook through the
    mirror, yanking out an emissary (a hostage?); something that,
    in its thin, flickering life was part of the mystery, a shifting
    flaw in the reflecting glass,
. . . . now flopping at your feet, turning dull
    in the sun, something you can eat, can understand, living,
    struggling, in pain, dying, caught.[32]

Here's a fine poem by a Vietnam War vet. You could call it a lament.

Grandfathers, Doug Rawlings

I watch my granddaughters grow up—
their heights measured by chalking the kitchen post—

So I think I know something about feet and inches

as I watch grainy footage from the war
of a Vietnamese grandfather, forearms of sinewy flesh,

swinging his hammer with the authority of long experience
being interviewed by some American journalist

staring into the hole of the camera through these five decades
I feel the agony of grandfathers so far removed from now

fashioning together coffin after coffin—each three feet long[33]

A poem by the Palestinian Taha Muhammad Ali. He fled to Lebanon with his family when he was seventeen after their village came under heavy bombardment during the 1948 Arab-Israeli War. The following year, he returned to Nazareth, where he lived until his death. In the 1950s and 1960s, he sold souvenirs during the day to Christian pilgrims and studied poetry at night. His formal education ended after fourth grade. He was owner of a small souvenir shop near the Church of the Annunciation, which he operated with his sons. Muhammad Ali wrote vividly of his childhood in Saffuriyya and the political upheavals he survived.

Twigs (excerpt), Taha Muhammad Ali

And so
It has taken me
all of sixty years
to understand
that water is the finest drink,
and bread the most delicious food,
and that art is worthless
unless it plants
a measure of splendor in people's hearts.[34]

This poem doesn't fit into any category of poems I know. So let's make a new category: ecstatic poems. The bold, direct, unabashed celebration of the poet's feelings is startling, outrageous, and funny. And we know why and what he means. Try it yourself with your own racial category, or religion, or ethnic group. "Everybody Ukrainian is my hometown team," or "Everybody Hindu is my hometown team," or "Everybody Yellow is my hometown team." We could all be savvy, exuberant poets in this way . . . with just a bit of winking and a sage smile on our lips. Thank you, Cortney.

I'm Rooting for Everybody Black, Cortney Lamar Charleston

Everybody Black is my hometown team. Everybody Black
dropped the hottest album of the year, easy. Everybody Black
is in this show, so I'm watching. Everybody Black is in this
    movie,
so I'm watching. Everybody Black wore it better, tell the truth.
Everybody Black's new book was beautiful. How you don't
know about Everybody Black?! Everybody Black mad
underrated. Everybody Black remind me of someone I know.
I love seeing Everybody Black succeed. I hope Everybody Black
get elected. Everybody Black deserves the promotion more than
anybody. I want Everybody Black to find somebody special.
Everybody Black is good peoples. Everybody Black been through
some things. Everybody Black don't get the credit they're due.
    I met
Everybody Black once and they were super chill and
    down-to-earth.
I believe in Everybody Black. There's something about Everybody
    Black.[35]

Then there's this brief and truly important poem by Langston Hughes, "Johannesburg Mines," most useful for thinking about how a simple poem like this (and a theoretical postrealist film) could produce dramatic results . . . and more useful poems and more useful films.

Johannesburg Mines

In the Johannesburg mines
There are 240,000 natives working.
What kind of poem
Would you make out of that?
240,000 natives working
In the Johannesburg mines.[36]

Here are some thoughts on the Hughes poem by Anne Boyer, from her "Actuary of the Apocalypse: The Anti-Extinction Engine" in the *Yale Review*:

> The poem isn't only a question for poets, though it is also that. It's one-third a question for poets, two-thirds the truth for everyone, and also, because one-third of the poem operates doubly, in that the question in the middle is also a kind of answer, one-third an answer for poets and anyone else who wonders what poems can do. The poem does not sentimentalize the suffering of the colonized workers in the name of politics and likewise does not aestheticize this suffering in the name of art. It also resolutely does not forget these workers or allow them to be forgotten, nor does it forget to mark its own place in the history of the class struggle.[37]

Kenneth Koch writes,

> Ordinary language is of course where the language of poetry comes from. It has the words, the usages, the sounds that a poem takes up and makes its own. It constitutes, along with thoughts and feelings, what may be called the raw materials of poetry. If you think of each word as a note, this ordinary language is like an enormous keyboard, and wherever it is, the poet has a medium, just as the painter has one wherever there are paints, the sculptor wherever there is wood, iron or stone. On the poetic keyboard, each note (each word) refers to or stands for something that is not physically present and that is not it itself.[38]

Start writing poems—start making poem-inspired films.

FIVE SUPERB HYBRID FEATURE FILMS TO STUDY

Most of the most successful hybrid (fiction/nonfiction) features are collaborations with social actors, individuals who have agreed to perform their experience by reenacting it for the camera. If you're thinking of a dramatic feature, here are five I suggest you study.

Coup Pour Coup

Watch Marin Karmitz's *Coup Pour Coup* (*Blow for Blow*, 1972), a fine collaboration with social actors and a fierce assault on the exploitative tendencies of bourgeois capitalism. It's performed by actual women strikers at a small textile plant in France and written by them collaboratively with Karmitz. When harsh work conditions become more than they can bear, the women occupy the factory, sabotage the machines, and take their male boss hostage. Though there had been male union leaders, they are bypassed or ousted for their lack of leadership and negotiating skills. The women on strike abandon their domestic obligations to their husbands, and there is a lively exchange about this role reversal, years before stay-at-home husbands became a possibility. The strikers' treatment of the factory director is riotously funny . . . he is humiliated and marched out of his own factory, but not before he has called in the police, who arrest the women strikers.

This film was a collective effort. Videotapes of upcoming scenes were discussed by the workers, and camera angles as well as dramatic refinements were agreed on before any film was exposed. The result portrays the strikers as intelligent actors in the process of planning and carrying out their plant occupation. This successful film could and should be screened not only in film production and gender studies courses but also for every union local in the country.

The Exiles

To further grasp the potential for collaboration, watch Kent MacKenzie's 1961 film *The Exiles*. Background: the Indian Relocation Act was passed by Congress in 1956 in order to reduce the costs of maintaining Native American peoples on reservations. It encouraged them to leave their reservations, acquire vocational skills, and assimilate into the general population in urban centers. Native Americans were offered some help in housing and jobs by the Bureau of Indian Affairs in exchange for relocating to urban centers. This act played a significant role in increasing the population of urban Native Americans in Los Angeles, Minneapolis, Chicago, Denver, Phoenix, and Tucson in the succeeding decades.

The Exiles is a hybrid, a collaborative fiction performed by social actors . . . a group of twenty-something Native Americans friends of the filmmaker who reperform their recent painful experience of being enticed off their reservation and brought to Los Angeles to wander through wild drunken nights in the city—that is, to become Americans. It is one of the most painful and most beautiful films I have ever seen. The Indigenous actors had left reservation life in the 1950s for the Bunker Hill district of Los Angeles, a run-down neighborhood of decayed Victorian mansions and skid-row apartment buildings. They were living marginal lives, boozing every night, playing poker, flirting, driving fast cars, and just hanging out. MacKenzie spent a year and a half sitting with them night after night before they agreed to reenact scenes from their transplanted lives. There was never any script. Filmed on nights and weekends, it took three years to complete.

MacKenzie called it an "anti-theatrical and anti-social doc film." No scene had anything to prove, and there is no narrative to be moved forward. Each sequence plays as long as needed. Completely unsentimental, it is unblinking, almost unbearably intimate, deeply respectful, tragic, and full of pleasures.

MacKenzie started this film with $579 in his bank account in 1955. When he ran out of cash, his barber gave him $1,200. The cinematographer/director Haskell Wexler gave him $5,000 near the end of filming. MacKenzie used short ends . . . leftover bits of film stock he could purchase from large expensive shoots. He went through three cameramen as, one by one, they were drafted for the Korean War. At last, *The Exiles* was released in 1961.

The Exiles premiered at the Venice Film Festival to much acclaim, played a few colleges and festivals, then fell into obscurity and vanished. In 1980 the film's negatives were discovered in the UCLA Film and

Television Archive, and the film was rereleased by Milestone Films to rave reviews. With Cassavetes' 1960 *Shadows* and Godard's 1961 *Breathless*, *The Exiles* completes a trilogy of astonishing feature films, marking the birth of the independent film movement. It's said that *Shadows* and *Breathless* reinvented cinema. Just as profoundly, so did *The Exiles*.

Close-Up

Another example of the hybrid feature is Abbas Kiarostami's film *Close-Up* (1990), an exemplary mix of nonfiction and reenactment. Based on a story Kiarostami read in the newspaper, the film introduces Hossein Sabzian, playing himself, an impoverished out-of-work bookbinder who loves the cinema, in particular the films of Mohsen Makhmalbaf. One day, in casual conversation with a rich woman sitting next to him on a bus, he claims to be that famous Iranian filmmaker whose screenplay he has been reading. Sabzian's impersonation is spontaneous, coming from his cinephilia and perhaps, in that moment, his desire to imagine escape from the labor that keeps him perennially destitute. Eventually he meets with the woman's family in their home and enlists their help in making his "next film." Sabzian's misleading pretext eventually is undone. He's arrested and tried for attempted fraud. The film follows the recorded courtroom procedures where he is being prosecuted for the impersonation. The family members are there in the courtroom tensely watching the proceedings. The courtroom footage alternates with dramatizations of the story Sabzian tells in court, also performed by family members, and others, playing themselves.

What's remarkable for Western viewers is to learn that in Iranian courts the aggrieved party is offered a chance to forgive the perpetrator. After the family had heard penniless Sabzian's story, he is forgiven and released. Soon after, the family and Sabzian agreed to participate in Kiarostami's dramatization of the events as themselves. I will not relate the last scene in the film, after Sabzian is released, because it is the most joyous sequence I know of in any film I have ever seen. Don't take my word for it, watch it and look for your own opportunity to mix actuality footage with reenactment. Kiarostami has shown us what can come of it.

The agreement to participate in the reenactments by Sabzian, the family, and even the reporter, Farazmand, who dashed off to be the first to report the crime, as well as their genuine humility and courage, is what advocates so strongly for collaboration with social actors.

> I like so much what Cristina Vatulescu has written about *Close-Up*. "In the process of making the film, we see Kiarostami redefine cinema as a medium whose primary task is precisely to mediate between law and its subjects, as between people and their clashing fantasies. To be able to do this, however, the film itself is transformed by the encounter with the law and its subjects, opening the way for a new type of documentary filmmaking—not just antimimetic, but blatantly interventionist, interpersonal and interactive. . . . More pointedly, filmmaking is here a way of being in the world for others, of acting for them while giving them a chance to act their best."[39]

Iranians voted *Close-Up* the best film in Iranian film history, and Kiarostami was voted the most important director of the 1990s by U.S. critics.

Born in Flames

Another hybrid, Lizzie Borden's *Born in Flames* (1983), perfectly fulfills Bertolt Brecht's admonition that *a work of art should always show the distance between what is and what could be.* Here is a futuristic tale of a small, racially diverse army of radical lesbian feminists in New York City after a peaceful social-democratic revolution. The lesbians have discovered that the situation for women, and especially women of color, has not been improved by the revolution—not at all. It's a world rife with violence against women, high female unemployment, sexism, racism, unfair labor practices, sexual assault, and government oppression. In response, the women take their defense into their own hands, mobilizing in the streets, in their clubs, and in their homes, preparing to educate themselves and to act. As you watch the film, you feel it's happening everywhere, that you are everywhere, witnessing a dyke bike brigade run down a sexist harassing asshole in the streets, broadcasting on short-wave pirate radio their *Radio Ragazza* and *Phoenix Radio* programs, and more. The film suggests that the time for civil disobedience has come and gone. The socialist government, which has bumped women and racial minorities to the bottom, calls their actions treasonous and attacks them in the media. In this film, Borden insists that liberation is not something linear and utopian on the horizon, but requires intimacy, militancy, solidarity, anticapitalist politics, as well as a complete reimagining of what constitutes "the future."

The film is narratively structured but contains mosaic-like, faceted sequences and follows many different story lines. In the final sequence, a group of women force their way into a television station, interrupt an on-air speech by the president of the United States, take over the microphones, and begin broadcasting their agenda, proposing that women be paid to do housework and more. They bomb the antenna on top of the World Trade Center to prevent destructive messages from reaching the mainstream.

Borden, on a shoestring budget, filmed *Born in Flames* over a period of five years. She adopted guerrilla techniques and filmed on real street corners and subway cars that capture the rot and grit of New York City. The film's documentarylike reality is the most important element: what keeps the improbable future mixed with the present feeling not only actual but almost as if it has *already* happened. The tensioned space between it did/could/will happen and it didn't/couldn't/won't happen is acute. The performances are unprofessionally effective, vibrating between the documentary in the present and the projected future. The women speak with conviction from a place of power. The distance between what is and what could be . . . that too is *Born in Flames*.

Ten Canoes

One more collaboration is worth studying—the superb *Ten Canoes* (2006), an Australian period drama codirected by the filmmaker Rolf de Heer and Indigenous Peter Djigirr in collaboration with the Aboriginal people of Arnhem Land in the Northern Territory of Australia. *Ten Canoes* is the first feature film to come completely from the Aboriginal culture—from Aboriginal aesthetics, morality, community organization, pace and rhythm and filmed entirely in an Australian Aboriginal language. Based on an ancient story from the Yolngu people from the time before Western contact, it relates a profound moral tale about a murder of the wrong culprit and the requisite retribution as self-sacrifice that must be offered by the guilty party.

We are immersed in superb photography and superb storytelling. A student of mine, Julian Owyong, characterized the address to viewers in this way:

1. You people . . . you came here to listen to a story, a story like you've never seen before, but it's not like your story—it's my story . . . but a good story all the same.
2. It is a story, a true thing about my people and my land, how we come from this land—we follow the law, which is the same law we have now—it's like that for my people.
3. We try to lift up the laws, how they used to sit a long way back, so anyone can see we've got laws . . . they can recognize us.
4. We try to teach about what happens when we die, how we all go back to our water hole—how all of us are the same that way.
5. You people . . . maybe now you can recognize us, our culture, all the systems . . . and maybe this story will help you live the proper way.

Then he wrote, "It's the first film from an 'away' culture that actually asks me to both be inside the away culture while seeing it as a story and laughing and crying with it."

De Heer has said, "People talk about what is a white director doing making an indigenous story? They're telling the story, largely, and I'm the mechanism by which they can. Surely that is one way to understand the role of the filmmaker working in collaboration with social actors from another culture—to be the mechanism by which their stories can be told."[40]

A BRIEF REVIEW OF THE 2017 BURNS/NOVICK PBS SERIES *THE VIETNAM WAR*

How does the Burns and Novick eighteen-hour PBS documentary series *The Vietnam War* degrade us as citizens? How could they get us to be *reconciled* with the fact that the U.S. conducted a genocidal war against the Vietnamese people for twenty years? We watch American GIs recalling, over and over, the buddies lost, the amputations, the terror of it all that they experienced in the jungles of Vietnam. Eighteen hours later, in the last episode's voice-over, we receive a kind of dreamy resolution of these unspeakable memories. *In Vietnam, the land has largely healed. Old animosities have mostly been buried. But ghosts remain. Americans and Vietnamese work together to clean up places where Agent Orange has poisoned the earth. Unexploded ordnance half hidden in the ground still takes lives each year. Aged mothers and fathers from northern Vietnam still roam the south seeking to discover what happened to their sons and daughters.* How reassuring! This is a kind of canonic *The End* title card like those that used to show up just before the final credits in Hollywood films, telling us that this drama is finished, all questions have been answered, there's nothing more to say, you've seen it all. Now you are educated, having lived the experience hyperefficiently, without pain. But there is so much more to say in the aftermath of the Vietnam War.

A few ghosts remain? Perhaps just a few missing sons and daughters. No. There are thousands of still missing sons and daughters. And there are thousands of children with missing arms, legs, and eyes from their parents' exposure to Agent Orange's dioxin, which causes stillbirths, cancers, anencephaly, spina bifida, skin lesions, severe impairment of the liver, along with immune, endocrine, nervous system, and reproductive system disorders. There are at least 350,000 tons of live bombs, artillery shells, rockets, and mines still left in the land, which could take hundreds of years to clear. Since the war ended, roughly 40,000 Vietnamese have died from these UXOs, (unexploded ordinance), shattering (mostly children's) lives through four generations and likely to continue. Here are photos of a 700-pound bomb discovered in Nghe An province on July 7, 2019 (figures 4.1–4.2).

There are still tens of highly contaminated Agent Orange sites in South Vietnam. The use of Agent Orange in Vietnam violated every international treaty the U.S. has ever signed. Only one site, the Danang Airport, has been cleaned up since the war ended in 1975. But now, thanks to Burns/Novick, all that has been examined and straightened out for good. Now we know how it happened, why it happened, and how we did our best but failed to win the war. And on it goes.

FIGURES 4.1–4.2 Vietnamese photos of recovering an unexploded 750-pound bomb discovered in Nghe An province on July 7, 2019

It's outrageous that Burns/Novick neglected to mention, among other things, that, in 2020, every day, about twenty Vietnam War veterans commit suicide in the U.S., and 70 percent of them do so using a gun, according to statistics from the U.S. Department of Veterans Affairs. As of this writing, the number of U.S. Vietnam veterans who have committed suicide has far surpassed the fifty-eight thousand U.S. soldiers killed in the war whose names are posted on the Vietnam Veterans Memorial in Washington, D.C. No such memorial exists for the veterans who died of suicide after the war. Today, in 2020, American service members are more likely to take their own lives than to perish in combat.

This documentary series demonstrates what I mean by pornography of the real. All the horrors of that war have been depicted in detail, organized for your entertainment, education, and, finally, your peace of mind! No lessons learned. Gates closed. Reconciliation? Burns/Novick stated intention for making the series? Not for me.

Sad to say, the PBS eighteen-hour film series *The Vietnam War*, financed by the Koch brothers and Bank of America, will probably be the record of choice for high school teachers and lazy college professors of American history.

We have not—not ever—learned the lessons of the Vietnam War, and after eighteen hours of the PBS series we certainly still haven't. As I write, we have been at war in Afghanistan for twenty years to destroy the Taliban and deliver democracy to the suffering Afghanis—and we have failed. The U.S is also helping to destroy the coherence of two more Middle Eastern countries, Syria and Yemen. The pornographic portrayal of the Vietnam War brought to us by Burns and Novick produces nothing but ignorance. Against our "forever wars," documentary war porn is illusionary and devastatingly destructive. It proposes to resolve the moral injury in the nation's soul and it fails.

In the cinema, as in the novel, you would have to refuse to represent, in Coetzee's term, "the state's vile mysteries" in order to educate in an antiwar way. And while Alain Resnais and Marguerite Duras do this effectively in *Hiroshima mon amour* and Harun Farocki does it on napalm with *Inextinguishable Fire, The Vietnam War* by Burns/Novick fails completely in this regard.

"KILL THE DOCUMENTARY AS WE KNOW IT," JILL GODMILOW, 2001

Here's something I wrote in response the Danish Dogme group's 1995 announcement elaborating the responsibilities and terms for their fiction filmmaking, which, somewhat strangely, duplicated the rules for cinema verité documentary filmmaking: the camera must be handheld—no tripods, no inauthentic props can be brought onto the set; no nondiegetic music can be added; no fancy lighting, etc. The Dogme films would thus be more truthful, more powerful, and more trustworthy, if they abided by these monastic principles and shunned the glamorous and seductive effects of Hollywood production. At least that was the theory.

In fact, the Dogme films needed no rationalization. The techniques the Dogme filmmakers employ are purely pragmatic—a reasonable-enough way to concentrate on performances and to avoid the burden of two hours of lighting per shot. But it is hardly a recipe for truth telling any more than the documentary-as-we-know-it, with its *pedigree of the real*, is a recipe for useful truth telling in nonfiction.

I wrote "Kill the Documentary as We Know It" in response to the Dogma declaration. I wrote it for myself, in jest, as a kind of black joke. Take a look at "Kill the Documentary as We Know It" to see if these eleven mostly *Don'ts* are still useful today.

1. Don't produce "real" time and space—your audience is in a movie theater, in comfortable chairs.

2. Don't produce freak shows of the oppressed, the different, the criminal, the primitive. Please don't use your compassion as an excuse for social pornography. Leave the poor freaks alone.
3. Don't produce *awe* for the rich, the famous, the powerful, the talented, the highly successful—they are always everywhere, and we feel bad enough about ourselves already. The chance to envy, admire, or hate them in the cinema doesn't help anyone.
4. Don't make films that celebrate "the old ways" and mourn their loss. Haven't you yourself enjoyed change? How are the "old ways" people different from you?
5. Don't produce the surface of things: have a real subject and a real analysis, or at least an intelligent proposition that is larger than the subject of the film. If you forget to think about this before starting to shoot, find it in the editing room, and then put it in the film, somehow.
6. Keep an eye on your own middle-class bias, and on your audience's. Don't make a film that feeds it. Remember that you are producing human consciousness in people who are very vulnerable . . . and alone in the dark.
7. Try not to exploit your social actors. Just being seen in your film is not enough compensation for the use of their bodies, voices and experience.
8. Don't address an audience of "rational animals." We haven't evolved yet beyond the primitive urges of hatred and exploitation of the poor and the weak, so don't address us as if we have.
9. Whatever you do, don't make "history". If you can't help yourself, try to remember that you're only telling a story—and at the very least, find a way to acknowledge your authorship.
10. Watch that music. What's it doing? Who is it conning?
11. Leave your parents out of this.

WHAT HAPPENED TO JILL IN POLAND AND HOW POSTREALISM ENTERED HER LIFE

In 1980 I was in Poland shooting a film about the theater director Jerzy Grotowski. As we were wrapping up the project, the strikes began at the Gdansk shipyards . . . strikes that eventually produced the Solidarity

Trade Union movement that, in a few months, organized 80 percent of Poland's workforce. I thought this developing Polish situation might be the beginning of the end of the sinister symmetry of the Cold War, which had dominated world's political systems my entire life (the arms race, the space race, the Cuban Missile Crisis, *the devil lives in Moscow*, etc.). I wanted to take my crew up to Gdansk and start filming the strikes. However, as we were officially guests of Grotowski's theater company, he warned me against the trip: it could get his company into trouble with the Communist regime that ran Poland at the time. Unhappily, I acknowledged the risk and soon went back to New York to apply for visas for myself and a crew, and to raise money and return to Poland to make a film.

The money came easily, but not the visas. The Polish government, overwhelmed with foreign film crews from the West, turned down my visa applications. For a few months, I moaned and groaned, until a composer friend, Michael Sahl, said in exasperation, "Just make it here, goddammit!" But what documentary film could be made in New York City about Poland's Solidarity movement? How could I make the film without, for instance (as I always tell it), interviewing Lech Wałesa in front of the Gdansk shipyards?

Bit by bit, I answered this question, inventing outrageous strategies in the face of access denied. I introduced my visa dilemma into the film and let it inform everything. With the help of some extraordinary collaborators, Susan Delson, Andrzej Tymowski, and Mark Magill, *Far From Poland* turned into a self-reflexive, multilevel work, utilizing a variety of visual sources and texts to create a unusual account of Solidarity: clips from American television newscasts; interviews with political Polish exiles in the United States; footage of Solidarity union workers smuggled out of Poland to New York; Polish jokes (by Poles); domestic soap operas in which I argue with my boyfriend, Mark, who kept asking, "Why are all these Poles sleeping on our sofa?"; and a fictional voice-over dialogue between myself and Fidel Castro debating the problems of the artist within the socialist state. Holding down the center are three superbly performed reenactments of important interviews published in the Solidarity press: with Anna Walentynowicz, the crane operator whose firing sparked the strike in the Gdansk shipyard; with a government censor K-62, now looking everywhere for a new job; and with a Polish miner being interviewed by a *New York Times* reporter who can't quite fathom the notion of a "workers' state." The film closes with an epilogue, a fictional set of letters from the daughter of ex-premier General Jaruzelski to her father, now under house arrest after he imposed martial law on his own people. Altogether, *Far From Poland* constructs a radically different version of the events in Poland than the one told on the evening news, as it interrogates the motives and undoes the conceits of documentary film from inside and outside.

I hadn't planned to make such a film. I got entangled in it and then I started to dig doing it this way. *Far From Poland* turned out to be my trial by fire and the start of a radical change in my own filmmaking practice. Later I began to call these "Polish" strategies *postrealist* . . . my name for a nonfiction film that is post-, or after, realism . . . whose meaning-producing system is dependent not on what I call the documentary's pedigree of the real and hidden pornography of the real, but rather one whose trustworthiness and usefulness is dependent on the strength of the performance of its ideas.

Who was I before all this? A nice middle-class Jewish girl from the Philadelphia suburbs, transformed by a 1960 American Friends Service Committee Quaker summer work camp, putting tin roofs on sharecroppers' houses in the tiny town of Lilbourn, Missouri, and politicized by three days on the boardwalk of Atlantic City trying to seat the Mississippi Democratic Party at the Democratic National Convention in 1964, then civil rights and antiwar work at the University of Wisconsin, Madison. After Goddard's *Breathless* showed everyone that you could make films shooting handheld in the streets of Paris, without a Doris Day and/or a Rock Hudson, without glamour of any kind, I began my first film. With many collaborators over the years, and sometimes solo, I've made thirteen films, and I'm still making more.

I WANT TO BE USEFUL

I want to be useful. Soon I want to make a film about drones. It seems urgent to do so. I assume everyone knows what a drone is, right? Without a declaration of war, we've already drone-killed over two thousand people in five countries—and we're still doing it. I'm also making a film called *For High School Students—Notes and Images from the Vietnam War*, forty-five minutes long to fit into the classroom schedule, one-half done as I finish this book. I hope it will be a useful film for the future.

I am comfortable being useful and I want to be comfortable. Almost all artists hope to be useful—it makes us feel a little more comfortable in our skins.

This is how I go about it, trying to be useful: the actions of my life are my films and my efforts to promote others. My enthusiasm for the graceful, intelligent, and useful labors of other artists produces the energy to make my films and to bring attention to others by making films about their work. My scatter-shot approach has been decidedly promiscuous. But it keeps happening.

Is this a woman's way—sharing, spreading enthusiasms? If it is, it is useful. Trying to be useful has kept me on course.

I have made a habit of this . . . this pushing other artists around, especially when I think their work is politically valuable, particularly unique, and inspiring or useful to other artists. I pressure them to circulate their work. For instance, I have been illegally circulating the first six short animated films of the South African artist William Kentridge. These films are profoundly political. In 1998, when I first saw them, I wrote to Kentridge's gallery in Johannesburg and naively offered to arrange for their worldwide distribution. I was snubbed, "This artist wasn't interested in 'distribution' . . . his work sells in galleries." I waited a few months, then wrote the gallery on some fancy stationary, claiming to be an American art buyer and asking to see the Kentridge films, which they sent me on Betacam, and which I have copied maybe one hundred times and mailed to friends and other filmmakers. (Of course, I returned the masters.) And I have written to Mr. Kentridge numerous times, told him what I was doing, asking him to make his films available in good formats. He is always interested in the idea, but for the moment I have to do this work for him. Yes, artists are thieves. They must borrow from other artists sometimes to speak.

The filmmaker Harun Farocki died, in July 2014. He was unknown in the U.S. for a long time, but in 1991, somewhat by accident, I saw his first film, *Inextinguishable Fire*, made in 1969. It's about how the Dow Chemical Corporation developed a "better napalm" for the war in Vietnam . . . an improved napalm that would be inextinguishable and stick to human skin. Farocki's film demonstrated how we could stop a war like Vietnam by not making napalm. How could we stop making napalm? By watching his film, *Inextinguishable Fire*. Even in 1991, long after the Vietnam War was finished, it seemed urgent and necessary to circulate Farocki's film, to encourage filmmakers to borrow or steal his strategies, his shorthand, his weak models, his German stand-ins for Dow executives and scientists, and his demonstrations in a high school chemistry lab. The way he put a stake in things, by which I mean to make it urgent to learn something . . . like how to stop a war. In 1998 I made a perfect replica of his black-and-white German film—in English and in color. I called it *What Farocki Taught*. It turned out to be useful . . . for me and other filmmakers. So I am comfortable being useful.

I'm a learn-by-doing kind of artist who was supposed to marry a dentist and have 2.5 kids. I started making films in the sixties because 1. Godard had made *Breathless* and 2. the promise of the civil rights movement and 3. the horror of war crimes in Vietnam. Fortunately for me, back then there were no art schools offering film courses . . . no theory courses . . . nothing that led me to think theoretically about what I was doing, which might have paralyzed me. Later, when I began teaching, I developed a caustic critique of the documentary-as-we-know-it and began to write about nonfiction cinema. I'm known now for two terms: "the pornography of the real" and "the pedigree of the real." Most documentaries trade in both.

We are stealing from each other because all artists are thieves, and I hope the replicas and thefts are useful and keep fresh blood circulating in the world. That's what I wanted to do.

Our strange species has invented art as a way of changing ourselves. Philosopher Susanne Langer calls art *the education of the senses*, the mind, as the Buddhists tell us, being one of the six. The cultural anthropologist Ernest Becker, in his famous book *Denial of Death*, says, "The most that any of us can seem to do is to fashion something—an object, or ourselves—and drop it into the confusion, make an offering of it, so to speak, to the life force."[41]

144 FEATURE FILMS YOU SHOULD SEE BEFORE YOU CROAK

Tomás Gutiérrez Alea	*Memories of Underdevelopment*
Pedro Almodóvar	*Talk to Her*
	All About My Mother
Michelangelo Antonioni	*L'Eclipse*
	The Passenger
Ingmar Bergman	*Persona*
	Shame
	The Devil's Eye
	Winter Light
Lizzie Borden	*Born in Flames*
Robert Bresson	*A Man Escaped*
	Diary of a Country Priest
	L'Argent
Alfonso Cuarón	*Roma*
	Y Tu Mamá También
Shirley Clarke	*The Connection*
Rolf de Heer, Peter Djigirr	*Ten Canoes*
Vittorio de Sica	*Umberto D.*
Carl Dreyer	*The Passion of Jean D'Arc*
	Ordet
	Day of Wrath
Ava DuVernay	*13th*
	When They See Us
Sergei Eisenstein	*Battleship Potemkin*
Rainer Werner Fassbinder	*Ali: Fear Eats the Soul*
	In a Year of Thirteen Moons
	Fox and His Friends
	The Stationmaster's Wife
	The Marriage of Maria Braun
	The Bitter Tears of Petra Von Kant
Federico Fellini	*8½*
	Nights of Cabiria
	Juliet of the Spirits
	La Strada
	La Dolce Vida

The Toolkit

Kleber Mendonça Filho	*Bacurau*
Miloš Foreman	*Amadeus*
	Loves of a Blonde
Jean-Luc Godard	*Breathless*
	A Woman Is a Woman
	Weekend
	Pierrot le Fou
	Je Vous Salue, Marie
Ashutosh Gowariker	*Lagaan*
David Gordon Green	*George Washington*
Hal Hartley	*Trust*
	Book of Life
Todd Haynes	*Safe*
Charles Laughton	*The Night of the Hunter*
John Huston	*The African Queen*
Shōhei Imamura	*Black Rain*
Miklós Janscó	*The Red and the White*
Jim Jarmusch	*Dead Man*
	Stranger Than Paradise
	Down by Law
Jon Jost	*All the Vermeers in New York*
Radu Jude	*Aferim!*
Aki Kaurismäki	*Match Factory Girl*
	Ariel
	La Vie du Boheme
	Man Without a Past
Buster Keaton	*The General*
Abbas Kiarostami	*Close-Up*
	Life and Nothing More
	Through the Olive Trees
Hirokazu Kore-eda	*Shoplifters*
Stanley Kubrick	*Dr. Strangelove*
	Paths of Glory
	2001: A Space Odyssey
	A Clockwork Orange
	Full Metal Jacket

Akira Kurosawa	*Seven Samurai*
	Ran
	Dersu Uzala
	Yojimbo
	Ikiru
	Rashomon
	Dodes'ka-den
Fritz Lang	*M*
Claude Lanzmann	*Shoah*
Spike Lee	*Do the Right Thing*
	Da Five Bloods
Ernst Lubitsch	*To Be or Not to Be*
Sydney Lumet	*Network*
	The Pawnbroker
Terrence Malick	*Badlands*
Louis Malle	*Lacombe, Lucien*
	Murmur of the Heart
Djibril Diop Mambéty	*Touki Bouki*
Gordian Maugg	*Olympic Summer*
Jiří Menzel	*Closely Watched Trains*
George Miller	*Babe*
Nino Moretti	*Mass Is Over*
Ermanno Olmi	*Il Posto*
	Singing Behind Screens
Yasujirō Ozu	*Tokyo Story*
	Late Spring
	Floating Weeds
Pier Paolo Pasolini	*Teorema*
	Mamma Roma
	The Gospel According to St. Matthew
	The Hawks and the Sparrows
Gillo Pontecorvo	*Battle of Algiers*
Satyajit Ray	*The Music Room*
	The World of Apu
Kelly Reichardt	*Meek's Cutoff*
Jean Renoir	*The Grand Illusion*
	Rules of the Game

Alain Resnais	*Hiroshima mon amour*
	Night and Fog
Carlos Reygadas	*Silent Light*
Leni Riefenstahl	*Triumph of the Will*
Eric Rohmer	*Pauline at the Beach*
Roberto Rossellini	*Rome, Open City*
	Germany Year Zero
Martin Scorsese	*Raging Bull*
	Taxi Driver
	Goodfellas
Ousmane Sembène	*Moolaadé*
	Black Girl
Abderrahmane Sissako	*Timbuktu*
Preston Sturges	*Sullivan's Travels*
Ming-Liang Tsai	*What Time Is It There*
	Goodbye, Dragon Inn
Jean-Marie Straub &	*Sicilia!*
Danièle Huillet	*Class Relations*
Andrei Tarkovsky	*Andrei Rublev*
	Nostalghia
Béla Tarr	*The Turin Horse*
	Satantango
Vittorio & Paolo Taviani	*Padre Padrone*
François Truffaut	*Shoot the Piano Player*
Pema Tseden	*Jinpa*
Gus Van Sant	*Drugstore Cowboy*
Agnes Varda	*Vagabond*
	Cleo from 5 to 7
Luchino Visconti	*Rocco and His Brothers*
	La Terra Tremble
Frantisek Vlácil	*Marketa Lazarova*
Andrzej Wajda	*Ashes and Diamonds*
	The Maids of Wilko
Apichatpong Weerasethakul	*Cemetery of Splendor*
William Wyler	*Best Years of Our Lives*
	The Children's' Hour

Edward Yang	*Yi Yi*
	A Brighter Summer Day
Krzysztof Zanussi	*Contract*
Jia Zhangke	*The World*
	Touch of Sin

FILMOGRAPHY

This list contains the titles of all films discussed in the text, as well as the name(s) of the producer(s), country and year of production, and running time of each film. The names given are typically those of the credited director or producer. Country of origin usually refers to the geographical site of production but may also reflect the source of funding or production personnel. This information is taken from a variety of sources, including onscreen credits, reviews, library records, and databases; not all sources agree on all details. Because different copies or versions of certain titles may be (or have been) in circulation, the given running times do not always correspond to extant versions. Except where the convention in English-language criticism is to preserve the original language of a foreign title, I have used the English translation of foreign-language titles.

100 N.Y., N.Y. 1989. Dir. Kyle Kibbe. USA. 1989. 17:40 min.

14.3 Seconds. Dir. John Greyson. Canada, 2009. 10:00 min.

The Act of Seeing with One's Own Eyes. Dir. Stan Brakhage, USA, 1971. 31:50 min.

Another Worldy. Dir. Leslie Thornton. USA, 1999. 28:40 min.

*Ausfegen (*aka *Sweeping Up)*. Dir. Joseph Beuys and Jurgen Boch. Germany, 1972. 26 min.

Black Film. Dir. Želimir Žilnik. Serbia, 1971. 14:51 min.

Blood of the Beasts. Dir. Georges Franju. France, 1949, 22:05 min.

Born in Flames. Dir. Lizzie Borden. USA, 1983. 90 min.

La Bouche. Dir. Camillo Restrepo. Guinea, 2017

Close-Up. Dir. Abbas Kiarostami. Iran, 1990. 98 min.

Coup Pour Coup. Dir. Marin Karmitz. France, 1972, 1:29 min.

Crossroads. Dir. Bruce Conner. USA, 1976. 37 min.

Dr. Strangelove, or How I Learned to Stop Worrying and Love the Bomb. Dir. Stanley Kubrick. USA, 1964. 1:35 min.

The Eternal Frame. Dir. collectives Ant Farm and T. R. Uthco. USA, 1975. 23:50 min.

The Exiles. Dir. Kent MacKenzie. USA, 1961. 72 min.

Fake Fruit Factory. Dir. Chick Strand. USA, 1986. 22 min.

First Comes Love. Dir. Su Friedrich. USA, 1991. 22 min.

The Fog of War: Eleven Lessons from the Life of Robert S. McNamara. Dir. Errol Morris. USA, 2003. 107 min.

From Gulf to Gulf to Gulf. Dir. Shaina Anand and Ashok Sukumaran of the Mumbai-based collective CAMP. India, 2013. 83 min.

Germany in Autumn. Omnibus film: Rainer Werner Fassbinder, Alexander Kluge, Edgar Reitz, Volker Schlöndorff, and seven others. West Germany, 1978. 119 min.

Harlan County. Dir. Barbara Kopple. USA, 1977. 103 min.

Hoop Dreams. Dir. Steve James, Frederick Marx, and Peter Gilbert. USA, 1994. 170 min.

How to Live in the Federal Republic of Germany. Dir. Harun Farocki. Germany, 1990. 83 min.

Hunger in America. Dir. CBS News. Prod. Martin Carr, co-produced, written by Peter Davies. USA, 1968. 51:24 min.

Las Hurdes (Land Without Bread). Dir. Luis Buñuel. Spain, 1933. 27 min.

An Image. Dir. Harun Farocki. West Germany, 1983, 25 min.

Inextinguishable Fire. Dir. Harun Farocki. West Germany, 1969. 25 min.

Juggling Gender. Dir. Tami Gold. USA, 1992. 26:56

Majorettes in Space. Dir. David Fourier. France, 1996. 6 min.

Mario Banana. Dir. Andy Warhol. USA, 1964. 4 min.

Media Burn. Dir. Ant Farm: Chip Lord, Doug Michels, Curtis Schrier, and Uncle Buddie. USA, 1975. 23:02

A Movie. Dir. Bruce Conner. USA, 1958. 12 min.

Nanook of the North. Dir. Robert Flaherty. USA, 1922. 79 min.

Night and Fog. Dir. Alain Resnais. France, 1956. 32 min.

Notes on the Circus. Dir. Jonas Mekas. USA, 1966. 12 min.

Of Great Events and Ordinary People. Raoul Ruiz. France, 1979. 65 min.
Paths of Glory. dir. Stanley Kubrick. USA, 1957. 57 min.
Perfumed Nightmare. Dir. Kidlat Tahimik. Philippines, 1977. 93 min.
Rat Life and Diet in North America. Dir. Joyce Wieland. USA, 1968. 16 min.
Reassemblage. Dir. Trinh T. Minh-ha. USA, 1982. 40 min.
The Route. Dir. Chen Chieh-Jen. Taiwan, 2006. 17 min.
S-21: The Khmer Rouge Killing Machine. Dir. Rithy Panh. Cambodia, 2003. 101 min.
Semiotics of the Kitchen. Dir. Martha Rosler. USA, 1975. 5:30 min.
Shoah. Dir. Claude Lanzmann. France, 1985. 566 min.
Shoplifting: It's a Crime? Dir. Sherry Millner. USA, 1979. 15 min.
Symbionese Liberation Army (SLA) Screed #16. Sharon Hayes. USA. 2002. 11:00 min.
Ten Canoes. Dir. Rolf de Heer and Peter Djigirr. Australia, 2006. 92 min.
A Time Lapse Map of Every Nuclear Explosion Since 1945. Dir. Isao Hashimoto. Japan, 2012. 14:24 min.
This Is Not a Film. Dir. Jafar Panahi and Mojtaba Mirtahmasb. Iran, 2011. 76 min.
Too Early, Too Late. Dir. Jean-Marie Straub and Danièle Huillet. France, 1981. 105 min.
Two Laws. Dir. Carolyn Strachan and Alessandro Cavadini. Australia, 1981. 130 min.
Videograms of a Revolution. Dir. Harun Farocki and Andrei Ujică. Romania, 1992. 146 min.
The Vietnam War. Dir. Ken Burns and Lynn Novick. USA, 2017. 17 hours.
Village, silenced. Dir. Deborah Stratman. USA, 2012. 7:15 min.
Waltz with Bashir. Dir. Ari Folman. Israel, 2008. 90 min.
What Farocki Taught. Dir. Jill Godmilow. 1998. USA, 30 min.
Winter Soldier. Dir. Winterfilm Collective. USA, 1972, 95 min.
Workers Leaving a Factory. Dir. Lumière Brothers. France, 1895, 1:55 min.

Notes

INTRODUCTION—A LETTER TO FILMMAKERS

1. James Agee, *Agee on Film,* (New York: Modern Library, 2000), 139; first published in the *Nation*, March, 24, 1945.
2. Agee, 139–40.
3. E. Ann Kaplan, *Rocking Around the Clock: Music Television, Postmodernism, and Consumer Culture* (New York: Routledge, 1989), 189.

1. ABANDON THE CONVENTIONAL DOCUMENTARY

1. Robert Bresson, *Bresson on Bresson: Interviews, 1943–1983*, ed. Mylène Bresson (New York: New York Review Books, 2016), 144.
2. Roger Munier, *Contre l'image* (Paris: Gallimard, 1963), 110; rev. ed. (Paris: Gallimard, 1989), 102.
3. Jean Rouch, from a recorded interview in *Cinema Verité—Defining the Moment*, ed. Peter Wintonick (Montreal: National Film Board of Canada, 1999).
4. Joel Agee, "See, Memory: The Nazi Era and the Challenge of Film," *Harper's Magazine*, January 2006, 88–92.
5. Hilary Roberts, "War Trophy Photographs: Proof or Pornography?," in *Picturing Atrocity: Photography in Crisis*, ed. Geoffrey Batchen, Mick Gidley, Nancy K. Miller, and Jay Prosser (London: Reaktion, 2012), 205.
6. Trinh T. Minh-ha, from her film, *Reassemblage* (1982).
7. Paul Rozin "Food Is Fundamental, Fun, Frightening, and Far-Reaching," *Social Research* 66 (Spring 1999), 66, 1; Wilson Social Sciences Abstracts, 9
8. Freddy Bauche, quoted in Francisco Aranda, *Luis Buñuel: A Critical Biography*, trans. David Robinson (Lebanon, IN.: Da Capo, 1976), 96.

1. Abandon the Conventional Documentary

9. James Baldwin, "Everybody's Protest Novel," from *Notes of a Native Son*, (Boston: Beacon, 1966), 14.
10. Thomas Frank, *Listen, Liberal: Or, What Ever Happened to the Party of the People?* (New York: Picador, 2016), 239.
11. Martha Rosler, "Moving Targets: The Work of Laura Poitras," *Art Forum* (February 2016), https://www.artforum.com/print/201602/moving-targets-the-work-of-laura-poitras-57463 2/5/2016 accessed 9/5/2020.
12. Amia Srinivasan, "The Uncertain Fate of the Whale," *New Yorker*, August 24, 2020, 68.
13. David Halperin, *Saint Foucault: Towards a Gay Hagiography* (Oxford: Oxford University Press, 1995), 13.
14. Ava Tomasula y Garcia, a friend, a graduate student, a fiction writer, a labor organizer.
15. Art Young, Art Spiegelman, and Frank Young, *To Laugh That We May Not Weep: The Life and Art of Art Young*, ed. Glenn Bray (Seattle: Fantagraphics, 2017), 36.
16. Ulla Dydo and William Rice, *Gertrude Stein: The Language That Rises, 1923–1934* (Evanston, IL: Northwestern University Press, 2008), 551.
17. Edward Said, *Culture and Imperialism* (London: Chatto and Windus, 1978), and from a radio talk, *Culture & Imperialism Program #SAIE012*, recorded in Toronto, Ontario on February 10, 1993.
18. Carl Sagan and Ann Druyan, *Pale Blue Dot: A Vision of the Human Future in Space* (New York: Random House 1996), 169.
19. Mark Fisher, *Capitalist Realism: Is There No Alternative?* (Winchester: O Books, 2009), 2.
20. Vivian Sobchack quotes Luis Buñuel in "The Dialectical Imperative of Luis Bunuel's *Las Hurdes*," in *Documenting the Documentary, Close Readings of Documentary Film and Video*, ed. Barry Keith Grant, Jim Leach, and Jeannette Sloniowski (Detroit: Wayne State University Press, 1998), 53.

2. TAKE ACTION—MAKE USEFUL POSTREALIST FILMS

1. Jean-Luc Godard, quoted in Emily Zants, *Creative Encounters with French Films* (Lewiston, NY: Edwin Mellen, 1993), 103.
2. David M. Halperin, *Saint Foucault: Towards a Gay Hagiography* (London: Oxford University Press, 1995), 145.
3. Giambattista Vico, *The New Science of Giambattista Vico* (New York: Cornell University Press, 2015), 27.
4. Russell Banks, *The Lost Memory of Skin* (New York: Harper Collins/Ecco, 2012), 31.
5. Jorge Luis Borges, "El idioma analítico de John Wilkins," in *Otras Inquisiciones, 1937–1952* (Austin: University of Texas Press, 1964), 31.
6. Susan Sontag, *Regarding the Pain of Others* (New York: Farrar, Straus and Giroux, 2003), 57
7. Viet Thanh Ngyen, *Nothing Ever Dies: Vietnam and the Memory of War* (Cambridge: Harvard University Press, 2016), 20.

2. Take Action—Make Useful Postrealist Films 179

8. Klaus Hofmann, "Poetry After Auschwitz—Adorno's Dictum," *German Life and Letters* 58, no. 2 (April 2005): 2.
9. Luis Buñuel, from his film *Land Without Bread* (1933).
10. Buñuel, *Land Without Bread*.
11. Freddy Bauche, *The Cinema of Luis Buñuel* (New York: A. S. Barnes, 1973), 32.
12. Dominique Russell, "Great Directors, Luis Buñuel," *Senses of Cinema*, no. 35 (April 2005): 5.
13. Luis Buñuel, *Documentary Film Classics*, ed. William Rothman (Cambridge: Cambridge University Press, 1997), 37.
14. Charles Bernstein, *Attack of the Difficult Poems: Essays and Inventions* (Chicago: University of Chicago Press, 2011), 133.
15. Kabir, excerpt from *The Kabir Book: Forty-Four of the Ecstatic Poems of Kabir*, translated by Robert Bly, English and Hindi ed. (Boston: Beacon, 1993 [1971]), 15.
16. Photo: *Saigon Execution*, 1968 (AP Photo/Eddie Adams). South Vietnamese Gen. Nguyen Ngoc Loan, chief of the National Police, fires his pistol into the head of suspected Viet Cong officer Nguyen Van Lem (also known as Bay Lop) on a Saigon street February 1, 1968, early in the Tet Offensive.
17. Alden Nowlan, "Witness to Murder," in *I'm a Stranger Here Myself* (Toronto: Clark, Irwin, 1974), 59.
18. Harun Farocki, from his film *Inextinguishable Fire*, 1969.
19. Farocki.
20. Farocki.
21. Franziska Buch, quoted in *Harun Farocki: Working on the Sightlines*, ed. Thomas Elsaesser (Chicago University Press, 2004).
22. Jill Godmilow, frame grab from her film *What Farocki Taught*, 1998.
23. Rosa Luxemburg, quoted in Immanuel Wallerstein, *The Decline of American Power: The U.S. in a Chaotic World* (New York: New Press, 2012), 72.
24. J. M. Coetzee, "Into the Dark Chamber: The Writer and the South African State," *New York Times*, January 12, 1986, § 7, 13, col. 1.
25. Julieta Aranda, Brian Kuan Wood, and Anton Vidokle, *Journal*, no. 59 (November 2014): eFlux editorial 76, https://www.e-flux.com/journal/59/61075/editorial-harun-farocki/.
26. Charles Baudelaire, "Be Drunk," in *Modern Poets of France: A Bilingual Anthology*, ed. and trans. Louis Simpson (Ashland, OR: Story Line, 1997).
27. Amy Sara Carroll, *11 Poems About Crossing The Mexican Border*, https://www.truthdig.com/articles/transborder-immigrant-tool-series-poetry-built-for-survival-on-the-u-s-mexico-border-multimedia/. The Desert Survival Series for Cellphones/The Transborder Immigrant Tool is a GPS cellphone safety-net tool for crossing the Mexico-U.S. border. It was developed by Electronic Disturbance Theater/b.a.n.g. lab in 2007 by artists Micha Cárdenas, Amy Sara Carroll, Ricardo Dominguez, Elle Mehrmand, and Brett Stalbaum.
28. Written in the early 1990s, this poem-manifesto was first published in 1992, following the announcement of the poet/activist Eileen Myles as a candidate to the presidency of the United States. Zoe Leonard's poem, "I Want a President," is in *Feminism-Art-Theory: An Anthology, 1968–2014*, ed. Hilary Robinson (Hoboken: Wiley Blackwell 2015), 95.

29. Ai Wei Wei, quoted in Charles Merewether, *Ai Wei Wei: Under Construction* (Sydney: University of New South Wales Press, 2009), 84.
30. Andrea Dworkin, "I Want a Twenty-Four-Hour Truce During Which There Is No Rape," in *Available Means: An Anthology of Women's Rhetoric(s)*, ed. Joy Ritchie and Kate Ronald (Pittsburgh: University of Pittsburgh Press; 2001), 334; first published as "Talking to Men About Rape," *Out!* 2, no. 6 (April 1984).
31. Private conversation with Ava Garcia y Tomasula, labor organizer in Chicago, Illinois.
32. Rita Giordano, "Updated," *Philadelphia Inquirer*, September 16, 2019.
33. Antonio Gramsci, quoted in James M. Russell, *A Brief Guide to Philosophical Classics: From Plato to Winnie the Pooh* (London: Constable and Robinson, 2015), 102.

3. FORTY POSTREALIST STRATEGIES TO LEARN FROM AND BORROW

1. Ernie Larsen and Sherry Millner, "Reclaim the Future," program notes for *Border-Crossers and Trouble-Makers*, Internationale Kurzfilmtage Oberhausen Film Festival, 2008.
2. Ursula K. LeGuin, speech at the National Book Awards, *Guardian*, November 19, 2014 https://www.theguardian.com/books/2014/nov/20/ursula-k-le-guin-national-book-awards-speech.
3. Martha Nell Smith and Mary Loeffelholz, eds., *A Companion to Emily Dickinson* (West Sussex: John Wiley, 2014), 334.
4. *The Vietnam War*, part 10, "The Weight of Memory," directed by Ken Burns and Lynn Novick, aired September 17, 2017, PBS.
5. Annette Michelson, "The Kinetic Icon in the Work of Mourning: Prolegomena to the Analysis of a Textual System," in *October: The First Decade*, ed. Rosalind Krauss, Douglas Crimp, and Joan Copjec (Cambridge, MA: MIT Press, 1987), 16–39.
6. *Ingmar Bergman Makes a Movie*, directed by Vilgot Sjoman, from *A Film Trilogy by Ingman Bergman*, DVD (New York: Criterion Collection, 2003).
7. Lewis Hyde, "Ars Oblivionalis," *Harpers Magazine*, June 2019, 12, https://harpers.org/archive/2019/06/ars-oblivionalis-a-primer-for-forgetting-lewis-hyde/.
8. William Hartung, in Tomgram: William Hartung, The Trillion-Dollar National Security Budget, posted July 25, 2017, https://www.opednews.com/articles/Tomgram-William-Hartung--by-Tom-Engelhardt-Budget_National-Security_Security_Security-State-170725-383.html.
9. Lewis Carroll, *Through the Looking-Glass* (New York: New American Library,1960), 192.
10. Joe Bellman, "A Crash Course on How to Handle Homelessness," TruthDig.com, November 15, 2019.
11. Susan Sontag, "Notes on Camp," in *Against Interpretation and Other Essays* (New York: Penguin Modern, 2018), 9.
12. Ant Farm, quoted in Linda Weintraub, *To Life! Eco Art in Pursuit of a Sustainable Planet* (Berkeley: University of California Press, 2012), 54.
13. From *Media Burn*, by Ant Farm, 1975.

3. Forty Postrealist Strategies to Learn from and Borrow 181

14. Jonas Mekas, "Statement by Jonas Mekas," *Film Comment* (Winter 1964): 28.
15. Stuart Jeffries, "Books, Tears, and Blood: Saad Eskander, Director of Baghdad's National Library," *Guardian*, June 8, 2008, https://www.theguardian.com/world/2008/jun/09/iraq.iraqandthearts.
16. Joseph Beuys, *What Is Art?: Conversations with Joseph Beuys*, ed. Volker Harlan (West Sussex: Clearview, 2004), 11.
17. Joseph Beuys, "Art = Human Being: A Lecture," Kaiser Wilhelm Museum, Krefeld, Germany, December 18, 1971.
18. Thomas Elsaesser, *Harun Farocki, Working on the Sight-Lines* (Amsterdam: Amsterdam University Press, 2004), 51.
19. John Berger, from his essay on Giacomo Leopardi, quoted by Lisa Appignanesi in "Berger's Ways of Being," *New York Review of Books*, May 9, 2019.
20. Chen Chieh-Jen, *Asia Society Presents Leading Taiwanese Artist Chen Chieh-Jen's Complete Video Works, Condensation: Five Video Works By Chen Chieh-Jen*, June 19–August 5, 2007, https://asiasociety.org/media/press-releases/asia-society-presents-leading-taiwanese-artist-chen-chieh-jens-complete-video-w.
21. Quote from Ford Foundation: "Report—Creativity Connects: Trends and Conditions Affecting U.S. Artists, Center for Cultural Innovation for the National Endowment for the Arts," September 2016, http://creativz.us/report-creativity-connects/.
22. Martin Luther King, quoted in Robert P. Jones, *White Too Long: The Legacy of White Supremacy in American Christianity* (New York: Simon and Schuster, 2020), 198.
23. Richard Schechner, *Between Theater and Anthropology* (Philadelphia: University of Pennsylvania Press, 1985), 109.
24. Trinh T. Minh-Ha, *Woman, Native, Other: Writing Postcoloniality and Feminism* (Bloomington: Indiana University Press, 1989), 48–49.
25. Adrian Martin, *Great Events and Ordinary People* (Des grands événements et des gens ordinaires: Les Élections) (Melbourne: Adrian Martin and Rouge, 2004), 1, http://rouge.com.au/2/great.html.
26. Raúl Ruiz, from the film *Of Great Events and Ordinary People*, 1979, Institut National de l'Audiovisuel (INA).
27. Vilém Flusser, *Towards a Philosophy of Photograph* (London: Reaktion, 2013), 10.
28. Murtaza Vali, "Lightning Strikes, On the Art of Kidlat Tahimik, " *Art Forum International*, November, 2019, https://www.artforum.com/print/201909/murtaza-vali-on-the-art-of-kidlat-tahimik-81073.
29. Carolyn Strachan and Alessandro Cavadini, *Experiencing Two Laws, Cinenotes* (Chicago: Facets Multimedia, 2008).
30. Loretta Todd, "What More Do They Want?," in Gerald McMaster and Lee-Ann Martin, eds., *Indigena: Contemporary Native Perspectives in Canadian Art* (Vancouver: Douglas and McIntyre, 1992), 45.
31. Jeff Skoller, *Shadows Specters Shards: Making History in Avant-Garde Film* (Minneapolis: University of Minnesota Press, 2005), 111.
32. Claude Lanzmann, quoted by Cathy Caruth, introduction to the special issue on Psychoanalysis, Culture, and Trauma, *American Imago* 48, no. 4 (Winter 1991): 204, https://www.bartleby.com/essay/Psychoanalysis-Culture-and-Trauma-FKLJX2YTJ.

33. Omer Bartov, *Murder in Our Midst: The Holocaust, Industrial Killing, and Representation* (Oxford: Oxford University Press, 1996), 169.
34. Primo Levi, *The Drowned and the Saved* (New York: Simon and Schuster, 2017).
35. The concept of moral injury emphasizes the psychological, social, cultural, and spiritual aspects of trauma. Distinct from psychopathology, moral injury is a normal human response to an abnormal traumatic event. According to the U.S. Department of Veterans Affairs, the concept is used in literature with regard to the mental health of military veterans who have witnessed or perpetrated an act in combat that transgressed their deeply held moral beliefs and expectations.
36. John Berger, "Brushes Standing Up in Jars," in *The Shape of a Pocket* (New York: Vintage, 2001), 202.
37. Andrei Tarkovsky, *Sculpting in Time: Reflections on the Cinema*, trans. Kitty Hunter-Blair (Austin: University of Texas Press, 1989), 50.
38. Gilberto Perez, "History, Then and Now: Paragons of Artistic Rigor, Jean-Marie Straub and Danièle Huillet Respect and Relive the Past by Keeping Their Distance," *Film Comment* (May-June 2016): 59.
39. Adrienne Rich, *Essential Essays: Culture, Politics, and the Art of Poetry*, ed. Sandra M. Gilbert (New York: New York Review of Books, 2018).
40. Daniel Mendelsohn, quoting Mary Renault in "The American Boy," *New Yorker*, January 7, 2013, 55.
41. Ron Padgett, "Ladies and Gentlemen in Outer Space," in *Collected Poems, Ron Padgett* (Minneapolis: Coffee House, 2013), 174.
42. Jean Daive, *Under the Dome: Walks with Paul Celan*, trans. Rosmarie Waldrop (San Francisco: City Lights, 2020).
43. Sylvia Plath, quoted in Janet Malcolm, *The Silent Woman: Sylvia Plath and Ted Hughes* (New York: Vintage, 1995).
44. Jorge Luis Borges, *Selected Non-fictions*, vol. 1, ed. and trans. Eliot Weinberger (New York: Viking Penguin, 1999), 483.
45. Toni Morrison, from her Nobel Prize acceptance speech, 1993.
46. Patrick Dahl, "Béla Tarr and Arbelos Films on Restoring *Sátántangó*," *Screen Slate*, October 18, 2019, https://www.screenslate.com/articles/176.
47. Leonard Cohen quoted in *Spirituality and Desire in Leonard Cohen's Songs and Poems*, Peter Billingham (Cambridge: Cambridge Scholars, 2017), 101.

4. THE TOOLKIT

1. Sharon R. Sherman, *Documenting Ourselves: Film, Video, and Culture* (Lexington: University Press of Kentucky, 1998), 3.
2. Richard Kilbourn and John Izod, *Confronting Reality: An Introduction to Television Documentary* (Manchester: Manchester University Press, 1997), 12.
3. Daniel Eagan, *America's Film Legacy: The Authoritative Guide to the Landmark Movies in the National Film Registry* (London: Continuum, 2010), 242.
4. Lee Grieveson and Haidee Wasson, *Inventing Film Studies* (Raleigh, NC: Duke University Press, 2008), 82.

4. The Toolkit   183

5. William Stott, *Documentary Representation and Thirties America* (New York: Oxford University Press, 1973), 14.
6. Raymond Spottiswoode, *A Grammar of the Film: An Analysis of Film Technique* (Berkeley: University of California Press, 1950), 289.
7. Jeanne Allen, quoted in Elizabeth Cowie, *Recording Reality, Desiring the Real* (Minneapolis: University of Minnesota Press, 2011), 45.
8. Marita Sturken, *Tangled Memories: The Vietnam War, The Aids Epidemic, and the Politics of Remembering* (Berkeley: University of California Press, 1997), 11.
9. Trinh T. Minh-ha, quoted in *Screen Writings: Texts and Scripts from Independent Films*, ed. Scott MacDonald (University of California Press, 1995), 197.
10. *Films for Women*, ed. Charlotte Brundson (Kiribati: Bloomsbury Academic, 1986), 9.
11. Paula Rabinowitz, *They Must Be Represented: The Politics of Documentary* (New York: Verso, 1994), 102.
12. Alexander Kluge, quoted in *Theorizing Documentary*, ed. Michael Renov (New York: Routledge, 1993), 98.
13. Elizabeth Cowie, *The Spectacle of Reality and Documentary Film,* documentary box no. 10 (Yamagata International Documentary Film Festival, 1997), 1–8, https://www.yidff.jp/docbox/10/box10-1-e.html.
14. Originally published in *Godard fait des Histoires*, in *Libération*, December 26, 1988; translation published in *Jean-Luc Godard son+image 1974–1991*, ed. Raymond Bellour (New York: Museum of Modern Art, 1992).
15. William Trowbridge, *Enter Dark Stranger: Poems* (Fayetteville: University of Arkansas Press, 1989), 23.
16. Allen Ginsberg, quoted by Sharin N. Elkholy, *The Philosophy of the Beats* (Lexington: University Press of Kentucky, 2012), 191.
17. Hafiz, quoted in Martha Bartholomew, *By Hand Unseen: A Poet's Words for a Reader's Pen* (Victoria, BC: Trafford, 2010), 16.
18. William Wordsworth, *British Studies on Wordsworth*, ed. Mohit K. Ray (New Delhi: Atlantic, 2003), 201.
19. Samuel Taylor Coleridge, quoted in *Best Words, Best Order: Essays on Poetry*, ed. S. Dobyns, 2d ed. (New York: Palgrave Macmillan, 2003), 153.
20. W. H. Auden, *Encounter* 44:92, ed. Stephen Spender, Irving Kristol, quoted in Hakim Bey (Peter Lamborn Wilson), *T.A.Z.: The Temporary Autonomous Zone, Ontological Anarchy, Poetic Terrorism* (Brooklyn: Autonomedia, 1991).
21. Lucille Clifton, "note, passed to Superman," in Barbara Hamby and David Kirby, eds., *Seriously Funny: Poems About Love, Death, Religion, Art, Politics, Sex and Everything Else* (Athens: University of Georgia Press, 2010), 6.
22. Ben, "Manhattan," P.S. 89, third grade. This was published on a small card in a series called Poem in a Pocket by Poets House in New York City. They have been unable to locate Ben since then.
23. Robert Bly, *The Winged Energy of Delight: Selected Translations* (New York: HarperCollins, 2004), 164.
24. Hafiz, *Drunk on the Wine of the Beloved: 100 Poems of Hafiz*, trans. Thomas Rain Crowe (Boston: Shambhala, 2001), 1.
25. Bly, *The Winged Energy of Delight*, 183.

26. Bly, 225.
27. "Haiku," in *The Essential Etheridge Knight* (Pittsburgh: University of Pittsburgh Press, 1986), 84.
28. Song of Songs, in *The NRSV HarperCollins Study Bible, with Apocryphal and Deuterocanonical Books*, ed. Harold W. Attridge (New York: Harperone, 2006), 53.
29. Ron Padgett, "The Drink," in *Collected Poems* (Minneapolis: Coffee House, 2013), 442.
30. Ben Mirov, "Automatic Teller Machine," in *Blessing the Boats: New and Selected Poems, 1988–2000* (Rochester: BOA, 2000).
31. Russell Edson, "A Performance at Hog Theater," in *The Childhood of an Equestrian* (New York: Harper and Row, 1973), later collected in *The Tunnel: Selected Poems* (Oberlin, OH: Oberlin College Press, 1994).
32. Dean Blehert, "Fishing," *Beltway Poetry Quarterly* (Fall 2002), http://washingtonart.com/beltway/blehert.html.
33. Doug Rawlings, "Grandfathers," unpublished MS, 2017, courtesy of the author.
34. Taha Muhammad Ali, *So What: New and Selected Poems, 1971–2005* (Port Townsend, WA: Copper Canyon, 2006), 115.
35. Copyright © 2018 Cortney Lamar Charleston, originally published in Poem-a-Day on January 15, 2018, by the Academy of American Poets.
36. "Johannesburg Mines," in Langston Hughes, *Good Morning Revolution: Uncollected Social Protest Writings by Langston Hughes*, ed. Faith Berry (New York: Carol, 1992), 13, first published in the *Crisis*, a publication of the NAACP, 1928.
37. Anne Boyer, "Actuary of the Apocalypse," *Harper's Magazine*, May 2021, 18.
38. Kenneth Koch, "The Language of Poetry," *New York Review of Books*, May 14, 1998.
39. Cristina Vatulescu, "The Face to Face Encounter of Art and Law: Abbas Kiarostami's *Close-Up*," *Law and Literature* 23, no. 2 (Summer 2011): 173–190.
40. Rolf de Heer, https://en.wikipedia.org/wiki/Ten_Canoes#Reception.
41. Ernest Becker, *Denial of Death* (Glencoe, IL: Free Press, 1973), 285.

Bibliography

Agee, James. *Agee on Film*. New York: Modern Library, 2000.
Agee, Joel. "See, Memory: The Nazi Era and the Challenge of Film." *Harper's Magazine,* January 2006, pp. 88–92.
Ali, Taha Muhammad. *So What: New and Selected Poems, 1971–2005*. Port Townsend, WA: Copper Canyon, 2006.
Appignanesi, Lisa. In "Berger's Ways of Being." *New York Review of Books,* May 9, 2019.
Aranda, J. Francisco. *Luis Buñuel: A Critical Biography*. Lebanon, IN: Da Capo, 1976.
Aranda, Julieta, Brian Kuan Wood, and Anton Vidokle. "Editorial—Harun Farocki." *e-flux journal #59* (November 2014). https://www.e-flux.com/journal/59/61075/editorial-harun-farocki/.
Baldwin, James. "Everybody's Protest Novel." In *Notes of a Native Son*. Boston: Beacon, 1966.
Bandis, Helen, Adrian Martin and Grant McDonald, eds. *Raúl Ruiz: Images of Passage*. Rotterdam: Rouge Press/Rotterdam International Film Festival, 2004.
Bartov, Omer. *Murder in Our Midst: The Holocaust, Industrial Killing, and Representation*. Oxford: Oxford University Press, 1996.
Bauche, Freddy. *The Cinema of Luis Buñuel*. New York: A. S. Barnes, 1973.
Becker, Ernest. *Denial of Death*. Glencoe, IL: Free Press, 1973.
Bellour, Raymond. ed. Originally published in *Godard fait des Histoires*, in *Libération*, December 26, 1988. Trans. *Jean-Luc Godard son+image 1974–1991*. New York: Museum of Modern Art, 1992.
Berger, John. "Brushes Standing Up in Jars." In *The Shape of a Pocket*. New York: Vintage, 2001.
———. "Leopardi." In *The Sense of Sight: Writings by John Berger*. New York: Pantheon, 1993.
Bernstein, Charles. *Attack of the Difficult Poems: Essays and Inventions*. Chicago: University of Chicago Press, 2011.

Beuys, Joseph. *What Is Art?: Conversations with Joseph Beuys*. Ed. Volker Harlan. West Sussex: Clearview, 2004.
Beuys, Joseph. "Art = Human Being: A Lecture." Kaiser Wilhelm Museum, Krefeld, Germany, December 18, 1971.
Blehert, Dean. "Fishing." *Beltway Poetry Quarterly* (Fall 2002). http://washingtonart.com/beltway/blehert.html.
Bly, Robert. *The Winged Energy of Delight: Selected Translations*. New York: HarperCollins, 2004.
Borges, Jorge Luis. "El Idioma Analítico de John Wilkins." In *Otras Inquisiciones,1937–1952*. Austin: University of Texas Press, 1964.
Borges, Jorge Luis. *Selected Non-fictions*, vol. 1. Ed. trans. Eliot Weinberger. New York: Viking Penguin Inc. 1999.
Bresson, Robert. *Bresson on Bresson: Interviews, 1943–1983*, ed. Mylène Bresson. New York: New York Review Books, Main edition, 2016.
Brunsdon, Charlotte, ed. *Films for Women*. New York: Bloomsbury Academic, 1986.
Buñuel, Luis. "Documentary Film Classics", ed. William Rothman. Cambridge: Cambridge Studies in Film, Cambridge University Press, January 1997.
Burns, Ken, Lynn Novick. *The Vietnam War*: part 10, *The Weight of Memory*. PBS. Aired September 17, 2017.
Carroll, Lewis. *Through the Looking-Glass*. New York: New American Library, 1960.
Caruth, Cathy. "introduction." *American Imago* 48, no. 4 (1991), *Psychoanalysis, Culture, and Trauma* 48, no. 1 (Spring 1991).
Chieh-Jen, Chen. *Asia Society Presents Leading Taiwanese Artist Chen Chieh-Jen's Complete Video Works, Condensation: Five Video Works By Chen Chieh-Jen*. June 19–August 5, 2007. https://asiasociety.org/media/press-releases/asia-society-presents-leading-taiwanese-artist-chen-chieh-jens-complete-video-w.
Clifton, Lucille. "note, passed to Superman." In Barbara Hamby and David Kirby, eds., *Seriously Funny: Poems About Love, Death, Religion, Art, Politics, Sex and Everything Else*, 6. Athens: University of Georgia Press, 2010.
Coetzee, J. M. "Into the Dark Chamber: The Writer and the South African State." *New York Times*, January 12, 1986.
Cowie, Elizabeth. *Recording Reality, Desiring the Real*. Minneapolis: University of Minnesota Press, 2011.
Dahl, Patrick. "Béla Tarr and Arbelos Films on Restoring *Sátántangó*." *Screen Slate*, October 18, 2019.
Dworkin, Andrea. "I Want a Twenty-Four-Hour Truce During Which There Is No Rape," originally published under the title "Talking to Men About Rape," *Out!* 2, no. 6 (April 1984).
Dydo, Ulla E., and William Rice. *Gertrude Stein: The Language That Rises, 1923–1934*. Evanston, IL: Northwestern University Press, 2008.
Edson, Russell. "A Performance at Hog Theater." In *The Childhood of an Equestrian*. New York: Harper and Row, 1973.
———. *The Tunnel: Selected Poems*. Oberlin, OH: Oberlin College Press, 1994.
Elsaesser, Thomas. *Harun Farocki, Working on the Sight-Lines*. Amsterdam: Amsterdam University Press 2004.

Fisher, Mark. *Capitalist Realism: Is There No Alternative?* Winchester: O Books, 2009.
Flusser, Vilém. *Towards a Philosophy of Photography.* London: Reaktion, 2013.
Frank, Thomas. *Listen, Liberal: or, What Ever Happened to the Party of the People?* New York: Picador, 2016.
Grant, Barry Keith, Jim Leach, and Jeannette Sloniowski, eds. *Documenting the Documentary, Close Readings of Documentary Film and Video.* Detroit: Wayne State University Press, 1998.
Grieveson, Lee, and Haidee Wasson. *Inventing Film Studies,* Raleigh, NC: Duke University Press, 2008.
Hafiz. *Drunk on the Wine of the Beloved: One Hundred Poems of Hafiz.* Trans. Thomas Rain Crowe. Boston: Shambhala, 2001.
Halperin, David M. *Saint Foucault: Towards a Gay Hagiography.* London: Oxford University Press, 1995.
Hofmann, Klaus. "Poetry After Auschwitz—Adorno's Dictum." *German Life and Letters* 58, no. 2 (April 2005).
Jay, Martin. *The Dialectical Imagination: A History of the Frankfurt School and the Institute for Social Research, 1923–1950.* Berkeley: University of California Press, 1996.
Kabir. *The Kabir Book: Forty-Four of the Ecstatic Poems of Kabir.* Trans. Robert Bly. English and Hindi ed. Boston: Beacon, 1993 [1971].
Kaplan, E. Ann. *Rocking Around the Clock: Music Television, Postmodernism, and Consumer* Culture. London: Routledge, 1989.
Kilbourn, Richard, and John Izod, *Confronting Reality: An Introduction to Television Documentary.* Manchester: Manchester University Press, 1997.
Knight, Etheridge. *The Essential Etheridge Knight.* Pittsburgh: University of Pittsburgh Press, 1986.
LeGuin, Ursula K. "Speech at the National Book Awards," *Guardian,* November 19, 2014. https://www.theguardian.com/books/2014/nov/20/ursula-k-le-guin-natio nal-book-awards-speech.
Levi, Primo. *The Drowned and the Saved.* Rev. ed. New York: Simon and Schuster, 2017.
MacDonald, Scott, ed. *Screen Writings: Texts and Scripts from Independent Films.* Oakland: University of California Press, 1995.
Malcolm, Janet. *The Silent Woman: Sylvia Plath and Ted Hughes.* New York: Vintage, 1995.
Merewether, Charles. *Ai Wei Wei: Under Construction.* Ed. Laura Murray. Sydney: University of New South Wales Press, 2009.
Michelson, Annette. "The Kinetic Icon in the Work of Mourning: Prolegomena to the Analysis of a Textual System." *October: The First Decade,* ed. Rosalind Krauss, Douglas Crimp, and Joan Copjec. Cambridge: MIT Press, 1987.
Mirov, Ben. "Automatic Teller Machine." In *Blessing the Boats: New and Selected Poems, 1988–2000.* Rochester: BOA, 2000.
Munier, Roger. *Contre l'image.* Paris: Gallimard, 1989 [1963].
Nguyen, Viet Thanh. *Nothing Ever Dies: Vietnam and the Memory of War.* Cambridge: Harvard University Press, 2016.
Padgett, Ron. "The Drink." In *Collected Poems.* Minneapolis: Coffee House, 2013.

Bibliography

Perez, Gilberto. "History, Then and Now: Paragons of Artistic Rigor, Jean-Marie Straub, and Danièle Huillet Respect and Relive the Past by Keeping Their Distance." *Film Comment*, May-June 2016, 58–65.
Rabinowitz, Paula. *They Must Be Represented: The Politics of Documentary*. New York: Verso, 1994.
Renov, Michael, ed. *Theorizing Documentary*. New York: Routledge, 1993.
Rich, Adrienne. *Essential Essays: Culture, Politics, and the Art of Poetry*. Ed. Sandra M. Gilbert. New York: New York Review of Books, 2018.
Roberts, Hilary. "War Trophy Photographs: Proof or Pornography?" In *Picturing Atrocity: Photography in Crisis*, ed. Geoffrey Batchen, Mick Gidley, Nancy K. Miller, and Jay Prosser. London: Reaktion, 2012.
Rosler, Martha. "Moving Targets: The Work of Laura Poitras." *Art Forum*, February 2016. https://www.artforum.com/print/201602/moving-targets-the-work-of-laura-poitras-57463 2/5/2016.
Russell, Dominique. "Great Directors, Luis Buñuel." *Senses of Cinema*, no. 35, April 2005.
Russell, James M., ed. *A Brief Guide to Philosophical Classics: From Plato to Winnie the Pooh*. London: Constable & Robinson, 2015.
Said, Edward. *Culture and Imperialism*. London: Chatto and Windus, 1978.
———. *Culture & Imperialism Program #SAIE012*. Toronto, Ontario, February 10, 1993.
Schechner, Richard. *Between Theater and Anthropology*. Philadelphia: University of Pennsylvania Press, 1985.
Sherman, Sharon R. *Documenting Ourselves: Film, Video, and Culture*. Lexington: University Press of Kentucky, 1998.
Sjoman, Vilgot. "Ingmar Bergman Makes a Movie." In *A Film Trilogy by Ingman Bergman*. New York: Criterion Collection, 2003.
Skoller, Jeff. *Shadows Specters Shards: Making History in Avant-Garde Film*. Minneapolis: University of Minnesota Press, 2005.
Sontag, Susan "Notes on Camp." In *Against Interpretation and Other Essays*. New York: Penguin Modern, 2018.
———. *Regarding the Pain of Others*. New York: Farrar, Straus and Giroux, .
Spottiswoode, Raymond. *A Grammar of the Film: An Analysis of Film Technique*. Berkeley: University of California Press, 1950.
Stott, William. *Documentary Representation and Thirties America*. New York: Oxford University Press, 1986.
Strachan, Carolyn, and Alessandro Cavadini. *Experiencing Two Laws*. Facets Multimedia, Cinenotes, March 2008.
Sturken, Marita. *Tangled Memories: The Vietnam War, the Aids Epidemic, and the Politics of Remembering*. Berkeley: University of California Press, 1997.
Tarkovsky, Andrey. *Sculpting in Time: Reflections on the Cinema*. Trans. Kitty Hunter-Blair. Austin: University of Texas Press, 1989.
Todd, Loretta. "What More Do They Want?" In *Indigena: Contemporary Native Perspectives in Canadian Art*. Ed. Gerald McMaster and Lee-Ann Martin. Vancouver: Douglas and McIntyre, 1992.
Trinh T. Minh-Ha. *Woman, Native, Other: Writing Postcoloniality and Feminism*. Bloomington: Indiana University Press, 1989.

Vali, Murtaza. *Lightning Strikes: On the Art of Kidlat Tahimik*. New York: Artforum International, 2019.
Vico, Giambattista. *The New Science of Giambattista Vico*. New York: Cornell University Press, 2015.
Wallerstein, Immanuel. *The Decline of American Power*. New York: New Press, 2012.
Wintonick, Peter. Interview with Jean Rouch. In *Cinema Verité—Defining the Moment*. Montreal: National Film Board of Canada, 1999.
Young, Art, Art Spiegelman, and Frank Young. *To Laugh That We May Not Weep: The Life and Art of Art Young*. Ed. Glenn Bray. Seattle: Fantagraphics; 2017.
Zants, Emily. *Creative Encounters with French Films*. Lewiston, NY: Edwin Mellen, 1993.

Index

Aboriginal people of Australia, 101–5, 159–60
à coté de, 24
The Act of Seeing with One's Own Eyes (1971), 105–7, 137, 173
Adams, Eddie, photo of execution of Viet Cong prisoner, 41–42
Adorno, Theodor, 35
advocacy filmmaking, 101–5
Afghanistan war, 30, 162
African Americans. *See* Blacks
Agee, Arthur, 18
Agee, James, 1–2
Agee, Joel, 12
Agent Orange, 161
agitprop, 48
Ai Wei Wei, 54
Alea, Tomás Gutiérrez, 169
Allen, Jeanne, 134
Almodóvar, Pedro, 169
American cultural colonialism, 99–100
American imperialism, 20–21
Anand, Shaina, 97, 174
animation in film, replacing unviewable realism, 99
Another Worldy (1999), 83–85, 137, 173
Ant Farm, 69–70, 90, 174

anthropophagy (borrowing) in filmmaking, 82–85, 96
antidocuments, 32
Antonioni, Michelangelo, 169
Apollo 11 landing on the moon, 22
Aranda, Julieta, 50
archives, destruction of, from war, 71–73
artist-in-exile, 23, 33, 115
arts: communicating the ineffable and inexpressible, 32; impossibility of, after World War II, 35; function of, 168; rights of, 71
asylum seekers and refugees, film to benefit, 80
atomic bomb tests, 64
Auden, W. H., 144
audience collaboration with filmmaker, 107
Auschwitz, arts after, 35
Ausfegen (aka *Sweeping Up*) (1972), 75–76, 123, 137, 173
Australia, 101–5, 159–60
autopsies, 105–7

Baldwin, James, 15
Bangoura, Mohamed, 120
Banks, Russell, 32

Bartov, Omar, 110
Bashō, 148
The Battle of San Pietro (1945), 35
Bauche, Freddy, 15, 39
Baudelaire, Charles, 50
Becker, Ernest, 168
Bellman, Joel, 68
Ben (eight-year-old poet), 146
Berger, John, 114
Bergman, Ingmar, 60, 169
Bernstein, Charles, 40
Beuys, Joseph, 75–76, 173
Black Film (1971), 66–68, 121, 138, 173
Blacks: basketball dreams, 17; oppression of, 19
Blehert, Dean, 151
Blood of the Beasts (1949), 5, 36–37, 122, 138, 143, 173
Bly, Robert, 40, 147
Boch, Jurgen, 75, 173
bombs, unexploded, 161
Borden, Lizzie, 158–59, 169, 173
Borges, Jorge Luis, 33, 124
Born in Flames (1983), 105, 158–59, 173
Borroloola territory of Australia, 101–5
Boyer, Anne, 154
Boyle, Deirdre, 114
Brakhage, Stan, 105–7, 173
Breathless (1961), 157, 168
Brecht, Bertolt, xiv, 158
Bresson, Robert, 7, 169
Breton, André, xii
Brown, Deborah, 73–74
Brunsdon, Charlotte, 134
Buch, Franziska, 45
Buddhist teaching, 168
Buñuel, Luis, 5, 36
Burgess, Anthony, 113
Burns, Ken, 27, 58, 175
Burns/Novick, 58–60, 160
butchers, 36–37
Butler, A. H. Reginald, 149

Cambodian genocide, 111–14
camcorder footage, 91
camp, 68–69
CAMP collective, 5, 97, 174
Canada, escape of U.S. draftees to, 63–64
Canyon Cinema, 60
capitalist realism, 23
Carroll, Amy Sara, 51
Carroll, Lewis, 66
Cassavetes, John, 157
Catholic Church, 39
Cavadini, Alessandro, 5, 101, 175
CBS News, 174
Ceaușescu, Nicolae, 91–92
Celan, Paul, 124
Charleston, Cortney Lamar, 153
Chen Chieh-Jen, 78, 80, 121, 175
Chicago, ghettos of, 17–19
cinema verité, 163
circus, 70–71
Clarke, Shirley, 169
class solidarity, 75
clichés, 146
Clifton, Lucille, 145
Clockwork Orange (book and film), 113
Closed Curtain (2013), 118
Close-Up (1990), 105, 157–58, 173
Coetzee, J. M., 49, 163
Cohen, Leonard, 125
Coleridge, Samuel Taylor, 144
collaboration with social actors, 101–5
common sense, 31, 56
The Communist Manifesto, xv
Confucius, 54
Conner, Bruce, 64, 97–98, 174
Coup Pour Coup (1972), 105, 155, 173
Cowle, Elizabeth, 135
criminal behavior in films, 80–81
Crossroads (1976), 64–66, 138, 174
Crowe, Thomas Rain, 147
Cuarón, Alfonso, 169
Cuban Missile Crisis, 65
cultural colonialism, 99–100
cultural imperialism, 22
Czech Republic, 118–19

Davis, Bryant, 143
DAWKI (term), 58. *See also* documentary-as-we-know-it
decolonizing, 19, 105
decontextualizing, 64–66

defamiliarization strategy of filmmaking, xiv, 62–64
de Heer, Rolf, 159–60, 169, 175
Delson, Susan, 165
demolition and burning, 69–70
Deren, Maya, xii
deserts, 51–53
"The Desert Survival Series" poems, 51–53
de Sica, Vittorio, 169
Dickenson, Emily, 58
digital filmmaking, 7
diminishment, 71–74
distribution systems for film, 60, 167
Djigirr, Peter, 159, 169, 175
dockworkers, 78–80
documentary: definitions of, 133–34; about documentary filmmaking (documenting itself), 96; questionnaire and close reading of, 128–33
documentary, conventional (liberal), 2–25; function of, 136–37; rules of, xiii, 58; short life of, 34
documentary, narrative, 18
documentary-as-we-know-it (DAWKI), 23, 27; pleasures of, 135–36
documentary filmmaking: film about, 96; interventionist and interactive, 28
Dogme95, xi, 163
Don'ts (Dogme 95), 163–64
Dow Chemical, 43–44
draftees portrayed by rats (gerbils), 62–64
Dreyer, Carl, 169
Drifters (1929), 2, 27
drones, 166–67
Dr. Strangelove, or How I Learned to Stop Worrying and Love the Bomb (1964), 35, 138, 174
drumming and dancing, 120–21
Duchamp, Marcel, "Fountain" readymade, 60–61
Duck Soup (1933), 98
Duras, Marguerite, 163
DuVernay, Ava, 169
Dworkin, Andrea, No-Rape speech, 55

Edson, Russell, 151
Eisenstein, Sergei, xi, xiv, 169
Ellsberg, Daniel, *The Doomsday Machine*, 66
empathy, 16
encyclopedias, 33
Engels, Frederick, 24, 115
enlightenment from postrealist film, 122
Eskander, Saad, 71
The Eternal Frame (1975), 90–91, 138, 174
ethnography in film, 11, 94–95; self- (by subject culture), 100, 120
evil, routine, 46
excessifying (putting excessive material in films), 97–98
The Exiles (1961), 105, 138, 155–57, 174
experimentation, 58

Fake Fruit Factory (1986), 74, 123, 138, 174
Far from Poland (JG), xiv, 165–66
Farocki, Harun, 5, 43–50, 62, 76–77, 87, 91, 163, 167–68, 174, 175
Fassbinder, Rainer Werner, 93, 169, 174
Federal Republic of Germany, 93
Fellini, Federico, 169
filmmakers: collaboration with other filmmakers, 93–94; presence of, in postrealist film, 62
filmmaking, forbidden, 116–18
films: pornography of, 83; transformative, 59; useful, 5
First Comes Love (1991), 88–89, 138, 174
Fisher, Mark, 23
Fisk, Robert, 99
Fitzcarraldo (Herzog), xvi
Flaherty, Robert, 2, 9–11, 13, 27, 174
Flaming Creatures (1963), 71
Flusser, Vilém, 98
The Fog of War: Eleven Lessons from the Life of Robert S. McNamara (2003), 22–23, 174
Folman, Ari, 99, 175
food preparation, 108
Ford Foundation, 86
Foreman, Miloš, 170

For High School Students—Notes and Images from the Vietnam War (JG, in progress), 167
formal film, 31
Fourier, David, 81, 174
14.3 Seconds (2009), 71–73, 123, 137, 173
France: peasantry, 115; Vichy, 36
Franju, Georges, 5, 36–37, 173
Frank, Thomas, 16
Friedrich, Su, 88, 174
From Gulf to Gulf to Gulf (2013), 97, 138, 174

Gates, William, 18
gay marriage, 89–90
gay sex, 68, 81
gender, biological and chosen, 85–86
gender relationships in film, 74
genocide, 111–14
Germany, 75–76, 93–94
Germany in Autumn (1978), 93–94, 138, 174
ghazal (Sufi song), 147
Ginsberg, Allen, 144
Gleeson, Patrick, 65
Godard, Jean-Luc, xi–xii, 7, 30, 98, 135, 157, 170
Godmilow, Jill, 164–66, 175; bio summary, 166; *Far from Poland*, xiv, 165–66; *What Farocki Taught*, 46–48, 141, 168, 175
Gold, Tami, 85, 174
Gowariker, Ashutosh, 170
Gramsci, Antonio, 56
Green, David Gordon, 170
Greyson, John, 71–73, 173
Grierson, John, 2, 27, 133
Grotowski, Jerzy, 164–65
Guinea, 120

Hafiz, 144, 147
Haig, Alexander, 92–93
haiku, 148
Halperin, David, 18, 30
Harlan County (1977), 15, 174
Hartley, Hal, 170
Hashimoto, Isao, 77, 175
Hayes, Sharon, 82, 175

Haynes, Todd, 170
Hearst, Patty, 82
hegemonic culture, 56
Herzog, Werner, xi, xvi
Hine, Lewis, 135
Hiroshima mon amour (1959), 163
history: loss of memory, 80, 92; recalibrating, 77; that should have been, 78–80
Holocaust, 109–11
homeless people, 66–68, 107
Hoop Dreams (1994), 17–19, 132–33, 174
horrorshows, 113
How to Live in the Federal Republic of Germany (1990), 87, 138, 174
Hughes, Langston, 153–54
Huillet, Danièle, 115, 172, 175
human body, dead, 106
humor in film, 81
Hunger in America (1968), 14–15, 174
Hussein, Mahmoud, 115
Huston, John, 35, 170
Huxley, Aldous, 125
hybrid films, 105, 155–60
Hyde, Lewis, 61
hymen-renewing, 20

ideology, 4
An Image (1983), 76–77, 138, 174
The Image Book (Godard), 98
images: making them new, 77; ubiquity of, in present world, 32
Imamura, Shōhei, 170
imperialism, 21–25
imperialism of the real, 24
impossible/unviewable subjects for filmmaking, 99, 109, 111–15
independent film movement, 157
indigenous viewpoint in film, 99–100
Inextinguishable Fire (1969), 43–50, 62, 123, 139, 163, 168, 174
International Longshore and Warehouse Union, 78
Inuit ("Eskimo"), 9
Iraq, archives, 72
Iraq Veterans Against the War, 30
Iraq War (2003), 30, 71–73
Isle of Flowers (1989), 139

James, Steve, 17, 174
Jancsó, Miklós, 170
Jarmusch, Jim, 170
Jennings, Humphrey, 119
Jia Zhangke, 173
jiggle it around (breasts), 85–86
Jim Crow, 19
Jim Kweskin's Jug Band, *Storybook Ball*, 70–71
Jost, Jon, 170
journalism, clichés of, 95–96
Jude, Radu, 170
Juggling Gender (1992), 85–86, 139, 174

Kabir, 40
Kaplan, E. Ann, 3
Karmitz, Marin, 155, 173
Kartemquin production group, 17, 19
Kaurismäki, Aki, 170
Keaton, Buster, 170
Kennedy, John F., 65; assassination of, reenactment film, 90–91
Kentridge, William, 167
Khrushchev, Nikita, 65
Kiarostami, Abbas, 157–58, 170, 173
Kibbe, Kyle, 107, 173
"Kill the Documentary as We Know It" (JG), 163–64
King, Rev. Martin Luther Jr., 94
Kluge, Alexander, 93, 134, 174
Knight, Etheridge, 148
koan, 90–91
Kobayashi, Issa, 148
Koch, Kenneth, 154
Kopple, Barbara, 174
Kore-eda, Hirokazu, 170
Korzybski, Alfred, xiv
Kubrick, Stanley, 170, 174, 175
Kurosawa, Akira, 171

La Bouche (2017), 120–21, 139, 173
landscape films, 27
Land Without Bread. See *Las Hurdes*
Lang, Fritz, 171
Langer, Susanne, 168
Lanzmann, Claude, 109–11, 171, 175
Larson, Ernie, 57

Las Hurdes (Land Without Bread) (1933), 5, 24–25, 34, 37–40, 123, 139, 174
Laughton, Charles, 170
Lee, Spike, 171
Le Guin, Ursula K., 57
Lenin, 48
Leonard, Zoe, *I want a president*, 53–54
Levi, Primo, 110
Lidice massacre, 118–20
limerick, 149
lists, making films from, 87
Lord, Chip, 174
Lorenz, Pare, 133
Los Angeles, 68
Lubitsch, Ernst, 171
Lumet, Sydney, 171
Lumière, August, 133
Lumière Brothers, 11, 175
Luxemburg, Rosa, 27, 47
lyric, 148

MacKenzie, Kent, 155, 174
Magill, Mark, 165
Majorettes in Space (1996), 81, 139, 174
male gaze, 84–85
Malick, Terrence, 171
Malle, Louis, 171
Mambéty, Djibril Diop, 171
manifestos: in cinema, xi–xii; political, xii
maps: "not the territory," xiv; of nuclear explosions, 77; in postrealist film, 27, 91–93
Marinetti, Filippo, xii
Mario Banana (1964), 68–69, 139, 174
Marx Brothers, 98
Maugg, Gordian, 171
May Day, 75
McKenzie, Scott, xi
McNamara, Robert, 22–23
Media Burn (1975), 69–70, 139, 174
Mekas, Jonas, 70, 174
memory loss, 113
Mendoza, Kleber Filho, 170
Menzel, Jiří, 171
Michelson, Annette, 59
middle-class viewers, 15–16
Miller, George, 171

Miller, Jennifer, 85–86
Millner, Sherry, 57, 80, 175
Minh-ha, Trinh T., 5, 13, 94–95, 134, 175
Mirov, Ben, 150
Mirtahmasb, Mojtaba, 117
Montez, Mario, 68–69
Moretti, Nino, 171
Morris, Errol, 22, 174
Morrison, Toni, 124
A Movie (1958), 97–98, 139, 174
Muhammad Ali, Taha, 152
Munier, Roger, 8
music clips, 88
My Lai massacre, 28

Nanook of the North (1922), 2, 9–11, 13, 27, 174
napalm B, 43–50, 168
narrative filmmaking: closure in, 18; pleasure of, 59
National Endowment for the Arts, 86
Native Americans, 155–56
neoliberalist regimes, 78, 79
Neptune Jade ship, 78
Nguyen, Viet Thanh, 34–35
Night and Fog (1956), 5, 34, 174
Nixon, Richard M., 22
not-a-film, 116–18
Notes on the Circus (1966), 70–71, 139, 174
not-understanding, 111
Novick, Lynn, 27, 175
Nowlan, Alden, 42
nuclear close calls, 65
nuclear explosions, 77

Of Great Events and Ordinary People (1979), 95, 122, 139, 175
Olmi, Ermanno, 171
100 N.Y., N.Y. (1989), 107, 123, 137, 173
Owyong, Julian, 160
Ozu, Yasujiro, 171

Padgett, Ron, 121, 149
Panahi, Jafar, 116–18, 175
Panh, Rithy, 5, 111–14, 175
Pasolini, Pier Paolo, 171

Paths of Glory (1957), 35, 175
patriarchy, 84–85
PBS, 160
Perez, Gilberto, 115
performance film, 108
performance with no-one watching, 79
performative film, 31
Perfumed Nightmare (1977), 99–100, 139, 175
pessimism, rejection of, 93–94
Philippine-American War, 100
Philippines, 99–100
Picasso, Pablo, 11
piracy of others' work, 82–85
Platform Diving (Brown, mosaic), 73–74
Plath, Sylvia, 124
play, 58
Playboy centerfold, 13, 76–77
poetry, 40–56; poets' thoughts about, 144; teach yourself to read and write, 141–54; useful, 124–25; what it does to waken the mind, 40–41; writing it, to loosen one's mind, 43
Poland, 164–66
Pontecorvo, Gillo, 171
pornography: absence of, 114; disregard for the subject in, 1; interrogating it, 76–77; of the real, 1, 162
postrealist film, 31, 166; as a koan, 90–91; longevity of, 34–35; usefulness of, 121–25; where to view or buy films, 137–41
preposturizing, 66–68
"private" art gallery, 60
privileged gaze, 97
prose poem, 149
Proudhon, P. J., 80

Rabinowitz, Paula, 134
rape, 55–56
Rat Life and Diet in North America (1968), 62–64, 140, 175
Rawlings, Doug, 152
Ray, Satyajit, 171
Reagan, Ronald, assassination attempt, 92–93

realism in film, 3–25; imperialism of, 21–25; pedigree of, 8–13; pornography of, 13–21
reality, delicacy of, 95
Reassemblage (1982), 94–95, 123, 140, 175
recast the terms, 81
Red Army Faction, 93–94
reenactments, film, 90–91
Reichardt, Kelly, 171
Reitz, Edgar, 93, 174
Renault, Mary, 116
Renoir, Jean, 171
replica films, 47–48, 168
resistance, 57–58
Resnais, Alain, 5, 163, 172, 174
Restrepo, Camillo, 120, 173
Reygadas, Carlos, 172
Rich, Adrienne, 116
Rich, Motoko, 66
Riefenstahl, Leni, 172
right action, 76
Riley, Terry, 65
Rilke, Rainer Maria, 147
Roberts, Hilary, 12
Rohmer, Eric, 172
Romania, 91–92
Rosler, Martha, 16, 108, 123, 175
Rossellini, Roberto, 172
Rouch, Jean, 11
The Route (2006), 78–80, 121, 140, 175
Rozin, Paul, 14
Ruiz, Raoul, 95–96, 122, 175
Russell, Dominique, 40
Russian formalists, xiv

S-21: The Khmer Rouge Killing Machine (2003), 111–14, 140, 175
Sabra and Shatila massacres, 99
Sabzian, Hossein, 157
Sagan, Carl, 22
Sahl, Michael, 165
Said, Edward, 21
Schechner, Richard, 94
Schindler's List (Spielberg), 110
Schlöndorff, Volker, 93, 174
Scorsese, Martin, 172

Scum Manifesto, 140
second track of meaning for spectators, 25
segregation, 19
Sembenè, Ousmane, 172
Semiotics of the Kitchen (1975), 108, 123, 140, 175
Senegal, 94–95
Shadows (1960), 157
Shoah (1985), 109–11, 122, 140, 175
shoplifting, 80–81
Shoplifting: It's a Crime? (1979), 80–81, 140, 175
showing the subject, not talking about it, 105–7
The Silent Village (1943), 119, 140
sincerity, 34
Sissako, Abderrahmane, 172
sixties, songs of the, 34
skid row, 68
slavery, 19
Smith, Jack, 71
Sobchack, Vivian, 24
social control, documentary and, 4
social imaginaire, 31–32; release from, 42
social rituals in films, 88–90
Solidarity movement, 164–65
Somebody, 134
Song of Songs, 148–49
songs of the sixties, 34
Sontag, Susan, 34
sound: absence of, 119; synchronized, 88
Soundie films, 83
soundtracks, 12; antierotic, 83; silence in, 119
South Africa, 49
Spain, impoverished villagers (Hurdanos) of, 37–40
spectators: collaboration with filmmaker, 107; not projected into the film, 115; on second track, 25
Spiegelman, Art, 20, 37
Spielberg, Steven, 110
Spottiswoode, R., 133
Stein, Gertrude, 21

Stolicy, Glos, 125
Stoller, Jeff, 110
Stott, William, 133
Strachan, Carolyn, 5, 101–2, 175
Strand, Chick, 74, 174
Stratman, Deborah, 119, 175
Straub, Jean-Marie, 115, 172, 175
strikes and picketing, 78
Sturges, Preston, 172
Sturken, Marita, 134
Sufi song, 147
Sukumaran, Ashok, 97, 174
Symbionese Liberation Army, 82
Symbionese Liberation Army (SLA) Screed #16 (2002), 82, 140, 175
syncopation and unwrapping, 70–71
Syria, 162

Tahimik, Kidlat, 99–100, 175
Taiwan, 78–80
Tarkovsky, Andrei, 114, 172
Tarr, Béla, 125, 172
Taviani, Vittorio & Paolo, 172
Taxi (2015), 118
Ten Canoes (2006), 105, 140, 159–60, 175
terrorism, 93–94
Thatcher, Margaret, 78
there/then realistic documentary, 24
thinking, films that inspire, 42
This Is Not a Film (2011), 116–18, 140, 175
Thornton, Leslie, 83–85, 173
thought without action, action without thought, 54
Three Faces (2018), 118
Through the Looking Glass (Lewis Carroll), 66
A Time Lapse Map of Every Nuclear Explosion Since 1945 (2012), 77, 141, 175
Todd, Loretta, 105
Tomasula y Garcia, Ava, 20
Too Early, Too Late (1981), 115–16, 141, 175
torture, 49
Transborder Immigrant Tool cellphone app, 51
Trowbridge, William, 142
Truffaut, François, 172
Tsai, Ming-Liang, 172

Tseden, Pema, 172
Two Laws (1981), 101–5, 123, 141, 175
Tymowski, Andrzej, 165

Ujică, Andrei, 91, 175
Uncle Tom's Cabin (Stowe), 15
understanding: and not-understanding, 111; obscenity of, 110
union workers, 78–80
useful films, 27–56, 111, 121–25, 166–68
us/them symmetries, 31
Uthco, T. R., 90, 174
utopia, 52–53
UXOs (unexploded ordinance), 161

Vali, Murtaza, 100
Van Sant, Gus, 172
van Trier, Lars, xi
Vard, Agnes, 172
Vatulescu, Cristina, 158
Vélodrome d'Hiver, 36
Vertov, Dziga, xi, xiv
Vico, Giambattista, 31
Video Data Bank, 60
Videograms of a Revolution (1992), 91–93, 141, 175
Viet Cong prisoner, execution of, 41–42
Vietnam syndrome, 22–23
Vietnam Veterans Against the War, 28
Vietnam War, 22–23, 28–30, 43–50, 58–60, 62–64, 161; how it was stopped, 59; war crimes committed, 28–30
The Vietnam War (2017), 27, 58–60, 111, 160–63, 175
Vietnam War veterans, suicides of, 162
viewers. *See* spectators
Village, Silenced (2012), 119, 141, 175
Vinterberg, Thomas, xi
Visconti, Luchino, 172
Vlácil, Frantisek, 172
Von Braun, Werner, 100

Wajda, Andrzej, 172
Waltz with Bashir (2008), 99, 141, 175
war/battle films, 1–2
Warhol, Andy, 68–69, 174

war porn, 163
wars, U.S., 30
Weerasethakul, Apichatpong, 172
Wexler, Haskell, 155
What Farocki Taught (1998), 46–48, 141, 168, 175
Wieland, Joyce, 62–63, 175
Wikipedia, 90–91
Williams, Raymond, 54
Winterfilm Collective, 175
Winter Soldier (1972), 28–31, 141, 175
woman, in the kitchen, 108
Women Make Movies, 86

Wordsworth, William, 144
Workers Leaving a Factory (1985), 11, 175
workers' strikes, 155
working class, 75
World Union for Documentary, 133
World War II, arts after, 35
Wyler, William, 172

Yang, Edward, 173
Yemen, 162

Zanussi, Krzysztof, 173
Žilnik, Želimir, 66–68, 121, 173

GPSR Authorized Representative: Easy Access System Europe, Mustamäe tee 50, 10621 Tallinn, Estonia, gpsr.requests@easproject.com

www.ingramcontent.com/pod-product-compliance
Lightning Source LLC
Chambersburg PA
CBHW022054290426
44109CB00014B/1099